Rethinking the Romantic Era

Rethinking the Romantic Era

Androgynous Subjectivity and the Recreative in the Writings of Mary Robinson, Samuel Taylor Coleridge, and Mary Shelley

Kathryn S. Freeman

BLOOMSBURY ACADEMIC
LONDON • NEW YORK • OXFORD • NEW DELHI • SYDNEY

BLOOMSBURY ACADEMIC
Bloomsbury Publishing Plc
50 Bedford Square, London, WC1B 3DP, UK
1385 Broadway, New York, NY 10018, USA
29 Earlsfort Terrace, Dublin 2, Ireland

BLOOMSBURY, BLOOMSBURY ACADEMIC and the Diana logo are trademarks
of Bloomsbury Publishing Plc

First published in Great Britain 2021
This paperback edition published in 2022

Copyright © Kathryn S. Freeman, 2021

Kathryn S. Freeman has asserted her right under the Copyright, Designs and
Patents Act, 1988, to be identified as Author of this work.

For legal purposes the Acknowledgments on p. ix constitute an extension
of this copyright page.

Cover design: Eleanor Rose
Cover image © Jane Freeman

All rights reserved. No part of this publication may be reproduced or
transmitted in any form or by any means, electronic or mechanical, including
photocopying, recording, or any information storage or retrieval system,
without prior permission in writing from the publishers.

Bloomsbury Publishing Plc does not have any control over, or responsibility for, any
third-party websites referred to or in this book. All internet addresses given in this
book were correct at the time of going to press. The author and publisher regret any
inconvenience caused if addresses have changed or sites have ceased to exist, but
can accept no responsibility for any such changes.

A catalogue record for this book is available from the British Library.

A catalog record for this book is available from the Library of Congress.

ISBN:	HB:	978-1-3501-6740-7
	PB:	978-1-3501-9493-9
	ePDF:	978-1-3501-6743-8
	eBook:	978-1-3501-6742-1

Typeset by Newgen KnowledgeWorks Pvt. Ltd., Chennai, India

To find out more about our authors and books visit www.bloomsbury.com
and sign up for our newsletters.

This book is dedicated to my son, Jordan, and my sisters, Jane, Linda, and Elizabeth, all of whom inspire me with their gifts and their commitment to their own recreative art.

Contents

Acknowledgments ix
List of Abbreviations x
Note on the Text xi

Introduction: Androgynous Subjectivity and the Recreative 1
    Coleridge Writing Wordsworth, Reading Wordsworth:
        A Reappraisal 7
    Spheres of Mutual Influence 9
    Gender as Nexus: Reintegrating the Poetic and Epistemological 12
    Reappraising Influence: Coleridge, Robinson, and Shelley 21

1 Coleridge's Gendered Revolt against Materialism: Textual Plasticity
    in "The Eolian Harp," *Rime of the Ancient Mariner*, and
    "Kubla Khan" 27
    Dilation and Contraction in "The Eolian Harp" 30
    Androgyny and Recreation in "Kubla Khan" 38
    Subverting Moral Binaries: *Biographia Literaria* and *Rime*
        of the Ancient Mariner 46

2 Coleridge and Robinson: "Sense Unchained" 57
    Dismantling Gender Binaries: "The Maniac," "Kubla Khan," and
        "To Coleridge" 60
    The Conversation between Robinson and Coleridge in
        Walsingham: Androgyny, Subjectivity, and the Perverse 68
    Coleridge after Robinson: The Paradox of Mourning Fellowship
        Founded on Nondualism 83

3 Secondary Imagination, Contamination, and
    Androgyny: Rethinking Coleridgean Fragmentation from "Kubla
    Khan" and *Christabel* to *Magnum Opus* 87
    Christabel: Subverting Masculinist Subjectivity 89
    Dejection's Layering Fragments of Selfhood 99

Dismantling Dualistic Systems of Morality in Order to
Recreate: German Philosophy, *Biographia Literaria*, and the
"Positive Negation" of *Magnum Opus* 102

4 The Plague of Storytelling: Mary Shelley through the Lens of
Robinson and Coleridge 113
Undercutting Masculine Subjectivity: *Walsingham*
and *Frankenstein* 116
Contamination and the Subversion of the Moral
Tale: *Frankenstein* and *Rime of the Ancient Mariner* 121
Daughters, Fathers, and Recreated Mothers: *Mathilda*
and *Christabel* 128
Narrative Contamination and Gender in *The Last Man*: Plague as
"Queen of the World" 136

Coda 147

Selected Bibliography 149
Index 159

Acknowledgments

I am grateful for the many forms of support that helped me shape this book.

For the opportunity to hone this project at its earliest phase through a research fellowship, I thank the University of Miami Center for Humanities. Two conferences, the 2016 BSESC Conference at Oxford and the 2018 Coleridge Conference at Cambridge, were invaluable in allowing me to present different phases of the project to colleagues in the field; for helping provide financial support to attend these meetings and for time to write and perform research, I am grateful to the University of Miami's College of Arts and Sciences and the Department of English. I thank Elizabeth Denlinger, curator of the New York Public Library's Pforzheimer Collection of Shelley and His Circle, who provided both her expertise and access to original manuscripts by Mary Robinson and Mary Shelley. For their scholarly insights, suggestions, and encouragement I thank Grevel Lindop, Stephen Berendt, and Frederick Burwick.

For meticulous editing and timely production, especially during the Coronavirus pandemic, I thank everyone at Bloomsbury involved with the project. I am grateful to the art department for using as the cover image the painting from the *Frankenstein* series by my sister, Jane Freeman.

As always, I thank my students for providing fresh perspectives and questions that have continued to motivate and challenge me.

Abbreviations

CL	*Collected Letters of Samuel Taylor Coleridge*. Ed. E. L. Griggs. 6 vols. New York: Oxford UP, 1956–71.
CN	*Coleridge's Notebooks*: A Selection. Ed. Seamus Perry. New York: Oxford UP, 2002.
CW	*The Collected Works of Samuel Taylor Coleridge*. Gen. Ed. Kathleen Coburn. Princeton: Princeton UP, 1969–2002.
Notebooks	*The Notebooks of Samuel Taylor Coleridge*. Ed. Kathleen Coburn. 5 vols. Princeton: Princeton UP, 1957–2002.

Note on the Text

References are given parenthetically following quotations. The author's name is only given parenthetically with page or line number if the name does not appear in the sentence. A key phrase from the title is given with the page number if the author or editor has more than one entry.

Unless otherwise indicated, line or page references to Coleridge's texts, including *Biogaphia Literaria*, are from Halmi et al., eds. *Coleridge's Poetry and Prose*. New York: Norton 2004.

References to *Rime of the Ancient Mariner* are taken from the 1834 edition unless otherwise noted.

Line references to Robinson's poetry, unless otherwise indicated, are from *Selected Poems*. Ed. Judith Pascoe. Orchard Park, NY: Broadview, 2000.

Page references to *Walsingham* are from Mary Robinson, *Walsingham; or, The Pupil of Nature*. Ed. Julie A. Shaffer. Orchard Park, NY: Broadview, 2003.

Page references to Mary Shelley's fiction are as follows:

Frankenstein [1818 edition]. 2nd ed. Ed. Paul Hunter. New York: Norton, 2012.
The Last Man. Ed. Anne McWhir. Orchard Park, NY: Broadview Press, 1996.
Mathilda. Ed. Michelle Faubert. Orchard Park, NY: Broadview Press, 2017.

Introduction: Androgynous Subjectivity and the Recreative

A male tale-teller who ostensibly sets out to redeem his auditor instead spreads contamination. For Mary Robinson, Samuel Taylor Coleridge, and Mary Shelley, this metanarrative device holds the tale-teller's moral sickening of his auditor in tension with the didactic message their readers have traditionally demanded from the poems and novels that contain the tales. In each case, the facile closure of a moral lesson fails according to what Kant refers to as the categorical imperative binding morality to systematic binaries. Such dualism undergirds British moral philosophy that in turn fuels the expectation of moral closure by late-eighteenth- and early-nineteenth-century British readers.[1] The tale-teller's narrative thus fails, whether he is disingenuous about his promise of redemption or lacks insight about the nature of tale-telling in the worlds these three writers recreate from the vestiges of the binary systems they variously dismantle. This study chooses the term nondual to describe such a literary impulse since it infers ambivalence about systematic binaries that the texts hold in tension rather than erase.[2] Each writer holds in tension the seemingly impermeable lines that constitute a range of binaries including good and evil; redemption and guilt; and perhaps most complicated, between the

---

[1] As Chapter 1 details, Anna Barbauld's response to *Rime of the Ancient Mariner*, claiming the poem did not have a moral, typifies the demand. Coleridge in turn responded that it had too much of a moral. See Chapters 1 and 3 for a fuller discussion of Kant vis-à-vis Coleridge's evolving nonbinary epistemology. The debate about whether there is a single, unified Enlightenment or a plurality of Enlightenments is taken up in Chapter 1. See Himmelfarb for a discussion of British moral philosophy as distinct from European and American forms of Enlightenment.

[2] Nondualism differs from pantheism, the term central to McFarland's study of Coleridge's epistemology; as detailed in Chapter 1, terms such as pantheism or monism are inaccurate when tracing the commonalities among Coleridge, Robinson, and Mary Shelley for a number of reasons, not the least of which is that the latter two remained outside the insulated masculinist educational system that engaged Coleridge in philosophical debates about materialism and transcendence.

heteronormative masculinity of the tale-teller and the nonbinary gendering of the recreated world he inhabits.

This pattern of undermining the redemptive thus speaks to a shared revolt among these three writers against the tradition of moral philosophy constituting what has been distinguished as a peculiarly British Enlightenment. Grouping these three writers, moreover, not only gestures to their common impulse to subvert, however ambivalently, the dualism at the heart of British moral philosophy but also underscores the role gender plays in this revolt. This commonality among Robinson, Coleridge, and Shelley challenges the long-held assumptions about Romantic lineage and the separate spheres of male and female writers. The term "influence" has long suggested the importance of generational relationships in tracing a literary history. Criticism emphasizing patriarchal inheritance, particularly in the field of canonical Romanticism, reached its peak with Harold Bloom's 1973 *The Anxiety of Influence*. As a variant of Freud's Oedipus complex, it describes literary lineage as an agonistic relationship between "strong poets, major figures with the persistence to wrestle with their strong precursors, even to the death" (5).[3]

The inroads made since the 1980s by feminist criticism are by now well established, its challenge to defining periodization through masculinist influence having had more than thirty years to crystallize. At this stage, questioning the divide between canonical male writers and noncanonical female writers has generated a new level of nuance to this history. Because women writers are often described through a parallel matriarchal lineage, canonical and noncanonical writers have remained segregated. One imbalance in the two sides of the field's gender binary is that, unlike the emphasis on textual discussions among those focusing on patriarchal influence, those that counter with matriarchal paradigms often focus on biographical mother–daughter relationships, prevalent in scholarship on Mary Wollstonecraft and Mary Shelley.[4] Reconfiguring these relationships ultimately helps rethink the

---

[3] Bloom places Coleridge in a lineage from Shakespeare, Milton, Poe, and Melville to Dostoevsky (*Visionary Company*, 208). In spite of the divergence of this study from Bloom, his observation of the etymological relationship between influence and influenza is a valuable connection to this study regarding the paradoxical relationship between traditionally linear ideas of influence and contamination.

[4] As Chapter 4 details, the scant attention to Robinson and Shelley's relationship is often viewed through the lens of Robinson's biographical acquaintance with Wollstonecraft. This study, by contrast,

contours of literary history at the pivotal turn from the late eighteenth into the nineteenth century. By reintegrating writers divided by the systematic binaries traditionally imposed upon them, nonlinear relationships emerge that trace androgynous movement among generations, circling among so-called precursors and descendants.

The shared pattern among these three writers to disrupt systematic binaries suggests an alternative to the long-held scholarly divides of gender, genre, and generation. Though all three of these writers wrestled with the structure of thought, Coleridge most directly contended with systematic philosophy due to the separate spheres of education for men and women. Ironically, Coleridge studies have maintained this segregation from that of his female contemporaries.

Discussion of Coleridge's representations of morality and motivation, for instance, has been entrenched in traditional religiophilosophical paradigms; however, that Robinson and Shelley share these epistemological and aesthetic concerns demands a dismantling of the traditional paradigm for a more integrated vision of the role gender plays in these emerging concerns. All three dismantle and reassemble constitutive elements of British materialism beginning with the relationship between self and other. This binary is the foundation of Western epistemology, connecting movements that otherwise appear antithetical to each other.[5] This study argues that the canonical/noncanonical binary that has dominated scholarship over more than thirty years thus descends from the same binary system underlying British Enlightenment thought that includes those of gender, race, subjectivity, and morality.[6] Romanticism, codified as a scholarly field in the late nineteenth century and continuing today, albeit contentiously, is likewise founded on systematic binaries beginning with the divide between self and other. This

---

argues that Robinson's textual relationship with Shelley is more radical than Wollstonecraft's with Shelley.

[5] See Chapter 1 for a fuller discussion of eighteenth-century British Enlightenment thought vis-à-vis German philosophy, especially regarding the conflicts these epistemological strains pose for Coleridge.

[6] It is important to note, however, that among these binary systems perhaps the most significant, the racial binary, emerges gradually in the seventeenth century. See Gallagher's discussion of this history: "As the slaves ceased to be 'Africans,' they became merely 'negroes,' while the masters, and even their Scots and Irish servants, started calling themselves 'whites.' The conditions were established for modern racial perceptions" (Gallagher, Introduction to *Oroonoko*, 12).

seemingly impermeable set of boundaries in scholarship has thwarted the potential for observing the shared resistance among those writers the field of Romanticism has largely isolated from each other.

While all three writers disrupt the dualistic thinking of both their contemporaries and ours, Coleridge thus requires the most attention because of his involvement, as a male writer, with the religiophilosophical debates of his time and because of the long-held biases in literary criticism regarding Coleridge's entrenchment in the literary canon. Since the nineteenth century, scholarship on Coleridge's poetics has largely concerned itself with the canonical Romanticism of the "Lake Poets," a triumvirate including Robert Southey and William Wordsworth, whose lives converged for a time in England's Lake District. The codifying of this insulated group of male poets began in their own time; in an important historical irony, it was Coleridge himself who initiated what was to be called canonical Romanticism in his shaping of Wordsworthian poetics by centralizing the poet's subjectivity in relation to external nature. In another historical irony, Byron, who notoriously satirized the "Lakers" in his 1818 "Dedication" to *Don Juan*, was included with Keats and Percy Shelley as a second generation of Romantic poets by late-nineteenth-century male poets and commentators (6). Perhaps the furthest extreme of this late-nineteenth-century ambivalence is Matthew Arnold's 1881 essay on Byron who, Arnold claims, "has no light, cannot lead us from the past to the future" despite Arnold's extolling Byron as "imperishable" (198). By the twentieth century, the critical school of Formalism, from F. R. Leavis to Harold Bloom, codified the literary canon of Romanticism with which scholarship continues to wrestle even as it perpetuates the dualism at its core.[7]

Beginning in the early 1980s, pioneering work such as Marilyn Butler's *Romantics, Rebels and Reactionaries* participated in the recovery of noncanonical texts.[8] This backlash against the "Romantic ideology"—a phrase

---

[7] See Wilson and Haefner's history of twentieth-century schools of criticism on Romanticism. They observe that Arthur O. Lovejoy, writing in 1924, was an early proponent of including the "literary productions" of women, though in 1949 Rene Wellek "rebutted Lovejoy ..., claiming to find a unifying style and philosophy that excluded all women except Madame de Stael" (3).

[8] The noncanonical designates a fuller spectrum of writers including men and women of the working class and those considered racially other, submerged in the creation of the literary canon during the early twentieth century by such male poets and critics as T. S. Eliot. Mellor and Matlak introduce their 1996 anthology by noting their "desire to give a comprehensive sense of the range of writing

coined by Jerome McGann in 1983—continues to challenge the historical vacuum created by the formalism that isolated textual analyses with little cultural or historical context. Submerged in literary history but recovered in a process that thus began over thirty years ago and continues today, noncanonical writers such as Charlotte Smith and Helen Maria Williams with whom Coleridge and Wordsworth engaged were often well-respected and influential in their own day.[9]

Though more than a generation of criticism has continued recovering literature of the period that had been casualties of canonization, the dismantling of the hierarchy crowned by a poetics of masculine subjectivity has brought with it a host of challenges. A spectrum of arguments has emerged from these early forays into rethinking how the recovery of women's writing during the period alters the Romantic paradigm.[10] In 1993, Anne Mellor diagnosed the problem by observing that the terms "masculine" and "feminine" Romanticism are not "binary opposites but rather the endpoints on a continuum"; however, Mellor observes that "there are important differences between the body of canonical masculine Romantic literature and the body of writing by women now excluded from this canon" (*Romanticism and Gender*, 11, 15). A year after Mellor's book, Isobel Armstrong argued that the philosophical systems upon which English canonical poetry is based were the impetus for women to look outside those systems; women poets, Armstrong writes, "did not take these [masculinist] philosophical traditions—the only traditions they had—as an inert model but reconstructed them through critique. This was a way of thinking through their relationship to knowledge" (16). Armstrong's essay articulates what has continued to be one of the greatest challenges in the

---

produced in England between 1780 and 1830" (2). They thus include women and men writing across social classes, differing races and ethnicities, and a wide range of genres.

[9] Stuart Curran pioneered the recovery of Charlotte Smith in the late twentieth century; he notes that Wordsworth, commenting on the importance of Smith's sonnets to his own poetry, prophesied that she was a poet "to whom English verse is under greater obligations than are likely to be either acknowledged or remembered" (Curran, xix).

[10] The Romanticism label has become so charged that many scholars opt for alternatives; introducing their anthology of the period, Mellor and Matlak write that they "have deliberately avoided using the terms 'Romantic' or 'Romanticism' to describe the historical period" as they are the "product of a specific historical and critical process that did not begin until the end of the nineteenth century" (2). For a promising late twentieth-century treatment of Coleridge's androgynous sublime, see Stevenson, who nevertheless keeps the systematic binaries of Western materialism intact as he treats the relationship of gender and creativity.

field: determining how and at what point the segregated treatment of canonical and noncanonical writers can give way to a new, integrated paradigm.[11]

The focus on women writers in their own terms over the past thirty years has led scholarship to an opportunity for looking afresh at canonical poets from the vantage point of concerns that emerge in women's poetry. Extending Armstrong's idea that women writers were seeking a paradigm free of the Western masculinist tradition, this study argues further that it was particularly the dualism at the basis of this tradition that these women resisted. This study argues that they share with Coleridge an androgynous poetics, portrayed through similar patterns of masculine and feminine subjectivities.

Romantic canonization has codified, as the dominant literary production of the period, a poetics whose dichotomous world revolves around a male subject positioning himself in relationship to nature objectified as feminine, a poetics passed onto male literary heirs. Coleridge's poetic and epistemological gifts to Percy Shelley have generated a plethora of scholarship focusing on such patriarchal legacies, for instance. The masculinist universe of the "Lake Poet" meant not only that a writer who did not fit into the paradigm was lost to history but that this insulation has likewise distorted Coleridge's writings. His idiosyncratic position among the canonical poets is founded on his having shaped Wordsworth's poetics based on British associationism, yet Coleridge subverts its very foundation through his nonbinary notion of the recreative.[12] Over the past few decades of scholarship on Coleridge's poetics, the canonical rubric has become as ill-fitting for Coleridge as the dragoon's uniform he wore during his brief stint as a soldier under the pseudonym Silas Tomkyn Comberbache.[13] These recent reappraisals, appearing more frequently since the late 1990s, have broken from tradition by historicizing Coleridge and, more specifically, have focused on the impact of Coleridge's literary correspondence

---

[11] Armstrong ends this 1995 essay with the caveat that, with the unearthing of women's writing, it was important to study them in segregation from their canonical contemporaries. This view counters that of Marlon Ross's 1988 study. Though Armstrong's caveat was compelling for late 1990s scholarship when, she argues, it was too soon to reintegrate women writers and their canonical contemporaries without the danger of subsuming them into the ideology of the Romantic canon. The time is thus ripe for reintegrating them in ways that do not compromise the original voices of these women but rather show their dynamic interactions with their male counterparts.

[12] Chapter 1 discusses the influence on Coleridge's early poetry of associationism, the last phase of British materialist philosophy, as well as the emergence of his androgynous notion of the recreative.

[13] See Holmes's transformative biography that has contributed to a richer understanding of Coleridge (1990, 4).

with noncanonical writers such as Robinson.[14] The newer focus on gender, however, has been confined to Coleridge's poetry to the exclusion of his prose; this study, by contrast, emphasizes the link between epistemology and gender in these writers' shared resistance to the implicit dualism of the British Enlightenment's categorical imperatives.

Coleridge Writing Wordsworth, Reading Wordsworth: A Reappraisal

In order to reintegrate Coleridge with Robinson and Shelley, this study dismantles what scholarship has treated as some of the most canonical Coleridgean ideas. Because there is a host of engrained assumptions about Coleridge in contrast to the relatively little attention scholarship has paid to his female contemporaries, two chapters, 1 and 3, are devoted to reinterpreting Coleridge vis-à-vis Wordsworth and the masculinist philosophical traditions into which Coleridge has been subsumed. While this choice may appear to perpetuate the emphasis on the masculinist tradition, each of these two chapters is prefatory to the chapters on Coleridge vis-à-vis Robinson, Chapter 2, and then Coleridge and Robinson vis-à-vis Shelley, Chapter 4. One of the best-known Coleridgean ideas, "motiveless Malignity," illustrates how confining him to a canonical lineage misses the opportunity to see how Coleridge is working against that lineage (*Lectures on Shakespeare*, 165). Beyond Coleridge's original use of the phrase in his discussion of Iago in his lecture on *Othello*, it resonates throughout his poetry and prose; Robinson's poetry and fiction; and Mary Shelley's fiction, from *Frankenstein* and *Mathilda* to *The Last Man*.[15] As Chapter 4 argues, each of the three writers represents the relationship between motive and malignity as deconstructing the very gender

---

[14] See, for example, Beavers; Cross, "Coleridge and Robinson"; Fulford, "Mary Robinson and the Abyssinian Maid"; and Hawley.

[15] As Chapter 3 discusses in greater detail, Coleridge originally used the phrase to describe Iago: "The triumph! Again, *put money* after the effect has been fully produced. The last speech: the motive-hunting of motiveless Malignity—how awful! In itself fiendish—whilst yet he was allowed to bear the divine image, too fiendish for his own steady view,—a being next to Devil, only *not* quite Devil,—and this Shakespeare has attempted and executed, without disgust, without Scandal!" (*Lectures on Shakespeare*, 165).

binary on which traditional Coleridge criticism has rested and which therefore has been missed in previous scholarship.[16] Reconfiguring Coleridge alongside Robinson and Mary Shelley exposes a literary conversation that deconstructs normative assumptions about evil.[17]

This study challenges the assumption of Coleridge's self-abnegation vis-à-vis various forms of patriarchy, including the church; the philosophical tradition leading to and including the Enlightenment; and the literary canon, culminating in the Wordsworthian poetics Coleridge himself had shaped. While Coleridge's dependence and irresolution, to invert the title of Wordsworth's "Resolution and Independence," are a characterization foundational to two centuries of Coleridge scholarship, his subjectivity is more expansive than this characterization suggests, even as it is reinforced by Coleridge's own poetry that represents himself as dependent and irresolute from the perspective of his male contemporaries, especially Wordsworth.[18] By contrast to Wordsworthian poetics, Coleridge's recreative agency dismantles, contaminates, disrupts, and fractures systematic binaries that have been described as culminating in associationism though, as Chapters 1 and 3 detail, they include even the German idealism that had helped extricate Coleridge from British empiricism. Coleridge neither names nor defines until the pivotal midpoint of *Biographia Literaria* the ideal artistic faculty as "secondary imagination"; nevertheless, he represents its recreative agency even in early poems, including the wind's subversive witchery in "The Eolian Harp." As

---

[16] For two 2017 essays, see Prickett's on Coleridge and Percy Shelley and Stabler's on Coleridge, Shelley, and Keats.

[17] A central shift that twentieth-century feminist psychoanalysis has brought to the masculinist philosophical tradition is the evolution of the aesthetic/psychological category of the uncanny that can be traced from Schelling to Freud. Kristeva's "abjection" is useful in exposing the commonality among Coleridge, Robinson, and Shelley in their resistance to the male philosophical tradition; abjection sets boundaries between subject and object, casting out that which disrupts order and identity. However, fragments of selfhood are found in that which has been cast out as other; hence the uncanny of Schelling and then Freud comes to be based on the mother as the primordial abject figure who must be cast out in order to form an identity. This redefining of the uncanny is important to poems such as *Christabel*. As Chapter 1 details, Geraldine subverts the will of Christabel's mother, contaminating her with her nonbinary subjectivity.

[18] A critical commonplace regarding "Resolution and Independence" is identifying Coleridge as the "He" in the lines, "But how can He expect that others should / Build for him, sow for him, and at his call / Love him, who for himself will take no heed at all? (ll. 40–2). Of the multiple biographies of Coleridge, Richard Holmes's nuanced two-volume biography (1990, 1999) has been crucial to challenging the assumption of moral failure as suggested by the title of Norman Fruman's 1971 *Coleridge, the Damaged Archangel*. By challenging the moral indictment implicit in Fruman's study, Holmes catalyzed the process of opening scholarship to possibilities for viewing Coleridge outside the canonical male poet paradigm.

Chapter 1 details, the androgynous Geraldine's metasexual contamination of Leoline's ancestral home and Coleridge's metatextual fragmentation of the poem further complicate Coleridge's representation of the recreative, even among its earliest iterations, as a nonbinary eroticism at odds with the patriarchal world it disrupts.

While scholarship has thus held Wordsworth himself to be Coleridge's greatest poetic creation, the agency that recreates is the culmination of a "life in writing" that wrestled with the philosophical school of associationism with which he had helped create Wordsworth's poetics of memory. This notion of the recreative emerges from Coleridge's revolt against traditional, masculinist materialism, ultimately even beyond German idealist philosophy. How Coleridge navigates such a thorny path is the focus of Chapters 1 and 3. To rephrase one of Coleridge's most famous coinages, this book seeks to suspend belief in the selective and distorting narrative—long perpetuated by biographers and filtered into scholarship—of Coleridge as a flawed and self-contradictory genius with Wordsworth holding a central place in such a narrative, emotionally and creatively supporting Coleridge.[19] Redescribing Coleridge through his literary relationships with Robinson and Mary Shelley, this study exposes his often ambivalent representations of feminine and androgynous subjectivities that his writings portray as contrary not only to the pull of the masculinist poetics of Wordsworth but to the Enlightenment dualism underlying it.

Spheres of Mutual Influence

Released from the stranglehold of a totalizing materialism embedded in Western philosophical systems, Coleridge thus emerges as an albeit ambivalent poet/philosopher/literary critic more deeply engaged with a spectrum of

---

[19] Everest, for instance, maintains that Wordsworth's "influence [on] Coleridge's abstract intellectual interests were joined with a truly remarkable transformation of his talents as a poet" (22). As Chapter 1 discusses, it is telling that Coleridge's coinage comes in *Biographia Literaria* XIV where he most directly distances himself from Wordsworth. He explains that it "was agreed, that my endeavours should be directed to persons and characters supernatural, or at least romantic; yet so as to transfer from our inward nature a human interest and a semblance of truth sufficient to procure for these shadows of imagination that willing suspension of disbelief for the moment, which constitutes poetic faith" (Engell and Bate II, 6).

nondual traditions sharing a feminine principle that, from the perspective of Western materialism, is demonic. As noted earlier, the term nondualism is used to describe the epistemology common to Coleridge, Robinson, and Shelley. This choice is not a case of mere semantics, but rather an attempt to convey more accurately the inherent struggle with dualism that other terms do not. Though none of these writers uses the term, nondualism speaks more accurately to their challenge to systematic binaries than such terms as monism or pantheism; most important, nondualism is a term that conveys the paradox of a system that dismantles systems, holding in tension the binaries with which each writer wrestles.[20] The alternative paradigm that emerges demands flexibility: the literary engagement among Coleridge, Robinson, and Mary Shelley exposes a sphere of influence not limited by the concept of patriarchal or even of matriarchal lineage. While these writers share a resistance to received concepts of lineage, they nevertheless represent distinctive forms of ambivalence regarding the struggle of a creative impulse in a world founded on linearity and dualism.

Underlying a mutual engagement among these three writers are shared artistic concerns involving the erotic and epistemological constraints of patriarchy. Coleridge's dynamic poetic relationship with Robinson, contributing to the poetic achievements of both writers, stands in ironic contrast to his decades-long struggle to extricate himself from Wordsworth's poetics of memory that Coleridge himself was central to creating and that increasingly marginalized Coleridge's voice. The sources that contributed to what emerges as Coleridge's ambivalently gendered subjectivity are a larger intellectual, spiritual, and poetic orbit including Robinson and Shelley.

---

[20] I have deployed the term as well in my previous studies of Blake and of late-eighteenth-century women writers and the Orientalists as a means to address the revolt against (in some cases) and ambivalence toward (in others) the inherited system of binaries that had reached its zenith in the Enlightenment. Regarding the theoretical scaffolding involved in this terminology, the terms have been important to feminist psychoanalytic theory, particularly that of Irigaray and Kristeva, as Chapter 2 discusses in detailing Robinson's literary relationship with Coleridge. Holmes notes that Coleridge was fascinated by female eros in a way that gestures toward a sensibility beyond the objectification of femininity prevalent among his male contemporaries. The theoretical component extends to the importance of eastern and Kabbalistic epistemology to Coleridge. Though Coleridge, even at his freest articulation of a state beyond materialism, is never fully unfettered from dualism, the term "immanentism" is problematic as well, since it is implicitly dualist. Chapter 1 develops the conflict between Coleridge and Wordsworth vis-à-vis their radically different attitudes toward their own moments of nondualism.

Though recent Coleridge studies focusing on gender have helped wrest Coleridge's poetics from the long-held critical commonplace of his insularity within canonical Romanticism, some problems have arisen that are potentially as reductive as the paradigm they counter. One such concern is that these newer studies have jettisoned the theological/philosophical focus of earlier scholarship because the male tradition excluded women, a concern raised by Armstrong who nevertheless posited in 1995 a future when criticism would be able to reintegrate women writers with their male contemporaries. The segregated treatment of the newly recovered noncanonical texts has been essential in allowing these women's voices to emerge and, as a consequence, to shape a countering epistemology to that of their canonical contemporaries. However, the result is often an equally restrictive paradigm that dismisses Coleridge as an essentialist out of touch with the nascent issue of women's rights. His representation of the female has commonly been reduced to either side of the objectification binary: the meek, pure, and domestic or the devouring, demonic female seen through the eyes of a repelled male subject equated with a poet thus labeled misogynistic.

By reintegrating male and female writers through their complication of systematic binaries, this study contributes to a growing counternarrative to this male subject/female object binary. The recent scholarship of Beth Lau, Tim Fulford, Katy Beavers, and Ashley Cross, for instance, has opened up nuances of Coleridge's writing that gestures toward his influence by and impact on a more complex literary world. Of the recent essays exploring Coleridge's literary relationship to Robinson, however, critical emphasis has largely been limited to the biographical importance of Coleridge and Robinson's literary alliance. These studies pave the way for re-evaluating Coleridge's participation in the watershed moment that redescribes this literary-historical narrative and for probing their relationship more deeply.[21] Coleridge's subjectivity incorporates the dominant masculine tradition only to dismantle and, however conditionally, reshape it. Through the lens of

---

[21] Elaine Showalter and Toril Moi highlight the twentieth-century revision of the feminist debate over essentializing the female, complicated more recently by the emergence of "gender studies" that can incorporate the case of male writers. This study in turn asserts that androgyny is a manifestation of a larger nondual epistemology among writers resisting patriarchal systems.

his literary relationship with Robinson and through his wrestling with the masculinist tradition in poetry and philosophy, Coleridge's voice emerges as richer and more ambivalent than previously described. Coleridge and Robinson's mutual engagement with female agency is detailed in Chapter 2 through such poetic dialogues as that between Robinson's "The Maniac" and "Kubla Khan"; while references to Coleridge's works have been widely cited in discussions of Robinson's "To the Poet Coleridge," Chapter 2 argues that Robinson not only celebrates a female nature in "Kubla Khan" but that she echoes its representation of the recreative, female nature not merely destroying Kubla's creation but reordering it through fragmentation and paradox. Coleridge's subjective voice, appearing in the final stanza of "Kubla Khan," is conditionally androgynous: the poet would—and, ironically, does—realize his vision by building paradox upon paradox, transforming the feminine power that has in turn transformed Kubla's creation through dissonance: the sacred as demonic; eros as epistemology; object as subject; and artistic failure as achievement.

Gender as Nexus: Reintegrating the Poetic and Epistemological

To undertake such a counternarrative, then, this study addresses not only the imbalance between Coleridge scholarship and that on Robinson and Shelley, but also the consequence of the split in Coleridge studies between those focusing on his poetry and those focusing on his religiophilosophical prose. Such a divide has meant ignoring the relationship between gender and epistemology both for Coleridge and his sources. The segregation of scholarship on his poetry and prose has also reduced the epistemological to a materialist-based philosophical system. The most important way this has occurred in Coleridge studies has been the continuing imperative to contend with Thomas McFarland's 1969 *Coleridge and the Pantheist Tradition* to address Coleridge's synthesis of philosophy and theology. In spite of the advances in our understanding of Coleridge's cultural context in nearly a half-century since McFarland's book, recent studies have largely continued placing Coleridge in the masculinist paradigm not only of the Lake Poets but of the larger Western philosophical tradition.[22] To take into account such discoveries as the influence of gender with the recovery of women's writing thus means needing to reconfigure the paradigm itself.

Scholars privileging the philosophical approach to Coleridge have tended to trace his evolution retrospectively through *Biographia Literaria*, the early chapters often reduced to David Hartley's influence, with chapters VI and VII regarded as refuting Hartley's system through the influence of German transcendental philosophy. Such accounts have ignored the importance, for Coleridge, of creativity that resists systematizing vis-à-vis Western philosophy. The divorce of monolithic, religiophilosophical scaffolding from Coleridge's poetics has meant ignoring his revolutionary approach to creativity, not only in his pull away from Hartley's associationism but in his ultimate rejection of German transcendental philosophy.

As Chapter 3 details, Coleridge's March 1801 letter to Thomas Poole describes his struggle with both Wordsworth and the German writers in gendered, poetic/epistemological terms. Describing Coleridge's "most intense study" of Kant and other German philosophers in having "overthrown the doctrine of Association, as taught by Hartley," the letter then connects his divorce from Wordsworth's poetics of associationism with *Christabel*: "Poverty was staring me in the face … I cannot express … the loathing, which I … felt, when I attempted to write, merely for the Bookseller, without any sense of the moral utility of what I was writing."[23] This sequence, sixteen years before *Biographia Literaria*, suggests not only the connection between Coleridge's poetics and epistemological explorations but his gendering of the sequence that is outside the philosophical system of cause and effect. Coleridge's corpus of poetry and prose, culminating in *Biographia Literaria* XIII, exposes the underlying connection between the two seemingly antithetical movements of

---

[22] In his 2007 polemic against McFarland, for instance, Richard Berkeley argues that the controversy over Coleridge's pantheism was not "an ontological dispute: an argument between those who took the self as the starting point … and those who took the external world as the starting point"; rather, Berkeley claims, "what was really at stake" was the problem of "reason" since, according to Berkeley, "Coleridge himself repeatedly minimized the appearance of dependency on pantheistic patterns of thoughts" (1–2).

[23] Halmi et al., 627. All further references to this edition of Coleridge's works, unless otherwise noted, are in the text.

associationism and German transcendentalism, namely, the Western philosophical tradition founded on a system of binaries that the two polarities of materialism and idealism represent. Underscoring the deeper roots of associationism as a culmination of Enlightenment humanism, this study thus argues that Coleridge resists the dualism inherent in Western philosophy that remains tenacious even in German idealism. Much scholarship mirrors the binary thinking with which Coleridge's writings grapple and from which he emerges with a subjectivity unlike any other among his male contemporaries. Thus, though scholarship on Coleridge's prose has treated associationism and German idealism as two antithetical poles, the common denominator between what has appeared to be Coleridge's shift from Hartley's memory-based philosophy to Kant and then Schelling, among others discussed in Chapter 3, is apparent in Coleridge's resistance to the dualism undergirding the Western tradition foundational to both these philosophical schools.

While Coleridge's notion of creativity is foundational to understanding his ambivalent revolt against the Enlightenment materialism that he appeared to embrace through associationism and to reject systematically by his writing of *Biographia Literaria* in 1817, this study argues that to suggest Coleridge merely replaced British associationism with German Romanticism—one masculinist tradition for another—is short-sighted in light of the revolt he shared with Robinson and Shelley against the masculinist subjectivity undergirding Western thought. Recent scholarship has suggested the readiness of scholarship to move beyond dualism. Danielle Follett, for instance, observes that "Coleridge's adoption of Kantian idealism and Trinitarian Christianity partially constituted a flight from the moral dangers of monism"; she identifies the more general movement of "post-Kantian German philosophers [such as] Schelling and Hegel, who undertook the difficult project of creating a subject based monism" (209).

However, as Chapter 3 details, this narrative is further complicated by the distinction between nondualism and monism that emerges through Coleridge's study of both the *Vedas* and *Kabbalah*. Both of these heterodox sources offered Coleridge liberation from systematic binaries, especially regarding their inclusion of a pervasive feminine principle that offered Coleridge liberation from the gender binary; in the pre-rabbinical *Kabbalah*, *Shekinah* is a feminine spirit in nature.[24] Thus, while McFarland identifies Coleridge's epistemological interconnections to Boehme, the Cabalists, Hermetics, Swedenborg, and others, more recently, scholars such as Alexander Schutz have noted the importance of the *Shekinah* as a female principle that Coleridge "carries … in his heart during his nightly wanderings in the wilderness, one that "can be seen alternatively as a source of salvation and a source of evil" (244, 245). That the *Shekinah* becomes "the symbol of individual guilt" for Coleridge will be seen in the subsequent chapters to be a fertile idea that bears not only on Coleridge's gendered nondualism but on that of Robinson and Shelley (Schutz, 246).[25] The term "nondualism," as discussed above, is thus not only distinct from monism but suggests a far-ranging struggle with the Western dualistic paradigm. That dualism and nondualism appear to constitute a binary but whose relationship dismantles the foundation of materialism becomes a useful means of avoiding the pitfall of that very materialism upon which the scholarly notion of the humanities has been built. McFarland's pantheism label, for instance, problematic in being filtered exclusively through the Western philosophical tradition, assesses Coleridge's "inability either really to accept or wholeheartedly to reject pantheism" as the "central truth" of his "philosophical activity" (McFarland, *Coleridge and the Pantheist Tradition*, 107).[26]

---

[24] Ironically, it was through German writers that Coleridge discovered the British Orientalists' translations of nondual Vedic texts from Sanskrit, including William Jones's poems on the Hindu deities. See Chapter 3 for discussion of the historical irony of Coleridge's interest in Vedic nondualism taking him beyond Kant, Schelling, and others, the very writers who introduced him to British Orientalism. For more on British writers' engagement with the translations of the Orientalists, the impact of gender studies on the field of postcolonial theory, and discussion of women writers in relation to the Asiatic Society vis-à-vis nondualism, see the introduction to my study, *British Women Writers and the Asiatic Society of Bengal*. Kabbalah held a fascinating position regarding the east/west binary in the late eighteenth and nineteenth centuries since, as Alun David's study has shown, the Bible was considered an Oriental text during the period.

[25] See the discussion of Coleridge's *Lectures on the History of Philosophy* at the end of Chapter 1, in which Coleridge attempted to connect the Shekinah to Messiah, suggesting not only Coleridge's desire to find the roots of the Judeo-Christian in nondualism but also to feminize Jesus.

[26] Though McFarland's 1969 study pre-dates the fields of postcolonialism and feminist literary theory, it is important to note his study's continued basis for scholarship on Coleridge's prose. The influence of Vedic nondualism via the Asiatic Society, the fluidity of gender in representations of subjectivity, and the importance of women writers to their male contemporaries all demand rethinking of the older paradigms. Note, for instance, the sexualized diction of McFarland's prose when he describes Coleridge's "dilemma" as he "moved from the concreteness of his poetic to the rigorous abstraction of his philosophical involvement, the alluring flesh of Schelling melted to the white and dreadful skeleton beneath: Spinoza! And the siren song of art's supremacy changed to the harpy rasp of moral horror" (123).

Coleridge's resistance to Western materialism underlies the various subjectivities informing his wide-ranging writings, from his earliest poetry to the late philosophical, theological essays and lectures, culminating in *Biographia Literaria*. Scholarship focusing exclusively on Coleridge's philosophy does so to the exclusion of Coleridge's representation of subjectivity as androgynous, an impulse that runs counter to the masculinist tradition out of which Wordsworth emerges.[27] Coleridge's ambivalent epistemology runs against the current of the dualistic Western philosophical tradition, a vision at once system and anti-system. Building and dismantling, it wrestles with the relationship among the creative, philosophical, and spiritual. Coleridge's evolving representation of ambivalence leads to this synthetic/fragmentary vision, itself a form of nondualism that rebels against materialism that insists on coherence and wholeness paradoxically founded on such binaries as male and female; subject and object; and good and evil.

Coleridge's lifelong struggle with the nature of creativity, the most serious casualty of segregating religiophilosophical studies from those treating gender in his poetry, binds together gender and the theological/philosophical in Coleridge's writings, his creation of modern literary criticism itself emerging out of this integrated vision.[28] His pull toward the nondual informs the arc of his career, held in tension with the dualism that he repeatedly finds inescapable. Schutz, concluding that Coleridge's imagination is "both a unifying and a disruptive and disseminating potential," moves toward this conclusion by identifying Coleridge's discomfort with Kant's representation of an agonistic relationship between the noumenal and phenomenal, which he describes as "a violent power struggle with the phenomenal world of the senses and imagination, in which the mind demonstrated to itself its own superiority at the expense of nature" (254, 216).[29]

---

[27] As many scholars have shown, even when William appropriates passages from the *Alfoxden* and *Grasmere Journal* of his sister, Dorothy, he inserts the masculine subjectivity conspicuously absent from her entries; most famous is her *Grasmere Journal* entry on the daffodils that William transmogrifies into "I Wandered Lonely as a Cloud," the title itself revealing the shift from the communal "we" in Dorothy's account, reflected in the "colony" of daffodils to William's "lonely" experience that is significant to him because of the later reflection that exemplifies the "spots of time" in *The Prelude* Book XII: moments that lift him out of poetic numbness, the mind "lord and master" (Dorothy Wordsworth, 85; William Wordsworth, 191, 345, l. 222).

[28] Among the ways Coleridge first systematized literary criticism, as we know it today, are his lectures on Shakespeare, widely celebrated as the first psychological treatment of the plays.

[29] By recontextualizing Coleridge's contention with philosophical precedents through his "life in literature," this study argues that imagination is more than a "unifying and mediatory power, which had found its strongest expression in the philosophical texts of the German Idealists" (Schutz, 216).

The confluence of Coleridge's poetic and religiophilosophical writing is thus tied to the equally interconnected concerns of gender and creativity. Although Coleridge does not use the term "secondary imagination" or define it until chapter XIII of his 1817 *Biographia Literaria*, he creates tension throughout his writings by superimposing a revolutionary impulse of recreative imagination onto the masculinist model of the British and European philosophical tradition. The following chapters revisit *Biographia Literaria* from several perspectives to explore the conflicting subjectivities between Coleridge's male narrators and an androgynously eroticized embodiment of recreative imagination. Chapter XIII, the structural center of *Biographia Literaria*, culminates with Coleridge's original definition and hierarchy of mental faculties, the recreative secondary imagination as its culmination. It stands as the pivotal moment on which the vision of his own "life in literature" turns, thus affording a more comprehensive view of his writings across genres. Chapters 1 and 3 of this study address Coleridge's dismantling of the male subjectivity in a bifurcated Western tradition that objectifies the feminine.

Reappraising Coleridge's relationship to German philosophy necessitates reappraising the problem of his plagiarism. Criticism has been at a stalemate over Coleridge's plagiarism of German philosophical writings in particular.[30] Evidence "in the privacy of the notebooks" has been cited regarding his consciousness about his "obligations" and "glaring resemblances" to German writers such as Kant and Fichte, Coleridge appearing at the very least self-deluded when he claims, "I seem to know, that much of the matter remains my own, and that the Soul is mine. I fear not him for a Critic who can confound a Fellow thinker with a Compiler" (K. Cooke, 3; quoting *CN* 2, 2375, 21.555).

Scholarship on Coleridge's epistemology confined to the "philosophical center" of *Biographia* that ends with chapter XII perpetuates the reading of Coleridge's plagiarism as the death knell of his imagination by distorting the sense of Coleridge's indebtedness to German writers. Coleridge's "imp of the perverse," however, reverses direction in chapter XIII.[31] Here, he follows the

---

[30] See McFarland's chapter on "The Problem of Coleridge's Plagiarisms" for a detailed history of scholarship on the subject, beginning with Rene Wellek's disparaging of him as a "purveyor of borrowed ideas, and, at worst, and in many cases, as an out-and-out plagiarist" (qtd. in McFarland, 1).
[31] The phrase "imp of the perverse" is the title of an 1845 short story by Poe, that most Coleridgean of nineteenth-century American writer plagiarists; it is thus proleptically useful in this reappraisal of Coleridge's plagiarism as well as its connection to his fascination with the nature of evil. In

plagiarisms with attributing to a friend that which is his original hierarchy of mental faculties, even providing a "letter" from that friend. Chapter XIII, the pivotal center of the work as a whole, explodes all that has come before. That Coleridge promised a "magnum opus" that would be "the system of all systems [through which] every possible philosophical perspective would prove to be relatable to the same underlying principles" suggests his sense of failure derives from his ambivalence about the goal of unity or wholeness (218). Reappraising the epistemological discussion by shifting away from the pantheism/Enlightenment materialism debate to the paradoxical interplay of dualism and nondualism thus brings into focus Coleridge's engagement with and ultimate liberation from German transcendental philosophy.[32]

In spite of the long-standing critical attention to Coleridge's plagiarisms, however, another apparently antithetical pattern of Coleridge's relationship to the creative process has not been addressed: Coleridge often follows plagiarisms by attributing to (often fictional) others what is in fact his original text, idea, or claim.[33] Reading suspiciously, in Ricouer's terms, exposes the perverse underlying Coleridge's statements that claim to seek unity while he undermines poetic wholeness and philosophical coherence.[34] Thus, while scholarship traditionally discusses Coleridge's plagiarism in the "philosophical

---

the story, Poe connects the self-subverting impulse, the perverse, to a "*mobile* without motive .... Through its promptings, we act without comprehensible object" (234).

[32] McFarland makes a nuanced comparison about the divergent contexts of Coleridge and his German influences, specifically regarding what Coleridge refers to as the tension of "I am"/"it is" that "kept Coleridge's philosophical bow bent throughout his life" (160). McFarland's image of the bent bow may be the closest articulation he gives of Coleridge's nondualism, precisely because of the tension it, as opposed to "monism," or even "pantheism," suggests. Distinguishing Coleridge from, among others, Schelling, Kant, Leibniz, and Spinoza, McFarland notes "the lines of their philosophical consequence start from different backgrounds and intersect in the Schelling translations of the *Biographia Literaria*, and then begin to diverge" (McFarland, *Coleridge and the Pantheist Tradition*, xxxvi). See also McFarland's Excursus (Notes III and IV) on the origin of the word "Pantheism" and Krause's systematic development of "Panentheism" that was a means of protecting oneself from charges of atheism, or for "having it both ways": "All Things are God, God is not equal to All Things" (McFarland, *Coleridge and the Pantheist Tradition*, 268). See Chapter 1 of this study for discussion of how the epistemological differences between Coleridge and Wordsworth intersect with gender and creativity.

[33] This pattern will be discussed below and detailed at various points in the book. See, for example, Chapter 1 that details the movement from chapters XII to XIV of *Biographia Literaria*. By revisiting Coleridge's preceding treatment of German writers in chapter XII and his subsequent criticism of Wordsworthian associationism, his articulation of secondary imagination takes on added significance in Coleridge's attributing it to "a friend."

[34] Ricoeur coined the phrase "the hermeneutics of suspicion" to articulate the common impulse among Freud, Marx, and Nietszche by which they seek to "unmask the lies and illusions of consciousness" (Ricouer, 356).

chapters" of *Biographia Literaria*, there is a relationship between Coleridge's plagiarism and his attributing to another his own ideas, seen for instance in chapter XIII. There, Coleridge credits his original definition of secondary imagination to "a friend"; likewise, in his Preface to *Kubla Khan*, Coleridge fabricates an elaborate ruse through which he pursues the androgynous ideal that he nevertheless represents himself as failing to realize.

Coleridge thus revolutionizes the relationship between originality and borrowing, scrambling this binary even, perhaps, beyond current standards. McFarland accounts for Coleridge's interplay of originality and borrowing by noting that originality, as a Romantic literary ideal, was still relatively new, its first articulation in Edward Young's 1759 *Conjectures on Original Composition*. McFarland sees Coleridge as able to straddle the two realms of originality and the old standard of imitation because "as a founder of English Romanticism, [he] was also a transitional figure from an earlier era"; McFarland perpetuates the poetry/philosophy binary by theorizing that "Coleridge, as not only a literary creator, but a philosophical systematist, was in the special position of being able to bestow his allegiance on whichever tradition suited the pressure of immediate circumstances" (31). Although it is apparent from the hindsight of a half-century of scholarship since McFarland made this statement that there are more ingredients for Coleridge's literary theory than this binary, recent studies have retained the paradigm.

This phenomenon is particularly important to Coleridge's wrestling with Schelling, often seen as the most important influence on Coleridge among German writers with Coleridge's plagiarism of Schelling in *Biographia Literaria* used to support the claim.[35] Though Schelling in particular provides Coleridge with a means of resisting patriarchy in the form of Enlightenment philosophy, Coleridge resists the binaries codified during the Enlightenment traceable

---

[35] According to Schutz, "Schelling provided Coleridge with a model of imagination, the self, and the philosophical system, which lent themselves much more readily to the development of a truly all-encompassing and palatable philosophical perspective" (217). To McFarland's credit, his chapter wrestles with "the curious mixture of frankness and of plain deceit," specifically in *Biographia Literaria* IX, in which Coleridge defends his use of Schelling that, McFarland says, "leads us, if we examine it even briefly, into a veritable labyrinth of paradox" (39). Paradox indeed is the ultimate challenge to dualism. The statement thus stands as a place to begin the process of wresting scholarship from its vise. Coleridge's use of the word "genial" to describe his discovery of Schelling is coincident with "much that I had toiled out for myself," (qtd. in Schutz, 217), yet his use of the term suggests a more profound spiritual affinity. Coleridge was thereby at liberty to employ his plastic power of imagination in adapting and indeed moving beyond Schelling.

through the relationship among that philosophical pull toward and ultimate emergence from German Romanticism. Contextualizing Coleridge's wrestling with Schelling vis-à-vis his contention with philosophical treatments of evil, his larger dismantling of systematic binaries becomes apparent, revealed in his commentary on Schelling's "Freedom Essay." Here, Coleridge contends that Schelling's theory of evil does "not do enough to elucidate his conception of the 'mysterious *Ground* of Existence'" (Struwig, 82). Coleridge's criticism of Schelling elucidates Coleridge's own struggle between the orthodox and the heterodox on multiple levels that manifest through the binary of good and evil. By examining Coleridge's plagiarisms in the context of his engagement with women writers and his pattern of representing the recreative imagination as a feminine power that subverts the male subject position, the German writers from whom Coleridge borrows provide a countering voice as he probes nondualism.[36]

Through analysis of Coleridge's early poetics, Chapter 1 argues that Coleridge's representation of gender and sexuality suggests a far deeper and earlier divorce from Wordsworthian poetics than acknowledged by McFarland and those more recent scholars who, though arguing against elements of his position, have maintained the narrative of Coleridge's early embrace of associationism—the culmination of this materialism—when he met Wordsworth and through which Coleridge influenced Wordsworth's nascent poetics. The retrospective view of Coleridge's early poetry through the hierarchy of mental faculties in chapter XIII of *Biographia Literaria* reveals the return of the early poet's repressed anger at Wordsworth and the masculinist epistemology of associationism; Coleridge himself had albeit ambivalently embraced this materialism at the time of his meeting Wordsworth until his exposure to German idealist philosophy.[37] Coleridge's shaping of Wordsworth's

---

[36] McFarland challenges the simplistic moral indictment of both Coleridge's contemporaries and modern biographers by noting that Schelling, from whom Coleridge translated, "did decline to make a charge of plagiarism" in spite of the accusations the British press made against Coleridge. See McFarland, xxxii–xxxv, regarding the "the nature and limitations of philosophical originality" as opposed to Northrop Frye's attack on the "terminological buccaneers" (xxxii) and Chapter 1 in which he addresses the origins of the plagiarism attacks. The title of Norman Fruman's study indicates the moral indictment of Coleridge, the "Damaged Archangel."

[37] Though Holmes's biography helps complicate Coleridge, it nevertheless perpetuates Coleridge's place in the masculinist poetics of the Romantic ideology discussed earlier. For instance, it assesses *Biographia Literaria* as "one of the characteristic monuments ... of English Romanticism; comparable in its way to Wordsworth's The *Prelude*, Keats's letters, Hazlitt's *Spirit of the Age* .... It

career into one that came to define canonical Romanticism in its meditative/descriptive focus on the poetic persona stands in stark and ironic contrast to Coleridge's own poetry and criticism as ambivalent about the very nature of what has defined canonicity: a dualistic relationship between its male-centered subjectivity dominating the phenomenal world of nature, as "The Eolian Harp" will be seen to demonstrate in Chapter 1.[38]

Reappraising Influence: Coleridge, Robinson, and Shelley

The most important difference between the education of men and women during the period, the immersion of male students in the field of Western philosophy and its absence in women's education, has informed scholarship's gendered separation among biographical, poetic, and philosophical treatments of male and female writers. However, to extend Armstrong's statement cited earlier, that women, segregated from the male philosophical tradition, "did not take these philosophical traditions—the only traditions they had—as an inert model but reconstructed them through critique," it is important to note that though Coleridge's philosophical struggles, including his resistance to British associationism and ultimately to German Romanticism, would not apply to Robinson and Shelley because of the differences in their gendered education, this study argues that Robinson and Shelley share with Coleridge a rejection of systematic binaries (16).[39] Central to that commonality is their representation of a feminine subjectivity as a principle of creativity at odds with an oppressive male figure of a monolithic patriarchy. By exploring Coleridge's nondualism, the resistance to masculinist binary systems behind his lyrical and narrative poetry can be seen as inextricably linked to Robinson's and

---

is the work that secures Coleridge in history"—the canonical literary history that buries Coleridge's bitterness toward Wordsworth and subsequent embrace of female erotic energy (37). Holmes goes on to claim that *Biographia Literaria* is "extraordinarily magnanimous to Wordsworth without the least hint of their personal difficulties" (38). Chapter 3 will take up the counterargument of Coleridge's dismantling of Wordsworthian poetics in *Biographia Literaria* XIII and XIV.

[38] See Berkeley, pp. 158, 214.
[39] Mary Shelley's education was idiosyncratic and complex, shaped by a father immersed in the male philosophical tradition yet a supporter of the polemical prose of her mother, Mary Wollstonecraft, herself an ambivalent advocate of women's rights. As Chapter 4 of this study argues, Shelley in turn shaped her fictional worlds from not only the ambivalent voices of her parents and her husband but from her intricate triangular literary relationship with Coleridge and Robinson.

Shelley's subversion of narrative tradition. The three writers have in common a feminine nondualism that runs counter to the masculinist tradition against which Coleridge consistently, if ambivalently, wrote.

Through this wider network of intellectual and artistic voices, a monolithic notion of literary tradition gives way to the mutual challenge to its systematic binaries. Coleridge, Robinson, and Shelley mutually illuminate not only a movement from unity to fragmentation but, more important, beyond fragmentation toward the tantalizing ideal of the recreative impulse that reorders the fragments. Rather than wholeness or unity, this nondual recreation conveys an active and unresolved play of perpetually recreative energy. That Coleridge shared these ambivalent impulses with other intellectuals of his day, especially women writers, thus becomes important in dismantling of the old canonical paradigm, freeing scholarship to explore Coleridge's struggle against and his ultimate rejection of British materialism.[40] This mutual engagement helps reorient the field through its relevance not only to women during this pivotal revolutionary period but also to those male writers resisting the masculinist poetics and materialist philosophy inherited from their Enlightenment precursors.[41] By tracing Coleridge's early subversion of traditional gender roles, Chapter 1 explores Coleridge's eroticized representation of a liberating epistemology, serving as a foundation for Chapter 2 that examines the literary dialogue between Coleridge and Robinson on their own terms rather than through the lens of canonical Romanticism; this chapter revisits both writers' texts complicating even the genre binary of the lyrical and narrative, including Coleridge's lyrical ballads vis-à-vis the embedded poetry in Robinson's novel, *Walsingham*. The chapter also rethinks Coleridge's "canonical" poems such as *Rime of the Ancient Mariner* and "Kubla Khan" through their relationship to Robinson's "The Haunted Beach" and "To Coleridge," respectively.

---

[40] Chapter 1 takes up this pivotal period through the discussion of *Christabel*'s textual history as an epistemological map to Coleridge's formulation of a poetics running counter to British associationist philosophy.

[41] Coleridge's female contemporaries recognized and admired his explosive representations of female subjectivity and sexuality; as noted in Chapter 3, one of his most ardent admirers, to Wordsworth's chagrin, was Dorothy Wordsworth, who loved *Christabel*, the very poem that William found repellant and unfit to include in *The Lyrical Ballads*. On 31 August of her 1800 *Grasmere Journal*, Dorothy Wordsworth writes that "Coleridge read us a part of *Christabel*. Talked much about the mountains, etc. etc" (39); on 4 October she writes "[e]xceedingly delighted with the second part of *Christabel*," and the following morning: "Coleridge read a 2nd time *Christabel*; we had increasing pleasure" (45).

After having explored in Chapter 2 the commonalities between Robinson and Coleridge regarding narrative and epistemological implications for the relationship between gender and contamination, the study returns to Coleridge's evolving representation of evil in Chapter 3 through the confluence of imagination, gender, and fragmentation in "Kubla Khan," *Christabel*, and *Magnum Opus*. By examining Coleridge's resistance even to the direction of their epistemology, particularly that of Spinoza, this chapter challenges the long-held assumption that Coleridge's discovery of transcendental philosophy during his trip to Germany between the two parts of *Christabel* was the source of his liberation from British materialist philosophy.[42] This third chapter reexamines Coleridge's late poems and the prose he produced long after his poetic career waned, as he honed the articulation of his struggle against the British Enlightenment's stubborn binaries: masculine/feminine, subject/object, good/evil, his later prose grappling with the "death of the I" so that to "make the object one with us, we must become one with the object—*ergo*, an object. *Ergo*, the object must be itself a subject .... God is Love—that is, an object that is absolutely subject."[43] The trajectory of Coleridge's fragmented texts toward the *Magnum Opus* is a willful rupture of systematic binaries that stands against both the poetic and philosophical masculinist lineages. Coleridge represents female eros as a nondual energy that threatens the self-proclaimed hegemony of patriarchy. This feminine energy as a threat to patriarchy is nowhere more apparent than in *Christabel* and "Kubla Khan," both of which speak to Coleridge's complicated sexual/textual identity; his self-representation is feminine in its sensibility, contrasting the masculinity of Wordsworth and Southey; in a letter, Coleridge not only describes his

---

[42] McFarland dismisses as "bargain-basement Spinozism" the eighteenth-century British materialism that stemmed from Newton and Locke and whose "avatars," Hartley, Priestley, and Godwin, were "diminishing in importance as they manifested themselves in time" (169). Coleridge's wrestling with them complicates their importance beyond their contributions to the history of philosophy since it became the basis of the Wordsworthian poetics that Coleridge shaped and from which he then struggled to extricate himself precisely through his exposure to Spinoza, Kant, Schelling, and others.

[43] *Anima Poetae*, 249. Coleridge extends this 1819 expression of nondualism the following year to underscore his rejection of Wordsworthian dualism: "nature-worship ... is the trait in Wordsworth's poetic works that I most dislike" (qtd. in McFarland, 271). Wordsworth embodies all that Coleridge 's own poetics rebels against, albeit ambivalently: Wordsworth's adherence to not only epistemological dualism but to binaries that anchor him firmly in the Western philosophical tradition, including those of gender, in which the subject is always masculine, nature feminized, and women objectified. Chapter 1 develops Coleridge's contention with the good/evil binary.

poetics of "feeling and understanding," but he does so through the maternal image through which he aligns the creative process with his "labor pains" in producing "every line" of *Christabel* (qtd. in Halmi et al., 161, *CL* I: 613).

Though his *Magnum Opus* never evolved beyond fragmentary notes, Coleridge challenges the traditional binary of good and evil throughout his corpus. Coleridge repeatedly struggles with systematic literary and religiophilosophical positions that he represents both poetically and decries in prose as multiple subjectivities laying claim to a universal or absolute moral compass. Coleridge writes that the self for which feelings are "alienated and estranged from their rightful objects" is "the phantom by which the individual misrepresents the unity of his personal being" (*CW* II, 72, 76). Though this statement that denounces assumptions of selfhood from various religiophilosophical perspectives comes late in his career, it informs his writing throughout. For Coleridge, by contrast to these systems, the perverse camouflages itself as that hegemonic claim to morality. Playing with subjectivity, Coleridge includes multiple orthodox views in both poetry and prose, resulting in a universe in which the illicit traffics with the moral, the masculine with the feminine, the notion of the real with the unreal.

Focusing on *Frankenstein*, *Mathilda*, and *The Last Man*, Chapter 4 traces the trajectory of Mary Shelley's fiction through the lens of Coleridge's and Robinson's writings discussed in the preceding chapters, namely, by complicating traditional notions of motive and malevolence.

When her literary sphere is reconfigured apart from the familial-literary relationships—posthumously with Wollstonecraft, with Percy Shelley, and less often with Godwin, Mary Shelley emerges as a writer engaged across her career in the relationship among narrative fragmentation, contamination, and androgyny. This chapter examines Mary Shelley's deepening exploration of the relationship between gender and narrative contamination. The trajectory from *Frankenstein* through *Mathilda* to *The Last Man* engages with many of the same elements present in the works of Robinson and Coleridge. Scholarship has seldom examined the relationship between Robinson and Shelley; when it has done so, it often projects Robinson's acquaintance with Wollstonecraft onto the relationship between Robinson and Shelley. Through a comparison of Robinson's *Walsingham* and Shelley's *Frankenstein*, however, this chapter argues that the two writers dismantle the systematic binaries foundational to traditional storytelling. More revolutionary than Wollstonecraft's didactic fiction, *Walsingham* and *Frankenstein* destabilize the narrative control of their male protagonists, in turn destabilizing masculinist assumptions about the relationship between morality and gender. Just as these two novels share epistemological concerns that go to the heart of Enlightenment dualism, *Rime of the Ancient Mariner* is likewise foundational to *Frankenstein*; the novel subverts traditional linear narrative and scrambles traditional gender binaries as it engages with Coleridge's poetics. Shelley's metanarrative represents influence as contamination, or influenza. This connection is closest to the surface in *The Last Man*, in which the difference between moral and mortal disease collapses through Lionel Verney's narrative. His series of stories within the larger narrative parallels the spread of the plague, the "cureless evil" that destroys the world.

A notable idiosyncrasy of this study, to which this introduction has alluded in the paragraphs above, is its structure: besides weaving two chapters on Coleridge (Chapters 1 and 3) with chapters on Robinson and Coleridge (Chapter 2) and then on the three writers (Chapter 4), several works are revisited from the chapters' different angles. For instance, "Kubla Khan" is discussed first in Chapter 1 as working against Wordsworth's systematic binaries, then in Chapter 2 in conversation with Robinson's poetry regarding subjectivity and gender; Chapter 3 adds new focus on the poem's incoherence vis-à-vis its subversion of categorical imperatives as Coleridge moves toward his later dissection of the systematic binary of good and evil.

Similarly, Robinson's embedded poetry in *Walsingham* is discussed in Chapter 2 in conversation with Coleridge's lyrical ballads, and then in Chapter 4 vis-à-vis *Frankenstein*. This structure is a means of challenging the assumption of influence as linear, thereby mirroring the study's argument. These three writers share a vision of the artist's work as subversive, a dismantling of received ideas of one's relationship to the world. Ultimately, the recreation they individually represent holds polarities in tension, embodied in various ways by an androgynous Life-in-Death.

1

Coleridge's Gendered Revolt against Materialism: Textual Plasticity in "The Eolian Harp," *Rime of the Ancient Mariner*, and "Kubla Khan"

In 1807, two events marked Coleridge's rejection of the stultifying binaries that informed his personal and literary relationships during his early years in the Lake District: his separation from his wife, Sarah Fricker, and his ambivalent "To a Gentleman" following Wordsworth's recitation of *The Prelude*.[1] While the 1795 "Eolian Harp" had already marked Coleridge's doomed new marriage to Sarah as the forced yoking of two disparate sensibilities, the poem "to" Wordsworth reflects the impossibility of Coleridge's literary union with Wordsworth who insisted upon a subjectivity "wedded to" the "goodly universe."[2] "To a Gentleman,"

---

[1] That Wordsworth asked Coleridge not to publish the poem suggests his own discomfort with the acerbic criticism underlying the hyperbolic praise that gives way to more explicit ambivalence. See Halmi et al. for a detailed textual history of the poem, including the early phase of Wordsworth's poem that was to become, posthumously, *The Prelude* (200, n. 1).

[2] *The Recluse*, l. 306; Wordsworth underscores this binary relationship lines later: "How exquisitely the individual Mind/... to the external World / Is fitted" (*The Recluse*, ll. 316–19). Blake's marginalia on these lines in his copy of *The Excursion* are excoriating: "How exquisitely the individual Mind ... to the external World / Is fitted.—& how exquisitely too ... The external World is fitted to the Mind," Blake writes. "You shall not bring me down to believe such fitting & fitted I know better & Please your Lordship," then, "does not this Fit & is it not Fitting most Exquisitely too but to what not to Mind but to the Vile Body only & of its Laws of Good & Evil & its Enmities against Mind" (*The Excursion*, ll. 666–7). While this study does not equate Blake's unequivocal damning of Wordsworthian dualism to Coleridge's ambivalent relationship to Wordsworth, it is important in the twenty-first century to revisit earlier studies of the Coleridge / Wordsworth relationship vis-à-vis nature. Even Raimonda Modiano's 1985 study, for instance, commendable in its time for articulating a more adversarial epistemological relationship between the two poets than had been previously argued, is itself embroiled in the Romantic ideology that claims, "No one would contest the fact that ... of the two, Wordsworth was by far the greater poet of nature" (3). Until one accounts for the representation of gender and selfhood vis-à-vis nature in Coleridge's poetry and prose, a factor to which Modiano would not have had full access in 1986, his agonistic relationship with Wordsworth cannot be fully represented.

Coleridge's poetic response to hearing Wordsworth read his then thirteen-book "Poem on the Growth of an Individual Mind," appears on the surface to extoll Wordsworth's genius and to excoriate Coleridge himself. However, his ambivalence surfaces gradually; he follows the hyperbolic praise of the opening line's epithets, "Friend of the Wise! And Teacher of the Good!" with a sequence of dubious characterizations of Wordsworth's poem: the "Theme hard as high!"—itself damning praise—emerges as the essence of Wordsworth's inner/outer binary: "Now in thy inner life, and now abroad, / When Power stream'd from thee, and thy soul received / The light reflected, as a light bestow'd" (*To a Gentleman*, ll. 17–19). When Coleridge's self-pity does emerge in the poem, it has already been problematized by the inherent criticism of Wordsworth: "Fears, self-will'd, that shunn'd the eye of Hope; / And Hope that scarce would know itself from Fear" (*To a Gentleman*, ll. 67–8). Perhaps nowhere does Coleridge better articulate his perverse self-destructiveness, marked by its disruption of the categorical imperative to choose the path of righteousness.

The poem ends in ambiguous prayer that further complicates the earlier self-pity: "I sate, my being blended in one thought / (Thought was it? Or Aspiration? Or Resolve) …. / And when I rose, I found myself in prayer" (*To a Gentleman*, ll. 109–12). Neither confirming nor negating self-pity, this parenthetical catalogue of questions throws into ironic ambiguity the final line, in which Coleridge finds himself "in prayer." Coleridge appears as troubled as the Wedding Guest of *Rime of the Ancient Mariner*, left by the Mariner stunned and solitary rather than embracing the pious community represented by the "kirk"; "To a Gentleman," in turn, looks ahead to the "secondary imagination" of *Biographia Literaria* XIII; there, Coleridge declares that the artistic impulse is one of disassembly and which, significantly, precedes Coleridge's most direct denunciation of Wordsworthian "fancy" in chapter XIV. Returning to the end of "To a Gentleman" from the vantage point of Coleridge's definition of secondary imagination, *Biographia Literaria* can be seen to complicate further rather than resolve the catalogue of questions, the continuum from chapters XII to XIV marking the trajectory from Coleridge's rejection of associationism to the focus on Wordsworthian imagination reduced to "mere Fancy." Coleridge uses this term in chapter XIII to dismiss the associationism Wordsworth himself learned from Coleridge as a lower faculty than either primary or secondary imagination. Ending "To a Gentleman" in prayer is a variation on a pattern in Coleridge's conversation poems of ending with a benediction that ostensibly provides resolution but is made ironic in the context of the poems, including "The Eolian Harp," "Frost at Midnight," and "Dejection."

Two years after he wrote "To a Gentleman," Coleridge wrote in his notebook that the "organs of motion & outward action perform their functions at the stimulus of a galvanic fluid applied by the Will, not by the Spirit of Life that makes Soul and Body one" (*Notebooks* II, 2557). The passive voice of this statement draws out its self-contradiction: If outward actions result from a "galvanic fluid," it would appear that Will is of little consequence to what appears an instinctively biological cause-and-effect phenomenon. Not only is Will paradoxically passive in applying such fluid to stimulate motion, but Coleridge distinguishes Will from the "Spirit of Life" that, by contrast to Will, makes "Soul and Body one." The statement thus epitomizes Coleridge's pull toward nondualism as a "Spirit of Life" held in contradistinction with mechanistic corporeality.

Coleridge not only rejects materialism, but he ultimately moves beyond the German transcendentalism that had been his means of rejecting associationism. The 1819 statement can thus be seen as a reiteration of the paradox at the heart of Coleridge's definition of the artist's recreative work in chapter XIII of *Biographia Literaria*. Secondary imagination, Coleridge writes there, is the faculty that "dissolves, diffuses, dissipates, in order to re-create" (Engell and Bate I, 304). The violence inherent in dismembering the world of phenomena as a means of recreation has more in common with Mary Shelley's 1816 *Frankenstein* than with Wordsworthian poetics or the German transcendental philosophy that Coleridge ultimately rejects by chapter XIII.[3] Indeed, *Frankenstein* enacts the central idea of Coleridge's 1798 notebook entry, for it is Frankenstein's monomaniacal will that stimulates the "galvanic" tissue of body parts to recreate life in a ghastly parody of the artist's work.[4] The interplay of these three textual meditations on the creative act—the notebook

---

[3] I follow McFarland here, who argues with regard to Chapter XIII that imagination is "conceived by Coleridge as functioning in a way that does not grow out of his Schellingian paraphrases, in a way that in fact frees him from dependence on such borrowings. For Coleridge the function of the imagination was to emancipate the poetic concern from any Spinozistic implications" (157).
[4] So too could *Biographia Literaria* be Coleridge's return to the implications of *Rime* through the lens of *Frankenstein*. See Chapter 4 for the full discussion of this sequence.

entry, *Frankenstein*, *Biographia Literaria* XIII—demonstrates the potential for a literary engagement that defies the binary systems inherent in segregated studies of gender, genre, and generation.

Attending to Coleridge's wrestling with systematic binaries from the hindsight of *Biographia Literaria* shifts the discussion of his literary biography. Doing so in turn challenges the scholarly binary implicit in the separate categories of Coleridge's poetry and philosophy. Articulating the frustration for scholars in the pursuit of a full representation of Coleridge, Alethea Hayter notes that privileging certain passages to support one's interpretation ignores those that do not: "Try as one may, no book like the present one is quite objective. Quotations chosen, as one thinks, to illustrate the tendencies of someone else's intellect may in fact back-project their light on to shallow, odd, or unseemly corners of one's own mind" (217). Of course, this dictum applies to all literary analysis in varying degrees; however, it resonates particularly for Coleridge's multifaceted oeuvre.[5] A double-edged consideration of his corpus does not mean blending the two disciplines as though they constitute a harmonious whole. Instead, a more accurate representation emerges of Coleridge's struggle to resist the common foundation upon which the Western traditions of poetry and the religiophilosophical rest, out of which, in turn, emerges his creation of modern literary criticism. This chapter returns to Coleridge's early literary productions to find the seeds of resistance to the very materialist traditions even as he ambivalently embraced them in poetry and prose.

Dilation and Contraction in "The Eolian Harp"

A starting point for studying Coleridge's early ambivalence toward British materialist philosophy and its attendant binaries is his 1795 poem, "Effusion XXXV," revised as "The Eolian Harp" in 1803, in which Coleridge describes

---

[5] This problem is even suggested by a plaque on a Coleridge residence that refers to him as "poet and philosopher"; through the lens of Coleridge's creation of modern literary criticism, one can see that Coleridge's nondualism brings together poetry and philosophy.

a momentary liberation from the constriction of a "world *so* hush'd" (l. 10). A tight-fitting subjectivity that opens this so-called honeymoon poem is the casualty of a marriage with erotic, epistemological, and artistic implications.

Though the most overt marriage in the poem is to his new wife, a "pensive" Sarah Fricker, there are even more vexed, albeit less explicit, marriages troubling Coleridge here that would take him more than two decades from which he would extricate himself: namely, those to materialist philosophy and, by extension, to William Wordsworth's poetics of memory. Here as well as in his other fragments, Coleridge revolts against rather than seeks to fulfill the classical standards of wholeness, harmony, and coherence, a view that runs counter to traditional readings such as that of J. C. C. Mays, who suggests that Coleridge revised "The Eolian Harp" in 1797, 1817, and 1828 "to wrestle its components into a more balanced whole by means of large excisions and interpolations," suggesting that "unsuccess … drove him onward to the end" (qtd. in Halmi et al., 10).

Coleridge's belated divorce decree is found buried midway through *Biographia Literaria*, twenty years later. At the end of the first volume, chapter XIII, Coleridge articulates in two brief paragraphs a dissection of imagination distinguishing that which exists in all human perception and that which is only to be found in the artist. Though secondary imagination has already been mentioned, it is worth examining in the entirety of its definition vis-à-vis primary imagination and fancy:

> The primary IMAGINATION I hold to be the living Power and prime Agent of all human Perception, and as a repetition in the finite mind of the eternal act of creation in the infinite I AM. The secondary I consider as an echo of the former, co-existing with the conscious will, yet still as identical with the primary in the *kind* of its agency, and differing only in *degree*, and in the *mode* of its operation. It dissolves, diffuses, dissipates, in order to re-create; or where this process is rendered impossible, yet still at all events it struggles to idealize and to unify. (Engell and Bate I, 304)

While secondary imagination is an "echo" of the primary, Coleridge distinguishes it as a recreative faculty. That the process may be "rendered impossible" is an ironic reference to his own inability to embody the poetical character as he represents it, for instance, in the final stanza of "Kubla Khan."[6] The statement that follows this definition of primary and secondary imagination is most damning of both Wordsworthian poetics and his own earlier embrace of associationism: the secondary imagination, that recreative faculty of artists, soars above the "fixities and definites" of mere fancy, relegated to a level below both primary and secondary imagination and therefore a derogatory term to which Coleridge finally reduces "the law of association"; Coleridge infers that Wordsworth's "ordinary memory," as mere Fancy, receives "all its materials ready made [sic]" (*Biographia Literaria*, 489).

The nature of the divide between Coleridge and Wordsworth can be foreseen in their earliest dialogues in prose and poetry. That Coleridge called his 1796 poems "Effusions" speaks to his early resistance to Wordsworth's poetics.[7] Coleridge's source for the term may be William Preston whom Halmi et al. quote as defining "love poetry as a 'spontaneous effusion of a mind wholly occupied by a single idea, careless of rules, little studious of poetic fame, and desirous only of expressing its emotions'" (5, n. 3). There are several ideas in Preston's statement that reverberate with irony as Coleridge and then Wordsworth echo them.

Defending his poems against charges of egotism in his 1796 Preface to *Poems on Various Subjects*, Coleridge distinguishes "effusion," or the outpouring of one's subjectivity, from egotism that, he claims, "is to be condemned then only when it offends against time and place as in an History or an Epic Poem. To censure it in a Monody or Sonnet is almost as absurd as to dislike a circle for being round" (qtd in Halmi et al., 4). Here Coleridge suggests that, whereas subjectivity should not enter narrative, it defines lyrical poetry. That he compares the latter to a circle is telling: Unlike traditional narrative, the lyrical is outside the realm of time and space. The circle image suggests that lyrical poetry is more than subjective; it is nonbinary, a merging of subject and object. In light of Coleridge's distinction between a nonbinary subjectivity and egotism, when one revisits Wordsworth's often-cited definition of poetry in the 1800 Preface to *Lyrical Ballads*, the "spontaneous overflow of powerful

---

[6] See the discussions later in this chapter and in Chapter 3 of Coleridge's nondual gendering of the poetical character in the final stanza of that poem.
[7] Although Wordsworth has "Effusion" poems as well, the sequence of these Prefaces suggests Wordsworth's resistance to an unfettered effusion of sensibility.

feelings" that "takes its origin from emotion recollected in tranquility," the distance between the two poets becomes pronounced (*Selected Poems and Prefaces*, 460).

Wordsworth's "overflow" can be seen as a pointed substitution for Coleridge's "effusion" that connotes outpouring, while Wordsworth's "overflow" suggests excess vis-à-vis a vessel of containment that would be a symbol for the discursive faculty that thinks "long and deeply" according to Wordsworth's definition of "good poetry" (448). That the poet "recollects" transgressive emotion in tranquility suggests the reasoning mind re-contains and therefore controls it.[8] Thus, whether or not a conscious allusion to Wordsworth's didacticism that reins in Wordsworth's own effusion, Coleridge underscores the gulf between their poetics when he decries "one species of egotism which is truly disgusting; not that which leads us to communicate our feelings to others, but that which would reduce the feelings of others to an identity with our own," then citing Churchill's "Effusion on Effusion *pour* away" (5).[9]

Framing "Effusion XXXV" (hereafter referred to as "The Eolian Harp") with this statement distinguishing egotism from the outpouring of subjectivity endows it with particular irony as it opens with a newly married couple sitting outside their small "cot," the shortened form of "cottage" suggesting the diminished life this new marriage represents by contrast to the expanding center of the poem when the persona takes imaginative flight. With his bride, Sarah, resting her head on his arm, at the opening of the poem, the narrator scans a tepid and stagnant vista whose "Jasmin and Myrtle" are conventional symbols of innocent love, Myrtle specifically associated in *Paradise Lost* with Eden.[10] It is a short-sighted gaze that moves only from this prelapsarian garden to the anticlimactic and neutered banality of "yon bean-field" (l. 10).

---

[8] Wordsworth typically swerves from moments of Coleridgean effusion with expository transitions, perhaps one of the most famous in "Tintern Abbey," just after his moment of intersubjectivity, "a sense sublime / Of something far more deeply interfused" (ll. 96–7). Lines later, he writes, "Therefore am I still / A lover of the meadows and the woods," determined to redraw the line between the subject and the outer world (ll. 103–4).

[9] As Halmi et al. explain, Churchill's reference to John Langhorne's *Effusions of Friendship and Fancy* is satirical. However, this tonal difference wouldn't diminish Coleridge's unironic use of the term in the thirty-six poems that follow this Preface, in spite of being grouped with a "separate title page and motto" (5, n. 3; 3).

[10] Book IV, 694–9. Cited in Halmi et al. (17, n. 2).

Suddenly, the sound of the Eolian Harp, "that simplest Lute" in the casement of the cottage window, shifts the speaker's awareness to an expansive, far more erotic marriage of subjectivities. The blending of breeze and harp creates "delicious surges [that] sink and rise"; at first the speaker appears to use the "long sequacious notes of the Eolian Harp" to seduce Sarah, hoping to melt her stiff reserve (l. 19). But as his vision expands, he leaves her behind along with the English garden, whose Jasmine and Myrtle give way to "birds of Paradise" (l. 25). Not only are the latter exotic, but the "Paradise" they represent is one associated with "witchery" as opposed to the subdued Myrtle's reference to Milton's Eden (l. 21).

Coleridge's replacement of the Judeo-Christian garden of prelapsarian innocence with a demonic realm goes beyond even the suggestion of the Miltonic story of the original fall to a more subversive shift from the piety embodied by Sarah, "Meek Daughter in the Family of Christ" (l. 46). The line between harp and breeze, subject and object, blurs as the poet is released from the quotidian parameters of cot and bean-field. This new gaze takes in a "Faery Land," a universe of "animated nature" moved by "one intellectual Breeze" (ll. 23, 39). Its "floating witchery" is demonic, suggested by the "sunbeams" that "dance like *diamonds* on the main" (ll. 20, 29, italics added). Defying the laws of materialism that rule the pious realm of cot and beanfield, this new subjectivity is not only a synesthesia blending sound, touch, smell, and vision in "*Melodies* of honey-dropping flowers"; it is a subjectivity for which the laws of materialism cannot account, indistinguishable from the phenomenal world (l. 23).[11]

As suddenly as the speaker's subjectivity dilates outward to a "plastic and vast" universe, however, this vision of a flexible universe contracts as Sarah darts an admonishing gaze at him (l. 39). By setting the "pensive" subjectivity of Sarah against the persona's poetic gaze, Coleridge complicates the idea of a "plastic" nature originated by the seventeenth-century philosopher Ralph Cudworth. Arguing against atheism, Cudworth had concluded that "there is a

---

[11] A variant of the Eolian Harp appears proleptically in Leibniz, who rejects Spinoza among "certain ancient and more recent thinkers [who] have asserted … that God is a spirit diffused throughout the whole universe, which animates organic bodies wherever it meets them, just as the wind produces music in organ pipes" (*Coleridge and the Pantheist Tradition*, qtd. in McFarland, 168).

plastic nature under" God "which, as an inferior and subordinate instrument, doth drudgingly execute that part of his providence"; Cudworth asserts that "it consists in the regular and orderly motion of matter."[12]

Contemporary scholarship has attributed Coleridge's revision of Cudworth's imagery of a plastic universe to Coleridge's influence by Joseph Priestley's materialism. Building on this assumption of Coleridge's influence by Priestley, it is commonly maintained that not until the 1817 *Biographia Literaria* did Coleridge express "skepticism of the use of the breeze and harp analogy by materialists, including probably Priestley," whose materialist philosophy "denied the common distinction among solid, impenetrable matter and spirit."[13] However, closer reading of the earlier poetry suggests that Coleridge's "plastic" universe is yet more radical than that in Cudworth and Priestley. Coleridge uses the term "monad" to describe "an energy in nature" in his early poem, "Religious Musings": "And ye of plastic power, that interfus'd / Roll thro' the grosser and material mass/In organizing surge! ... (And what if Monads of the infinite mind?)" (qtd. in Halmi, et al., ll. 424–6). The term suggests Coleridge's early pull away from the dualism of the materialist influence. Ironically, Coleridge seeks to divorce himself from the early phrase in an 1814 letter to Cottle in which he writes that it "may easily be misconstrued into Spinosism [*sic*]; and therefore, though it is susceptible of a pious and justifiable interpretation, I should by no means now use such a phrase. I was very young when I wrote that poem, and my religious feelings were more settled than my theological notions" (*CL*, iii, 467). Coleridge's use of the Eolian Harp image underscores that, in spite of what will be seen as a disclaimer in Coleridge's letter, Cottle may have held a similar function here for Coleridge to Sarah Fricker's in "The Eolian Harp," namely, projecting the self-censorship of the "unregenerate" mind.[14]

Although Coleridge may be serious regarding his self-flagellation here, there is irony in the word "unregenerate," as it is linguistically twice removed from

---

[12] Halmi et al., 19, n. 7. See also n. 15 of this chapter, below, elaborating the genealogy of the term "plasticity."

[13] This scholarship cites Priestley's argument that matter was composed of "physical points only" and that "nature and human consciousness were moved by God's energy" (Halmi et al., 19, n. 7).

[14] Halmi et al. note that, despite the fact that Bruno and Leibniz used the term before Coleridge, they instead trace the early use through Cudworth whose writing referred to Pythagoras's use (34, n. 4). This terminological genealogy suggests yet another level of influence/contamination that fascinated Coleridge.

creation, or generation: he should be "reborn" but he is not so. What makes Coleridge unregenerate is his pull toward nondualism that he represents as a sexual deviance from Sara's chaste path. Coleridge's subversive gendering of the nondual is a concern that has not been incorporated into theological/religious/philosophical studies because they tend to ignore the poetic intersection of subjectivity and gender that are, for Coleridge, inextricably related. Coleridge moves past the traditional binaries of the honeymoon poem that echo the Petrarchan sonnet's male subject trying unsuccessfully to woo the female object. He thereby plunges the reader into a radical shift in sexual dynamics. Doing more than reverse the gender roles, Coleridge likens himself to the traditionally female instrument played by the breeze: the breeze itself is liberated from the feminine role of the male poetic tradition, with "witchery" that is the agent of subversion.

In what Coleridge represents as her cold disdain toward her new husband, Sarah's reticence now appears to suggest more than passive resistance. The poem is the earliest of the "conversation poems," a genre whose creation has been attributed to Coleridge. Though scholars have noted the androgyny of the harp image at the center of this poem, the ostensible meaning of conversation as discourse would be ironic if it only pertained to the two humans in the poem, their only communication exclusively nonverbal and at cross-purposes at that. Instead, Coleridge plays on the connotations of both erotic and spiritual converses.[15] The last lines of "The Eolian Harp" thus do not merely return to the simplicity of the muted world before the expanded vision; they rather give way to the speaker's self-flagellation for his unregenerate mind that could tread so dangerously into unhallowed terrain, far from the humble path Sarah represents. Her leaning on him at the opening of the poem now appears less the passive "Maid half-yielding" to her lover, a gesture that had spurred him to personify the Harp which would, wishfully, seduce her. Now, her earlier "pensiveness" is not just the distraction of a lover who is not fully engaged with her new husband; her own subjectivity is reduced to the pious materiality of

---

[15] See the *Oxford English Dictionary's* (*OED's*) multiple definitions of the noun "converse" related to both spiritual conversation and sexual consorting. http://www.oed.com/view/Entry/40760?rskey=5IMsNl&result=1#eid (accessed August 5, 2020). A commonality among Coleridge's conversation poems is, in fact, that there is no conversation as discourse taking place; rather the spiritual and erotic converse break free of the speaker's solitariness in such poems as "Frost at Midnight" and "This Lime-Tree Bower My Prison."

the nonimaginative mind. As her subjectivity diminishes that of the speaker to a passive and "indolent" instrument for demonic thought, her leaning on him now suggests a prop to keep him upright (ll. 10, 39). Referring to Sarah's "silent but active presence in the poem," Alan Richardson reads her look of "mild reproof" as "inspiring him to abandon [the harp's] intimations of pantheism"; however, I prefer to work against the linearity of such reading so that, even at this early phase of Coleridge's career, he can be seen to experiment with structure, the center of the poem contaminating the frame, which now rings hollow (69).[16]

The poetic trajectory of contraction, expansion, and contraction as early as "The Eolian Harp" thus suggests the discord underlying even Coleridge's early weddedness to materialist philosophy. Coleridge's early embrace of associationism has traditionally been demonstrated by the 1798 "Frost at Midnight" in which "the stranger," a flap of soot on the fireplace grate, triggers Coleridge's memories of lonely school days when he had hoped for a visitor.[17] Looking back to Coleridge's 1795 "Eolian Harp" three years before "Frost at Midnight," however, a yet more complicated relationship with associationism emerges. The sound of the Eolian Harp triggers not memory but the release from this tripartite, repressive marriage: to Sarah's lack of erotic responsiveness, to the materialism that is the hallmark of associationism, and to the dualistic foundation of a patriarchal notion of creativity that sets male subjectivity against the objectified female. Thus, even at this early phase of his poetic vocation, when he is writing "The Eolian Harp," Coleridge paradoxically works against materialism even as he is honing it. Tracing his ambivalence toward materialism to "The Eolian Harp" exposes the triple valence of erotic, epistemological, and creative "plasticity" for Coleridge. In spite of his early

---

[16] Though McFarland's study has been criticized for referring to pantheism as a tradition, it seems to me that McFarland's label stems from the perspective of late eighteenth-century German philosophy. See Colmer's 1971 review of McFarland, in which Colmer notes McFarland's simplifying such "complex philosophical background" such as the "contrasting systems of Spinoza and Jacobi" (287). As detailed in the Introduction, this study distinguishes nondualism from pantheism based on their conflicting implications about systematic binaries: in nondualism they are held in tension, while pantheism suggests a unifying consciousness or energy underlying discrete objects.

[17] The retrospective irony of the poem becoming the inspiration for *Tintern Abbey* adds yet more complexity to Wordsworth's struggle with intersubjectivity (see n. 8 above). Wordsworth's meditation on the relationship between memories of an idyllic "thoughtless" youth and the paralyzing self-doubt of his adult state in turn become the prototype for his subsequent odes upon which he dilated in *The Prelude* for over thirty years.

claims to admiring Newton, Coleridge's plasticity is the anti-Newtonian, anti-Deistic upheaval of a universe in motion.

Such plasticity not only defies patriarchy and Newtonian fixity but also overturns Wordsworth's poetics founded on patriarchy, dualism, and the associationism with which Coleridge himself had shaped Wordsworth's career. Coleridge's revisions of *Christabel* straddle these periods of early associationism, the influence of German Romanticism, and the creation of an original poetics. Its textual history is thus pivotal in understanding the nature of his emerging poetics, particularly the part gender comes to play. Coleridge's 1799 description of starlings in flight emblematizes the plasticity of a universe in motion, closer to the Vedic notion of *spanda*, etymologically linked to the English "expand," than it is to the Newtonian fixity of time and space:

> Born along like smoke, mist—like a body unindued with voluntary Power / –now it shaped itself into a circular area, inclined—now they formed a Square—now a Globe—now from complete orb into an Ellipse—then oblongated into a Balloon with the Car suspended, now a concave Semicircle; still expanding, or contracting, thinning or condensing, now glimmering and shivering, now thickening, deepening, blackening!
>
> (*CN*, 39)

Coleridge here plays with geometric figures associated with the mathematics of the late eighteenth century in its mapping of the universe. His starlings are shape-shifters, as Gavin Sourgen has noted, their flight suggesting the freedom from the space/time continuum the narrator of "Eolian Harp" can only imagine fleetingly, returning chastised to the material realm at the end of the poem.

Androgyny and Recreation in "Kubla Khan"

Female figures in Coleridge's poetry, both human and symbolic, are androgynous by conventional standards. As powerful and often violent recreators, their nondual subjectivity contrasts the masculinist objectification of the feminine as either nurturing creators and sustainers of life or sexually devouring. These androgynous figures share a subversive nondualism that Coleridge at times sets against an ironically prudish male narrator, whose subjectivity is eclipsed by the subverting female. Though in some poems, including "The Eolian Harp," the self-deprecating male persona returns in an end-frame to assert an unconvincing and conventional closure, Coleridge's authorial presence in his texts is thus distinct from male subjectivities that are pulled toward the powerful feminine but tragically divided from it. This is the case of the belatedly introduced poet figure of "Kubla Khan."

In turn, Coleridge complicates these representations of ambivalence through a fictitious textual layering in such works as *Rime of the Ancient Mariner*, whose marginal glosses added to the 1834 edition deflect attention from the text by the often-obtuse fictional editor of a pretended ancient text. With this device, the ironic flip side of plagiarism, Coleridge attributes to fictional characters either his original and subversive ideas or censoring voices as is the 1834 "editor" of *Rime*.[18] The two most important of these textual red herrings are the visitor from Porlock, whom the equally fictitious editor of "Kubla Khan" blames for the fragmentary nature of the poem and, with significance for Coleridge's anxiety about articulating his notion of the artist's recreative faculty vis-à-vis the lesser Fancy that relies on associationism, the "friend" whom Coleridge credits for the hierarchy of mental faculties in chapter XIII of *Biographia Literaria*, sweeping away all the plagiarisms of German philosophy that precede it.

Coleridge's authorial presence eludes detection through the multiple personae in both Preface and poem that comprise "Kubla Khan." That the fictional editor of "Kubla Khan" refers to the poem as a "fragment" leads him to his rationale for publishing a work fundamentally flawed, "rather as a psychological curiosity, than on the ground of any supposed *poetic* merits" (qtd. in Halmi et al., 180). The fictional editor of the Preface describes a self-effacing poet, the object of great interest by an unnamed famous poet. Coleridge's authorial voice creates an ironic slippage in that first sentence among three figures in the opening statement. He builds on this decomposed subject by inviting the reader to challenge the binary between the poetic and the psychological/philosophical that was beginning to form in Coleridge's day and remains entrenched in Coleridge scholarship, as the introduction

---

[18] See the Introduction to this study for discussion of the relationship between Coleridge's plagiarism and the creation of a pseudotextual history.

above details.[19] Read ironically, then, Coleridge's authorial voice behind that of the editor of the Preface suggests that the fragment is a paradoxical achievement in what the conventional editor describes as his failure to find coherence. Coleridge further suggests that the fragment's poetic merits are not separable from the psychological. It is thus more than what the editor dismisses as a mere "curiosity." Coleridge was to systematize this paradox in *Biographia Literaria*, the year after he added the Preface and the poem's final stanza culminating in an androgynous figure of failure/achievement, wholeness/fragmentation.

The Preface to "Kubla Khan" expands on the "psychological curiosity" of the fragment by telling of the poem's birth, a dream parented by laudanum and two sentences from "Purchas's Pilgrimage" that produce the opening stanza of the poem. The editor's point of view on the interruption of the author's writing is pity, suggested by Coleridge's appending yet another fragment by way of consolation: a stanza from his own "The Picture, or the Lover's Resolution":

> Stay awhile,
> Poor youth! Who scarcely dar'st lift up thine eyes—
> The stream will soon renew its smoothness, soon
> The visions will return! (l. 181)

The promise of a return of the vision remains unfulfilled in the poem that follows, however. That Coleridge added the third stanza along with the Preface containing this extract suggests his intention to create their tension.

Reading back from *Biographia Literaria* XIII, on secondary imagination, to the final stanza of "Kubla Khan," this extract from "The Picture" suggests that it is not a mirror image that returns but a recreation that assembles the fragments paradoxically, seemingly incoherent though uncontrollable from the perspective of the male poet as a "poor youth." Indeed, following the stanza from "The Picture," the editor relays to the reader that the author "purposed to finish for himself what had been originally, as it were, given to him"; but, he adds, "to-morrow is yet to come" (l. 181). The editor suggests the failure of the author

---

[19] Coleridge's writing on Shakespeare is one of Ernest Jones's literary sources for his concept of decomposition (26).

to "finish" the poem, "the fragments dim of lovely forms," is thus impossible to bring "trembling back [and] unite" to make the pool a mirror (l. 181).

Coleridge often associates nondual nature with androgyny toward which he is pulled even as he resists it. His identification with the nonbinary in gender is not one of passivity, therefore, but a powerful eros that disrupts patriarchal repression, as seen in "The Eolian Harp," where this androgyny emerges through the harp image at the center of the poem. Comprising the original poem, the first two stanzas describe Kubla's creation of the pleasure dome, a masculinist enterprise of domination in which he seeks to control nature that he measures and "girdles" round. However, in the second stanza, an erotically feminized nature erupts explosively in the form of the "sacred river," wailing like a woman for her demon lover. This second stanza of "Kubla Khan" overtly represents nature not only as a female erotic energy but as nondual. She is both sacred and demonic, by contrast to Kubla's objectifying point of view toward nature in the first stanza, where she appears as passive in apparently giving up the beauties of her "fertile ground" (qtd. in Halmi, et al., l. 6). Comparing the first of the two stanzas of "Kubla Khan" to Wordsworth's "Nutting" illustrates Coleridge's argument with associationist psychology in general and Wordsworth specifically. Kubla, the male aggressor, shares with the narrator of "Nutting" an eroticized desire to dominate nature. In "Nutting," the poet-figure details a memory of his boyhood adventure to look for hazelnuts. When he gets to "one dear nook," however, he ravages nature's bower in thinly disguised terms of rape:

> Forcing my way, I came to one dear nook
>
> Unvisited …. A virgin scene!—A little while I stood,
>
> Breathing with such suppression of the heart
>
> ….
>
> Then up I rose,
>
> And dragged to earth both branch and bough, with crash
>
> And merciless ravage: and the shady nook
>
> Of hazels, and the green and mossy bower,
>
> Deformed and sullied, patiently gave up
>
> Their quiet being. (*Selected Poems and Prefaces*, ll. 16–48)

The most striking difference between this moment in "Nutting" and Kubla's dominion over nature is that Wordsworth's poem is a memory of being a boy who violently desecrates the passive virginal bower. Wordsworth ends his poem with a coda in which the male persona, strangely, turns to a "Maiden," uttering a warning that she should "move along these shades / In gentleness of heart; with gentle hand /Touch—for there is a spirit in the woods (*Selected Poems and Prefaces*, ll. 54–6). By contrast to the Coleridgean pattern of male personae inadequate to the recreative power of the feminine, Wordsworth simultaneously calls attention to his difference from his auditor in gendered terms (the Maiden is closer to the virgin landscape than to him, her human companion), yet ironically conflates her with him by warning her not to behave as he has, thus creating the dissonance of the final lines.[20] There is no indication until this moment that she apparently has been walking with him as he reflects on the memory. He warns her to "move along these shades / In gentleness of heart … for there is a spirit in the woods." This male subjectivity is so authoritarian that he even projects, ludicrously, the possibility of this "dearest Maiden" going on a rampage whose imagery so vividly subscribes to the traditional gender binary that would have her in the object rather than subject position.[21]

"Kubla Khan," by contrast to Wordsworth's "Nutting," shifts the subjectivity in the second stanza from Kubla to a powerful female nature he likens to a "woman wailing for her demon–lover!" When a "mighty fountain" bursts from its "deep romantic chasm," this paradoxically holy and savage energy does not merely destroy Kubla's pleasure dome but reconfigures it to its own paradoxical and androgynous vision, "a miracle of rare device /A sunny pleasure dome with caves of ice" (qtd. in Halmi et al., 35–6). This is no virginal bower in Wordsworth's nature, but rather a representation of the sublime that is distinctly female. The power of such a recreative feminine principle

---

[20] The "dearest Maiden," a young virgin, in other words, who is probably his sister, Dorothy, follows the pattern of "Tintern Abbey" in which the reader is not aware of Dorothy's presence until the end of the poem. There, she is described as "wild" in her innocence, a state in which Wordsworth would have her remain (*Selected Poems and Prefaces*, l. 119).

[21] Similar to the end of "Nutting," "Tintern Abbey" oddly eroticizes nature vis-à-vis the maidenly Dorothy, saying "Nature never did betray / The heart that loved her," the difference being that Wordsworth suggests nature is a lover rather than a virgin in "Tintern Abbey" (*Selected Poems and Prefaces*, ll. 122–3).

is thus not only antithetical to Wordsworth's poetics but to Burke's notion of the sublime as a masculine aesthetic. In this way, as Chapter 4 details, "Kubla Khan" is closer to Mary Shelley's *Frankenstein* in its complicating notions of masculinist subjectivity vis-à-vis creativity than it is to the Wordsworthian poetics insisting upon masculinist subjectivity defined in relationship to a passively feminized nature.

Coleridge not only defers the introduction of the poet's subjectivity until the third and final stanza but does so with the conditional "could I revive" the song of the Abyssinian maid; Coleridge returns to this undercurrent of poetic failure in *Biographia Literaria* XIII's definition of secondary imagination, an ideal "when rendered impossible, yet still at all events it struggles to idealize and to unify" that which it has "dissolved, diffused, and dissipated" (Engell and Bate I, 304). Here, in stanza 3 of "Kubla Khan," he can only hope to embrace the powerful, feminine energy suggested with the image of his "flashing eyes and floating hair," as a means to embody a poetical character who would inspire "holy dread," simultaneously daemonic and divine (qtd. in Halmi et al., 50, 52).[22]

Paradoxically, then, Coleridge's poem about poetic failure captures the complexity of what he would come to call secondary imagination in *Biographia Literaria*. Coleridge "grasped the notion of a subconscious mental life and varying levels of consciousness," writes Kathleen Coburn, attributing to him the coinage of the term "psycho-analytical"; yet she nevertheless compartmentalizes Coleridge's texts into separate vocations: poet, "critic of science," "social and political critic"; "educationist" and theological critic (4–5). "Kubla Khan" epitomizes Coleridge's plumbing the depths of the human psyche but also challenges such a notion of Coleridge as Renaissance man; instead, he portrays a male subject who refuses identification with patriarchy and whose poetic ideal is androgynous defiance of the categorical imperative. "Kubla Khan" thus traces a pattern that recurs in Coleridge's poetics, from the dualistic arrogance of patriarchy that casts out and represses the feminine to its disruption by female nature's unleashed power, to his own ambivalence toward the ideal poet's harnessing of the paradoxical sacred and demonic potential as

---

[22] As Halmi et al. point out, the floating hair is traditionally associated with Apollo in Virgil's *The Aeneid* and Horace's Odes. However, the classical allusion does not preclude Coleridge's overlaying it with significance from within his own poem, in this case, with the female figures that come to dominate the poem.

a means to unite eros and epistemology. The evolution of Coleridge's poetic structure evolves from "The Eolian Harp" to the fragmentary "Kubla Khan," a developing rejection of the earlier frame that controlled the opening out of the center's androgynous vision.

Yet Wordsworth haunts Coleridge's imagination in the very failure of Wordsworth's poetics to embrace the female. One can see Wordsworth's recurring presence as an element of Coleridge's own divided subjectivity, a crisis of imagination that Coleridge's enigmatic 1800 dream vision about a woman identified in the dream as "Ebon Ebon Thalud" betrays:

> Morning–a most frightful Dream of a Woman whose features were blended with darkness catching hold of my right eye & attempting to pull it out—I caught hold of her arm fast—a horrid feel—Wordsworth cried out aloud to me hearing my scream—heard his cry and thought it cruel he did not come / but did not wake till his cry was repeated a third time—the woman's name Ebon Ebon Thalud—When I awoke, my right eyelid swelled. (*Notebooks* I, November 28, 848)

Before turning to the problem of interpreting the dream itself, it is useful to examine the surrounding notebook entries as they reveal the dream's deeper, epistemological significance than has hitherto been discussed, framing it with blankness in the surrounding descriptions of snow and fog. The day following the dream, for instance, Coleridge writes of the "uniformity of the Snow every where [*sic*]—The sameness of Grasmere Sombrous—"; the following entry, apparently the same day, Coleridge writes, "Losing all sight of Land, & still meeting the Billows working out of the West" (*Notebooks* I, November 28, 849, 850). Taken together, Coleridge's recreative impulse emerges out of erasing landscape, a stark contrast from Wordsworthian poetics in which objects in material nature trigger memory, a distinction Coleridge was to articulate seventeen years later in *Biographia Literaria*.

There has been a range of interpretations of this brief notebook entry about "Ebon Ebon Thalud," many returning to the influence of opium, much as the readings of "Kubla Khan" have.[23] The name "Ebon Ebon Thalud," specifically, has been broken down as darkness (repeated in "ebon"), "thalud" as suggesting

---

[23] See Ward, Wayans, and Hayter. Holmes, following Coburn (*Notebooks* VI, 848), traces the "sinister name" to "a drug-dealer Ebn Thaher" in *The Arabian Nights* (*Early Visions*, 293; on Coburn and

"Talmud" or for some, "salud," Spanish or Italian for "health." Blending "Talmud" and "health" in this subconscious coinage suggests the irony of patriarchal law's repression of this dark female power, an agonistic struggle manifesting through the orthodox Wordsworth and the powerfully dark, female energy that echoes Coleridgean nature in "Kubla Khan." That Coleridge awakens with his right eye swollen shows not only how opium can unleash the forbidden but how the pain itself plays a part in the psychodrama.[24]

But as in the case of the Preface to "Kubla Khan," the pretext of opium is relevant as a catalyst to liberate Coleridge from the constrictions of late eighteenth-century Enlightenment patriarchy and its host of binaries.[25] Here, he attempts to hold back the woman who is trying to pull out his right eye whereupon Wordsworth, whose scream blends with Coleridge's, does not come to Coleridge's aid. The missing subject in these fragments, separated by dashes, is central to interpreting the dream. Particularly significant is the sequence, "Wordsworth cried out aloud to me hearing my scream—heard his cry ..." As with the Preface to "Kubla Khan," whether pretext or not, the daze of being woken out of sleep or a narcotic stupor is an opportunity to dispense with traditional subjectivity: he does not write, "'I' heard his cry" nor does he write, "but 'I' did not wake." Coleridge understands what psychoanalysis would theorize a century later about the self being decomposed in dreams.[26] Without the centrality of ego, Coleridge thus splinters into Wordsworth, whom

---

others, see Grant, 128, n. 29). Though the literary allusion may be the starting point, the question this study addresses is what the dream comes to represent in Coleridge's "secondary imagination" that recreates with the fragments of textual life and human relationships. Thanks to Grevel Lindop for suggesting the importance of this dream fragment for my argument.

[24] Freudian reading of the poem suggests castration through the Oedipal image of blinding as castration; that Coleridge's right arm cannot successfully fend off the pain may not necessarily gesture to a masculinist psychology in the vein of Freud but rather the diffusion of Coleridge's sense of self in pain, narcotic, and its resulting poetry.

[25] According to Hayter, Coleridge "insisted, over and over again, that it was not, and never had been, the hope of pleasure, but always the fear of pain, that made him take opium" (196). The phrase "late eighteenth-century Enlightenment" is used throughout this study to distinguish the specific revolt among Coleridge and many of his contemporaries, particularly Robinson and Shelley, from a monolithic Enlightenment, a distinction well made by such scholars as Gertrude Himmelfarb and Ian Hunter, the latter beginning his study by noting, "Despite the recognition of different national, cultural, and religious enlightenments, and regardless of recurrent doubts about the utility of the concept itself, a dominant form of intellectual history remains committed to the reality of a single process or project of Enlightenment, even if this is something that has to be synthesized from diverse intellectual expressions, institutional settings, and historical locales" (Hunter, 1).

[26] See Ernest Jones for the psychoanalytic use of the term, "decomposition" and its literary implications.

at this time Coleridge understands to be bound by a "natural piety" founded on associationism; himself; and the female, Ebon Ebon Thalud.[27]

The androgynously splintered subjectivity in this dream provides an opportunity to revisit Coleridge's statement, "a great mind must be androgynous," often quoted out of the context of the essay in his 1832 *Table Talk*. Returning the phrase to its context reveals how gender and epistemology inform each other in Coleridge's poetics:

> I have known *strong* minds, with imposing, undoubting, Cobbett-like manners; but I have never met a *great* mind of this sort. And of the former, they are at least as often wrong as right. The truth is, a great mind must be androgynous. Great minds—Swedenborg's, for instance—are never wrong, but in consequence of being in the right, but imperfectly. (199)

Coleridge disavows strength of mind as unintegrated, intellectual virility, the polemical correctness embodied by William Cobbett, the radical reformer. Yet Swedenborg, exemplifying a great and androgynous mind, can only be imperfectly right since Swedenborg expounded upon his counter-empirical visions in the pseudolanguage of Bacon and Locke.[28] Thus, Coleridge writes in the next paragraph, "A philosopher's ordinary language and admissions ... are as his watch compared with his astronomical timepiece. He sets the former by the town-clock, not because he believes it right, but because his neighbours and his cook go by it" (199). Coleridge equates the androgynous mind with greatness because it rejects the masculinist ideal of strength that is self-limiting when connected to the "philosopher's" need to be correct according to the status quo rather than his paradoxically nonlinear/nonspatial place in the cosmos.

Subverting Moral Binaries: *Biographia Literaria* and *Rime of the Ancient Mariner*

Biographia Literaria has been criticized for many apparent failings, especially its borrowings from German philosophers and its lack of expository coherence,

---

[27] See Ward on the relationship between psychology and imagination in Coleridge's access to "the inherited forces which underlie our sense of self" (23).
[28] See his *Heaven and its Wonders and Hell* for his use of materialist philosophy influenced by Newton, Locke, and Bacon to argue that there is an equilibrium between heaven and hell.

Leslie Stephen most famously having pronounced it "put together with a pitchfork" (qtd. in Engell, 62). The formalist perception of the text's failings has been revisited through postmodernism that in turn gestures toward a genre-fusing autobiography, philosophy, and poetics and a structure that refuses coherence or unity of voice. However, what has not been considered is perhaps most enigmatic: an authorial voice deferring to fictional authors what is original even as it is charged with plagiarism. In the spirit of nondualism, one can thus redescribe the structure of *Biographia Literaria* as plastic in its freedom from discursive modes of cause and effect as it takes on the history of European thought.

The text's plasticity is marked by Coleridge's shifting account of his relationship with Wordsworth from the opening chapter, in which Coleridge opens with an ostensible defense of Wordsworth against the criticism of contemporaries, praising Wordsworth's translation of "prose thoughts into poetic language" (Engell and Bate I, 21); to chapter IV, in which Coleridge distances himself from what one contemporary reviewer called "the School of whining and hypochondriacal poets that haunt the Lakes" for which, in chapter IV, Coleridge blames Wordsworth's own Preface to the *Lyrical Ballads* as responsible for the "opposition" he has "been since doomed to encounter" (Coleridge's note qtd. in Halmi et al., 408, n. 3); and to chapter XIV, in which the criticism of Wordsworth comes to the surface. That Coleridge replaces his initial praise of Wordsworth with criticism that dismantles the foundation of Wordsworth's poetics is central to *Biographia Literaria*'s textual logic *sui generis*.[29]

As early as chapter IV, however, Coleridge prepares for chapter XIII's breakdown of Fancy and Imagination, the hierarchy that allows him to invert the relationship between the memory-based poetics of Wordsworth and the recreative impulse that subverts it. The textual path Coleridge forges in chapter IV begins with Coleridge's discussion of the etymological differences between the Greek *Phantasia* and the Latin *Imaginatio*, a distinction he then draws in XIII between Fancy and Imagination (Engell and Bate I, 305). Taking up the

---

[29] According to Halmi et al., the reviewer was Francis Jeffrey, editor of the *Edinburgh Review*; Coleridge "himself embraced Jeffrey's view that Wordsworth was most successful when he abandoned his system" (408, n. 3). See the detailed "Editors' Introduction" to Engell and Bates's edition of *Biographia Literaria*.

history of the "law of association" from Aristotle to Hartley, chapter V prepares to reduce association to the "mechanism of the reproduction of impressions ... the universal law of the *passive* fancy and *mechanical* memory," while chapter VI connects this passivity to the responsibility for the subject/object dualism that Coleridge traces from Aristotle to Hartley (*Biographia Literaria*, qtd. in Halmi, et al., 421–2). Chapter VII, on the "necessary consequences of the Hartleian theory," (*Biographia Literaria*, qtd. in Halmi, et al., 427) leads to chapter VIII's analysis of Cartesian dualism (433ff). It is this "despotism of outward impressions, and that of senseless and passive memory," that is the foundation of Wordsworth's "spots of time," the lynchpin of his poetics that Coleridge disassembles in chapter XIV (*Biographia Literaria*, qtd. in Halmi, et al., 426).

Coleridge interrupts this trajectory from chapters IX to XII, however, turning to his "obligation to the Mystics;—to Emanuel Kant" and to Schelling (*Biographia Literaria*, qtd. in Halmi, et al., 439). His description of the danger of an "irreligious PANTHEISM" to which German idealist philosophy may be "converted" appears disingenuous, Coleridge going further from the security of a pious materialism even than they do (*Biographia Literaria*, in Halmi, et al., 443). When he defends himself against the charges of plagiarism by claiming that "all the main and fundamental ideas, were born and matured in my mind before I had ever seen a single page of the German Philosopher," the criticism of the German writers as "irreligious" may appear especially ironic; yet looking back at the seeds of his ambivalence from his earliest writings, this criticism of those he plagiarizes is not as outlandish as has been suggested (*Biographia Literaria*, 447).[30]

By chapter XIV, Coleridge not only joins the fray of Wordsworth's critics but does so far more incisively, denouncing what he himself had shaped in Wordsworth: a poetics founded on associationism. In ironic contrast to Wordsworth's claim for having helped write *Rime of the Ancient Mariner*, Wordsworth blamed the poor sales of the second edition of *Lyrical Ballads* on

---

[30] While much of the philosophical discussion of Coleridge's influences has emphasized the differences between Kant and Schelling, it is notable that Coleridge himself collapses differences among them at this point. Katharine Cooke identifies the "German Philosopher" as Fichte, yet she rightly takes issue with the plagiarism label, noting that Coleridge may "owe a debt to his reading, but he is also saying that he has read critically" (94–5). From a twenty-first century perspective, however, Coleridge's unspecified "German philosopher" statement offers a yet more radical challenge to

Coleridge, specifically, on *Rime of the Ancient Mariner*. What had begun as a joint venture in 1798 became increasingly a platform for Wordsworth's poetry.[31] Coleridge waited until 1817 to respond to Wordsworth's claims about the poem. Having concluded chapter XIII with the climactic paragraphs delineating the hierarchy of mental faculties, Coleridge demotes Wordsworthian memory-based poetry to the lowest rung, adding as a bridge between chapters XIII and XIV the sentence that is Coleridge's most overt criticism of Wordsworth. Of Fancy, Coleridge writes, "But equally with the ordinary memory it must receive all its materials ready made from the law of association" (Engell and Bate I, 305).

Coleridge's subsequent promise of an essay on the "Supernatural in poetry" to serve as preface to *Rime of the Ancient Mariner* is significantly vague: "Whatever more than this, I shall think it fit to declare concerning the powers and privileges of the imagination in the present work, will be found in the critical essay" (Halmi et al., 489). There did not turn out to be "more than this"—presumably those two paragraphs on Imagination and Fancy. However, that Coleridge both connects the hierarchy to *Ancient Mariner* and uses it as a bridge into chapter XIV suggests the need to revisit the poem with an eye to its subversion of that principal binary of self and other to which Coleridge claimed Wordsworth was wedded.

In the context of its appearance in chapter XIV, the phrase "willing suspension of disbelief" crystallizes Coleridge's amalgamation of selfhood. Though the phrase remains in the lexicon today, it is understood largely as meaning the choice to set aside better judgment, as though with a sly wink to the auditor. However, for Coleridge, this presumption of better judgement is precisely the arrogance of British moral philosophy that he resisted throughout his literary life though he articulates it explicitly only at this late stage. The nuances underlying the phrase become apparent in its context, *Biographia Literaria* XIV, in which Coleridge describes the original plan of the *Lyrical Ballads*:

---

the charge of plagiarism. Coleridge's choice of a generic German philosopher suggests that he is emerging from a composite of competing German influences to arrive at secondary imagination which, in turn, allows him to wrest his own poetics from Wordsworth's.

[31] On Wordsworth's complaint about *Rime* and subsequent omission of Coleridge's poems, see Halmi et al. (54–5); on Wordsworth's suggesting the killing of the albatross, see Halmi et al. (64, n. 4).

[I]t was agreed, that my endeavours should be directed to persons and characters supernatural, or at least romantic: yet so as to transfer from our inward nature a human interest and a semblance of truth sufficient to procure for these shadows of imagination that willing suspension of disbelief for the moment, which constitutes poetic faith. (Engell and Bate II, 6)

Many questions arise about each term in this statement, all of which revolve around the problem of point of view: Whose disbelief must be suspended? To prefix "dis" onto "belief"—a term that connects with the poetic "faith" that constitutes this process—inverts the traditional binary of the heterodox and orthodox when talking about "poetic" faith. The inversion is thus an important reminder for readers who insist on separating Coleridge the poet from Coleridge the religiophilosophical essayist. How much weight should we put on the "will" of this disbeliever? Coleridge's 1809 notebook entry, discussed at the opening of this chapter vis-à-vis Coleridge's early meditation on a nonbinary notion of creativity, likened Will to a "galvanic fluid" stimulating "organs of motion & outward action"; the phrase "willing suspension of disbelief" can be seen as a yet more complex articulation of Coleridge's paradoxical rejection of Wordsworth's rejection of his own nondualism.[32]

In the context of the "willing suspension of disbelief" as he states it in chapter XIV, Coleridge is talking about the plan of *Lyrical Ballads* in which he, as opposed to Wordsworth, was to write about objects and events that do not appear in nature but whose textual life occupies creative, moral, and psychological dimensions. Thus, the willingness of the reader suggests a choice to take a leap of poetic faith into the nondual realm constituted by a level of intelligence in which the artist recreates by "dissolving, diffusing and dissipating," an act of secondary imagination that stands above mere "fancy," bound by the law of association, as Coleridge defined it in chapter XIII (488).

Coleridge thus demands that one willingly suspend the disbelief in a permeable self that fragments, shares identity with that which Western materialist philosophy has cast out as the other, and ideally reorganizes in a

---

[32] Wordsworth's self-censorship can be seen throughout his corpus—a topic for another study—though perhaps most visibly in "Tintern Abbey," in which a rare moment of nondual vision is censored by the discursive faculty. Thus, the persona's revelation, "And I have felt/A presence that disturbs me with the joy/Of elevated thoughts; a sense sublime/Of something far more deeply interfused" is followed by "Therefore am I still/A lover of the meadows and the woods" (ll. 93–103).

process he names in chapter XIII as secondary imagination. Returning, then, to this passage with the hindsight of the hierarchy of imaginative levels Coleridge articulated in chapter XIII, "suspend" is a verb with two potentially antithetical pulls: to temporarily cease and to hold up or hang, possibly for examination. The terms he uses conditionally are asking for but evading precision: "supernatural" but if not, then "romantic," which in either case, requires a complex process, a "transfer from our inward nature a human interest and a semblance of truth" that can "procure" this "willing suspension of disbelief" for these "shadows of imagination"; finally, this process "constitutes poetic faith."[33] "Procure" is a curious verb to use in this context; the Oxford English Dictionary (OED) shows that in the nineteenth century, it could have various shades of meaning, including "To prevail upon, induce, persuade, get (a person) *to* do something"; "To acquire or obtain, esp. with care or effort; to gain, get possession of (now the usual sense)"; and, most intriguing, "To obtain (a person, usually a woman) as a prostitute or illicit sexual partner for another person."[34] I wish to suggest that all the shades of meaning are potential in Coleridge's attempt to describe his "poetic faith" as he sets it against Wordsworth's "historic faith": it is tinged with the illicit in its trafficking with disbelief—willingness to take as true that which is not true according to Newtonian laws of science.

That "suspension" has two meanings further complicates the statement: We willingly suspend our disbelief by putting it on hold, thus a temporary act; but we also suspend our disbelief in the sense of allowing it to hang before us, to have it appear before us so that we may study and perhaps judge it. The two meanings would be contradictory for the English reader: Coleridge calls the bluff of the rationalist who claims knowledge through discursive detachment, but to ask that we suspend judgment of that which can't be proven empirically is also to force us to observe it with detachment accorded to objects of scientific study.

---

[33] This last phrase appears earlier, in the transcript of Coleridge's lecture on Shakespeare's *The Tempest* in which Coleridge compares poetic faith to "historic faith"; according to Halmi et al., "Coleridge's own notes for [the first three lectures] do not survive" (307); the transcript is that of John Payne Collier, one of the paid notetakers at Coleridge's lecture series. Coleridge's return to the phrase at this critical moment in *Biographia Literaria* suggests that the earlier lectures were sketches for his response to Wordsworth; by using Shakespeare as the embodiment of poetic faith and by contrasting it to historic faith, Coleridge further diminishes the Wordsworthian poetics of association and rustic life to a lesser pursuit.

[34] The earliest example of this meaning in the OED is later in the nineteenth century.

However, the phrase does not exist in a vacuum; its significance to the work as a whole is intensified by its appearance after Coleridge's treatment of German transcendental philosophy in chapter XII, in which he paradoxically plagiarizes Schelling's *System of Transcendental Idealism*. With the willing suspension of disbelief, one hears a subversion of Kant's opening salvo in the third section of his *Groundwork of the Metaphysics of Morals*: "A *will* is a kind of causality of living beings in so far as they are rational, and *freedom* would be that property of such a causality, as it can be efficient independently of alien causes *determining* it; just as *natural necessity* is the property of the causality of all nonrational beings to be determined to activity by the influence of alien causes" (56). Juxtaposing the statement with Coleridge's phrase, one is struck by Kant's systematic binaries: will is allied with the rational, whereas natural necessity is allied with the nonrational. Through secondary imagination, Coleridge dismantles the Kantian imperative by demanding of his reader a nonbinary suspension of reason through his/her will.

As the opening of chapter XIV, the phrase is pivotal not only in following Coleridge's rejection of Kant but in its own bridge between chapter XIII's rejection of Wordsworthian poetics in XIV. Coleridge had ended chapter XIII with both an exaltation of the recreative faculty that disrupts and fragments received modes of perception and, following, the disparagement of "Fancy," the Wordsworthian poetics of memory founded on the law of association. Having brought this distinction to the surface, Coleridge is therefore ready in XIV more fully to dissect both the problems of Wordsworth's poetics and the ideal of what he calls a "poetics of faith." Coleridge thus goes on to say that while Wordsworth was writing his poetry "to give the charm of novelty to things of every day," he was "preparing among other poems, the 'Dark Ladie,' and 'Christabel,' in which [he] should have more nearly realized [his] ideal" (*Biographia Literaria*, qtd. in Halmi, et al., 490). However, he goes on, Wordsworth's "industry" proved "so much more successful, and the number of his poems so much greater" that an imbalance was created, made worse because Wordsworth appended his Preface to the second edition that he extended "this style to poetry of all kinds, and to reject as vicious and indefensible all phrases and forms of style that were not included in what he … called the language of *real* life" (*Biographia Literaria*, qtd. in Halmi, et al., 490–1).

That "willing suspension of disbelief" is thus the endpoint of the brief but significant trajectory that begins with chapter XIII's definition of secondary imagination, the faculty that recreates by dissolving, diffusing, and dissipating, through the reference to *Ancient Mariner*. If one applies the phrase to the poem, the reader is in the position of the Wedding Guest whose interjections throughout the poem suggest his unwillingness to suspend disbelief. The moments the Wedding Guest appears most uncomfortable in the thrall of the Mariner's story involve orthodox religious beliefs; such a moment appears in the 1834 edition with lines added in 1800 in which the Wedding Guest exclaims, "I fear thee, ancient Mariner!" when the bodies of the dead crew rise up to man the ship. The Mariner responds,

> Be calm, thou Wedding-Guest!
> 'Twas not those souls that fled in pain,
> Which to their corses came again,
> But a troop of spirits blest (ll. 345–9)

Coleridge's irony behind the Mariner's ostensibly comforting words is comical here, the poem having scrambled moral binaries from the beginning, with the Mariner's perverse shooting of the albatross to what may appear a cosmic irony in which the albatross drops off the neck of the Mariner.

Among the changes Coleridge made to the poem between 1798 and 1834, one of the most striking is the addition of marginal glosses. Such a change has been cited as evidence of Coleridge's growing conservatism, implying that the glosses are to be taken at face value. However, a different interpretation appears more consistent with Coleridge's subversiveness: by adding an editorial voice to the poem, Coleridge forces the reader to question her own interpretation of the poem and, in so doing, consider where authority lies, as he suggests in his wry response to Anna Letitia Barbauld's complaint that there was not enough of a moral to the poem:

> Mrs. Barbauld once told me that she admired the Ancient Mariner very much, but that there were two faults in it,—it was improbable, and had no moral. As for the probability, I owned that that might admit some question;

but as to the want of a moral, I told her that in my own judgment the poem had too much; and that the only, or chief fault, if I might say so, was the obtrusion of the moral sentiment so openly on the reader as a principle or cause of action in a work of such pure imagination. It ought to have had no more moral than the Arabian Nights tale of the merchant's sitting down to eat dates by the side of a well, and throwing the shells aside, and lo! a genie starts up, and says he must kill the aforesaid merchant, because one of the date shells had, it seems, put out the eye of the genie's son.[35]

While the anecdote about Barbauld's criticism of *Rime* and Coleridge's response are often cited, Coleridge's miniature tale of the merchant from the *Arabian Nights* speaks yet more deeply to Coleridge's deconstruction of "motiveless malice" that has been equated with evil in scholarship on *Rime*.[36] By unconsciously tossing the date shells "by the side of a well," the merchant brings to life the dormant, subconscious world of the supernatural, the "daemonic" realm of "The Eolian Harp" that Sarah reproves the Coleridgean persona for pursuing. In more direct connection to *Rime*, the genie's supernatural threat of retribution suggests Coleridge's problematizing evil: The well hints at the entrance to a subliminal realm that bursts into the natural world with the merchant's unconscious wounding of the genie's son; it is the merchant's motivelessness more than the act itself that makes him guilty. However, the very unconsciousness of the act is the source of the recreative for Coleridge, exposing the subterranean level of imagination that takes the artist deeper than mere memory.

The story of the merchant and the genie encapsulates Coleridge's "willing suspension of disbelief" that is central to *Rime* and that a reader seeking a pious lesson will either miss (Barbauld here) or chastise (Sarah in "The Eolian Harp"). Just as Death and Life-in-Death gamble for the soul of the Mariner, one might say on a metatextual level that the compulsion to inform the tale with piety, as seen through the Barbauldian glosses of the 1834 version of the

---

[35] *Table Talk*, 86.
[36] See the discussion in Chapter 3 of Coleridge's use of the phrase "motiveless malice" in his marginalia to Shakespeare's plays; referring to Iago's soliloquy in *Othello* I. iii, just after Iago parts from Roderigo, saying, "Thus do I ever make my fool my purse," Coleridge writes, The triumph! again, *put money* after the effect has been fully produced.—The last Speech, the motive-hunting of motiveless Malignity—how awful! In itself fiendish—while yet he was allowed to bear the divine image, too fiendish for his own steady View.—A being next to Devil—only *not* quite Devil—& this Shakespeare has attempted—executed—without disgust, without Scandal!—(*Lectures on Shakespeare*, 165).

poem, battles for the soul of the Wedding Guest who represents the reader. Thus, as the poem moves toward its close, the Mariner says,

> O Wedding-guest! This soul hath been
> Alone on a wide wide sea:
> So lonely 'twas, that God himself
> Scarce seemed there to be.
>
> (1798, ll. 630–3)

The 1834 gloss for these last stanzas seems to be an ironic nod to Barbauld herself: "And to teach, by his own example, love and reverence to all things that God made and loveth." The poem appears to support this claim with the Mariner's last words to the Wedding Guest: "He prayeth best who loveth best, / All things great and small: / For the dear God, who loveth us, / He made and loveth all." (1798, ll. 647–50). Yet they do not "walk together to the Kirk" as the Mariner has advised, nor does the poem end with the "goodly company" in which "all together pray"; rather the solitary man—no Wedding Guest at all—"went, like one that hath been stunn'd ... A sadder and a wiser man" (1798, ll. 655–7).

Returning to Part I of the poem with an eye for Coleridge's subversion of binaries, one can detect the Mariner's contamination of the Wedding Guest in the stanza-long dialogue between them:

> "God save thee, ancient Mariner!
> From the fiends, that plague thee thus!—
> Why look'st thou so?"—With my cross-bow
> I shot the Albatross.
>
> (1834, ll. 79–82)

The caesura in line 81 both divides and joins their words, as though the Wedding Guest apprehends the story both subliminally and immediately, taking the length of the poem to comprehend it consciously. Among the marginal glosses that Coleridge added to the 1834 edition, the gloss for this stanza underscores with notable irony the distance between the poem's meditation on the seepage between traditional binaries and the glib piety of the fictitious editor, entrenched in the facile boundaries between good and evil: "*The ancient Mariner inhospitably killeth the pious bird of good omen*" (*Ancient Mariner*, qtd. in Halmi, et al., 65).

While the Mariner promises to tell a tale that will be his redemption and, indirectly, that of the auditor, it is thus actually a tale of contamination, perhaps the source of Barbauld's discomfort with the poem. Chapter 2 addresses Coleridge's far more harmonious literary relationship with Mary Robinson as a fellow writer and reader sharing Coleridge's defiance of such pieties in the spirit of plumbing a deeper consciousness.

2

Coleridge and Robinson: "Sense Unchained"

Coleridge's poetic conversation with Mary Robinson has seen increasing scholarly attention since the late twentieth century when focus on the Romantic canon began to make way for the recovery of writers outside its ideology. The evolution has been gradual, however. Scholars of the last decades of the twentieth century debated how and when to integrate these recovered writers into the canon, thereby redefining it. On the one hand, for instance, Marlon Ross insisted, "As we recover their place in history, we must be sure not to examine them in isolation" (*Contours*, 6). Isobel Armstrong, on the other hand, made a compelling case for the counterargument, warning that it would be premature to integrate women into the critical discussion alongside the canonical male poets before considering them in their own terms.

These women, she argued, would be subsumed into the masculinist poetics of the Romantic paradigm: "It will take some time for this work to become fully visible, and this may justify a one-sided study of women's poetry in isolation from male poetry. The next step will be to look at the interaction of the two—but let us postpone this until women's work is known better" (31).

Particularly in the case of Robinson and Coleridge, early attempts to integrate noncanonical and canonical writers generated productive discussion about the trajectory of a field whose very name has been contested, as discussed in the Introduction; Armstrong's 1995 caveat against immediately subsuming noncanonical writers into the Romantic paradigm appears prescient from the hindsight of twenty-first-century scholarship. Much of that early commentary that attempted such a reintegration now appears denigrating to the noncanonical writers. For instance, Stuart Curran's 1994 essay, "Mary Robinson's *Lyrical Tales* in Context," an important first step in drawing attention to Robinson both in the context of and against the "Lake

Poets" vis-à-vis the literary marketplace, suggests that it would have been "highly flattering" for Robinson to "find herself linked with this group of young, talented poets," thus betraying what Armstrong identified as the problem of this early integration (21). Granting Robinson access to the canon while keeping her separate from the "young talented poets" appears premature through its implicit reinforcement of the gender binary.[1]

The Romantic paradigm's central binary of masculine subject, feminine object not only misrepresents Robinson but also Coleridge, who is relegated to the male half of the binary implicit in the label "young talented poets." The interplay of gender and subjectivity in his poetry and prose is thereby lost to the reductive paradigm of canonical male poetics. Other early attempts to reintegrate the two poets in this early phase ironically entrenched them even more deeply in the gender binary by separating Coleridge's response to the biographical Robinson from his engagement with the textual Robinson. One 1994 essay, for instance, distinguishes Coleridge's public praise for Robinson as a poet from his private attitude toward her as "avuncular and condescending" (Luther, 393). According to this argument, Coleridge perpetuates "gender stereotypes" by wanting to protect Robinson as a "fallen but repentant woman," a position that projects misogyny onto Coleridge when he privately conveyed his anger to Robinson's daughter for her plan to publish her mother's writings alongside gothic writers as damaging to her reputation (Luther, 394).[2] Nevertheless, the 1990s also produced treatments of the literary relationship between Coleridge and Robinson by eschewing biographically based textual analysis, exemplified by Lisa Vargo's 1995 essay focusing instead on the relationship between sensibility and the political conversation of their poetry.

More recent studies, discussed in the Introduction, demonstrate the distance the field has come since the 1990s. Aligning Robinson with the poetics of her male contemporaries and, in turn, demonstrating her influence on their poetics, for instance, Cross reassesses Robinson's career as one that

---

[1] One might contrast this perspective to Airey's 2016 discussion of Robinson's "economics of authorial labor," particularly regarding the empathy Airey finds in Robinson's depiction of Chatterton in her "Monody," to be discussed in relation to Coleridge's monody later in this chapter.

[2] See *Collected Letters* II (904). Another such instance, Daniel Robinson's 1995 treatment of Coleridge and Robinson as fellow poets, concludes that the "conventional meter" and "patronizing emphasis on Robinson's physical beauty" in Coleridge's "Alcaeus to Sappho" are "dismissive" of Robinson (7).

does not "fit the model of feminine and masculine Romanticism that Anne Mellor posits in *Romanticism and Gender*" (Coleridge and Robinson, 43).[3] This chapter extends Cross's reappraisal that they "shared an investment in reconfiguring traditional poetic imagery and a concern for poetic reputation" by examining the mutual influence of Coleridge and Robinson as a shared resistance to systematic binaries (67). Just as it was apparent to Armstrong in 1995 that women poets used sensibility to challenge and remake the "male philosophical traditions," it should now be equally apparent that Coleridge turned from the same masculinist tradition whose subjectivity was multifaceted and permeable (15).

The aim of this chapter is thus to bring together gender and epistemology in the mutual representation of androgyny in Coleridge and Robinson's poetic dialogue.[4] Their androgynous subjectivities prove symbiotic, a shared resistance to the dualistic foundation of the masculinist literary tradition. Just as Chapter 1 deploys the concept of nondualism to indicate Coleridge's ambivalence rather than merely a reversal or blending of binaries, this chapter extends the term to Robinson's poetics as well. Robinson shares with Coleridge a recreative impulse that finds comparable expression in androgyny and contamination.

The topic of androgyny in Romantic-era literature, particularly that of Coleridge and Robinson separately, has garnered scholarly attention in recent years. However, the segregation of gender and epistemology has meant that the gender arguments have focused on Coleridge's biographical relationship with Robinson, while the religiophilosophical scholarship has ignored gender

---

[3] See also Cross's essay, "Romantic Flies, Insect Poets, and Authorial Sensibility," that challenges the binaries on which previous scholarship itself has been founded. The wry irony of Robinson's poem, "May Fly," Cross observes, results from tension between the "witty playfulness of Robinson's newspaper poetry in the late 1780s and the seriousness" of her paralytic and deteriorated state (342). Fulford's 2015 *Literary Coteries* has added a significant perspective to the developing field of literary alliances that cross the boundaries of the canonical and noncanonical through the topic of print culture. While he places Robinson among the writers important to the developing "tribe," however, Fulford nevertheless reduces Robinson's poems to being "themselves influenced by Coleridge's"; further, the study perpetuates the sexualized persona to which Robinson has been subjected by her contemporaries and scholars since her time, Fulford writing that Robinson "carried on a flirtatious verse correspondence with the Della Cruscan poets" and that she "put her experience of manipulating newspaper reports to literary use" (45, 30).

[4] For a discussion of the larger implications of their literary legacy, see Chapter 4, whose premise traces Robinson's and Coleridge's linking androgyny and contamination through Mary Shelley's fiction.

as it has remained entrenched in Coleridge's relationship to the masculinist tradition of philosophical and theological precedents.[5] The dearth of attention to commonalities among male and female writers in representing androgyny can be explained when one revisits discussions of androgynous figures in Coleridge's poems. The claim is often that these representations derive from Coleridge's "fear and hatred of women," as in the case of Geraldine in *Christabel* (Hoeveler, 1990). As the Introduction has argued, however, the poetics of androgyny flies in the face of Coleridge as "Lake Poet," the label suggesting the Wordsworthian poetics of description and reflection in which a masculine subject projects his imagination upon the other in the form of an objectified nature.

Dismantling Gender Binaries: "The Maniac," "Kubla Khan," and "To Coleridge"

This chapter thus views Robinson and Coleridge through the lens of their artistically productive confluences that challenge the divorce of gender and epistemology. As the following explorations of poetic dialogue between them seek to show, Robinson not only shared but may even have helped generate Coleridge's notion of a recreative artistic agency that he came to identify as "secondary imagination" in *Biographia Literaria*. Though poetic dialogue between "Kubla Khan" and "To Coleridge" has been the most frequently discussed comparison of Coleridge and Robinson because of the overt echoes of "Kubla Khan" in Robinson's poem,[6] the overreliance on biography among these treatments has been particularly reductive with the focus on Coleridge's and Robinson's use of opium, the "anodyne" for debilitating pain as well as a source of poetic inspiration that Coleridge refers to in his Preface to "Kubla Khan."

Scholars have recently extended the opium-focused approach to the relationship through the commonalities between Robinson's "The Maniac"

---

[5] For the reasons discussed in the Introduction, Robinson does not engage directly with philosophical systems as does Coleridge.
[6] The comparison was first made by Lowes in 1927. According to Hayter, Robinson's is the first printed reference to *Kubla Khan* (218).

and Coleridge's "Kubla Khan"; it is well documented, for instance, that, as an invalid later in her life, Robinson wrote her 1793 "The Maniac" under the influence of opium. Not only did her poem pre-date Coleridge's 1798 "Kubla Khan," but even the later account by Robinson's daughter of Robinson's writing the poem pre-dated "Kubla Khan." Her daughter writes that Robinson dictated "with her eyes closed, apparently in the stupor which opium frequently produces"; her daughter continues, "On the ensuing morning 'she' had only a confused idea of what had past" (qtd. in Pascoe, 123, n. 1). Opium appears to have provided both poets with a catalyst to dismantle the dualistic scaffolding imposed by Western epistemology, especially the gendered basis of that materialist paradigm.

Based on Robinson's references to specific lines in "To Coleridge," Paula Byrne suggests that Coleridge showed Robinson the unpublished "Kubla Khan" in 1800, Byrne surmising that "it is highly probable that Coleridge and Robinson discussed the imaginative effects of opium when they met" (268). The more important commonality, however, appears in Byrne's subsequent observation: "The sense of unconscious composition, the inability of the writing pen to keep up with the dreaming mind, the vanishing of the vision once the poet awakes: in all these respects there is an uncanny resemblance between Robinson's account of the origin of her poem and Coleridge's of the origin of his" (268–9). Their shared commitment to exploring the relationship between layers of consciousness and the poetic process is further complicated by the equally important representation of their resistance to traditionally dualistic approaches to the poetic process. Thus, though for both writers opium may have helped liberate what Coleridge would refer to in *Biographia Literaria* as the faculty that recreates, it is not the sole avenue to liberation from patriarchal oppression.[7] By expanding and complicating their conversation across three texts, their shared concerns with the relationship between gender and creativity become more pronounced. In this conversation, Coleridge's "Kubla Khan" stands chronologically between Robinson's two poems, "The

---

[7] As Chapter 4 discusses through the relationship among Coleridge, Robinson, and Shelley, with or without the aid of opium, the emphasis on this deep layer of consciousness is represented through the aesthetic sublime. See Chapter 1 for detailed discussion of *Biographia Literaria*, chapter XIII, in which Coleridge referred to this recreative agency as secondary imagination, a mental faculty distinct from mere memory. In it, the artist actively rearranges elements in nature whose result is a tension between the world of binaries and the ideal of freedom from them.

Maniac" and "To the Poet Coleridge." The three together make up a sequence in their larger conversation that began earlier in their poetic correspondence and that reveals their common concerns with gender and epistemology.[8]

Robinson's "The Maniac" was inspired not only by opium but by an occurrence Robinson witnessed and wrote about in her memoirs, in which an old man known as Jemmy was "hurried by a crowd who pelted him with mud and stones" (Pascoe, 123, n. 1). Robinson organizes the poem around a series of questions the narrator directs toward a character based on Jemmy, who appears a madman out of the tradition of gothic hyperbole. The first two stanzas begin with familiar gothic imagery: "What art thou, whose eyeballs roll" (l. 1); "Why dost thou rend thy matted hair" (l. 7). Robinson is not merely perpetuating what had become a cliché, however. Hers is the "new gothic," in which gothic machinery is used to represent psychological depth; Robinson shares the new gothic style with Coleridge and Shelley, as Chapter 4 discusses.[9]

As the poem proceeds, the narrator's questions become more complicated in ways that connect his madness to a struggle with the binaries of Enlightenment reason. The poem's subjectivity shifts as the gap narrows between speaker and Maniac. By the third stanza, Robinson brings this nondualism to the surface: "Why doest thou from thy scanty bed / Tear the rude straw to crown thy head?"; Robinson elevates the "rude straw" to subvert the connotations of both aristocracy and reason in her ironic use of the familiar metaphor of the "crown of [the] head" (ll. 13–14). The Maniac's behavior makes less and less "sense" from the perspective of the so-called sane: the narrator notices that the Maniac's spatial orientation appears to have gone awry.[10] She asks, "Why doest thou climb yon craggy steep, / That frowns upon the clam-rous deep" (ll. 19–20). The Maniac's apparent confusion between beauty and the grotesque is

---

[8] For a discussion of the earlier poetic dialogue in the Snow-drop poems, see the later section of this chapter focusing on *Walsingham*.

[9] Though most scholarship has used the term "new gothic" to refer to later uses of the genre, this study argues that it is already evident in Coleridge, Robinson, and Shelley, among other writers. See McGrath on the psychological complexity of the genre beginning with Poe.

[10] Robinson's Maniac may be compared to the speaker of Blake's "Mad Song" who says, perversely, "Like a fiend in a cloud ... I turn my back to the east, / From whence comforts have increas'd; / For light doth seize my brain / With frantic pain" (ll. 17–24). Whereas Blake takes his reader into the diseased mind of the speaker, Robinson develops the narrator's relationship with the Maniac from a distance between the uncomprehending interrogator and the Maniac to one that dissolves difference.

yet more disturbing for the narrator, who then asks, "why dost thou strip the fairest bow'rs, / To dress thy scowling brow with flow'rs" (ll. 25–6); Robinson suggests in this stanza that the narrator sees the Maniac's self-adornment as a perversion of art since it takes what was whole and, as the narrator notes, "round thy naked limbs fantastic fragments bind?"

The narrator's discomfort with the grotesqueness of the Maniac leads her to a shift in the poem. Here, she introduces a "Minstrel of the witching hour" (l. 35), a figure who evolves through "Kubla Khan" and then "To the Poet Coleridge," and who is here "congeal'd with fear, to hear thy dismal moan" (l. 36). This "minstrel of the witching hour" is a poet-figure whose art reflects the "dismal moan" of one whose "sense [is] unchain'd," leading the narrator to celebrate a mental state liberated from the binaries imposed by Enlightenment reason (41). The poem shifts away from the narrator's horror to one of empathy: "I will share thy pangs, and make thy griefs my own" (l. 54). Thus, the narrator makes a pact with the Maniac that she will provide a voice for him that does not objectify him but rather provides the double vision in which subject reflects subject, both horrifying and familiar.

This representation of tearing apart an epistemology founded on binaries and recreating its elements was to become an essential element of Coleridge's notion of secondary imagination, as Chapter 1 has argued. Coleridge resists the dualism underlying his own early embrace of British associationism even as he extolled this philosophical school founded on empiricism that shaped his early poetics of memory. As Chapter 1 discusses, that Coleridge simultaneously rebelled against this materialism even as he used it calls for the need to qualify the emphasis on Coleridge's use of associationism in "Frost at Midnight" influencing Wordsworth's "Tintern Abbey," hence keeping Coleridge locked in the role of heralding the new canonical poetry as one of meditation and reflection. It took Coleridge decades—with his writing of *Biographia Literaria*—to reject as mere Fancy both his early and Wordsworth's continued reliance on memory. Merely playing with objects that are "essentially fixed and dead," Coleridge writes, Fancy is simply "Memory emancipated from the order of time and space," receiving "all its materials ready made from the law of association" (Engell and Bate I, 305). Though this strong assertion may be belated in Coleridge's career, it did not emerge without precedent. This chapter adds to the previous one Robinson's centrality to that precedent. This shift in focus helps explain why it is not enough to see this mental hierarchy as emerging from German romanticism.[11]

The 1816 "Kubla Khan" shares with "The Maniac" the unfortunate status of a poem dismissed for more than a century as the hallucinogenic and thereby incoherent effect of opium. Yet the discovery in 1934 of an earlier draft of the poem, known as the Crew manuscript, provides evidence of Coleridge's careful crafting of the poem to create such an effect.[12] Thus, adding both the Preface and final stanza to his earlier fragmentary poem between 1816 and 1829, Coleridge heightens the effect of the opium-induced vision. Whether fictional or not, such a pretext liberated both Robinson and Coleridge from the expectations of coherence expected of traditional poetics. The nondual results for the two poets are similar: a double vision that embraces the dissolution of binaries even while holding them in tension.[13]

Coleridge's fictional editor of the fragment describes the dream's catalyst as a confluence of laudanum and the fragmentary images in Purchase's *Pilgrimage*, the book the poet had been reading before he fell asleep. Though the editor of the Preface notes that the fragment is "a psychological curiosity" rather than a work to be judged by "poetic merit," there is an ironic distance between Coleridge's voice and that of the editor. While most readers have dismissed the statement as a variant of the humility topos, typical of Coleridge's self-denigration, that it is a "psychological curiosity" is no trifling matter for Coleridge, who looks ahead to a psychological complexity at odds with the associationist philosophy of his time. Thus, interrupted while recording the dream by a knock on the door, the poet discovers to his horror that he cannot remember the rest of the dream. Byrne links the poem to "The Maniac," noting that "it then could be that Coleridge made up the story about the person from Porlock in order to give his poem the same kind of authenticity as 'The Maniac'" (269). In their shared exploration of a yet unplumbed psychophilosophical depth, Robinson and Coleridge refute "poetic merit" based on the materialist philosophical tradition.

---

[11] See Chapter 3 for the development of this component of *Biographia Literaria*'s wrestling with German philosophy.
[12] See Halmi et al., on the textual history of the poem (180, n. 1).
[13] Chapter 3 revisits "Kubla Khan" through a larger view of Coleridge's poetic fragments.

The frame created by the 1816 Preface thus alerts the reader about the problem of subjectivity that intensifies in the two stanzas to follow the original poem, and that comes to the surface in the third stanza also added in 1816. The reversal of gender between Kubla's patriarchal point of view in the first stanza and the female erotic power in nature that takes down Kubla's walls and towers in the second stanza leads to a paradoxical recreation that brings contraries together, with pleasure domes made of ice by the end of the second stanza, a forceful depiction of nondualism's tension between contrary states.

Coleridge's addition of the poet's subjectivity in the third and final stanza of "Kubla Khan" is a significant means of subverting the gender binary that may otherwise have equated the poet with Kubla. However, the effect of echoing the second stanza's imagery in the third is the creation of a poetic subjectivity gendered nonbinary. Readers have been tempted to regard the two contrasting female figures of the erotically powerful nature of the second stanza and the demure Abyssinian maid of the third stanza as evidence of Coleridge, canonical male poet, objectifying the feminine as either virgin/muse or whore/destroyer. However, this "Abyssinian maid" is far from Wordsworth's objectified maidens that he represents in "Nutting" and "Tintern Abbey" as Chapter 1 discusses; the Abyssinian maid sings both "symphony and song," a complex/simple nonbinary that suggests other nonbinary qualities, including her roles as would-be muse to the poet and a creator herself of a music he would emulate as it is liberated from tradition. She is also an innocent with sexual knowledge, singing of a nonwestern source for the Judeo-Christian paradise that complicates Milton's Eden in *Paradise Lost*.[14]

Even as the Abyssinian maid of stanza 3 transfigures nature's wailing in stanza 2, the poet's own artistic frustration is central to the final stanza. The conditional "could I revive" her "symphony and song" suggests his failure to channel her as a muse (ll. 42–3). Coleridge returns to this undercurrent of anxiety in *Biographia Literaria* XIII's definition of secondary imagination as an ideal; "when rendered impossible, yet still at all events it struggles to idealize and to unify" (Engell and Bate I, 304). Here, in stanza 3 of "Kubla

---

[14] See Halmi et al., who trace the name of the mountain to James Bruce's 1790 *Travels to Discover the Source of the Nile* to account for Coleridge's changes to the name in the Crewe manuscript from Amora to Amara to Abora (183, n. 1). See also Alun David on the Romantic-era view of the Bible as oriental text, cited as well in the Introduction to this study.

Khan," the poet is already far removed from the masculine tradition of English poetry that Wordsworth perpetuates by centralizing his subjectivity that he divides unambiguously from a feminized and objectified nature. By contrast to Wordsworthian poetics, Coleridge in "Kubla Khan" delays the appearance of the poetic persona in a swerve from the traditional framing of a lyric poem with the subject's point of view.

The third stanza thus transmutes the raw power and sounds of feminine nature in the second stanza through the Abyssinian maid; her dulcimer suggests both Eastern and Western music that, as symphony and song, is both complex and lyrically simple. One might even hear the homonym "made" in "maid," suggesting that even in his failure to recreate her music he has recreated her from the fragments of his vision. Thus, though he frames the vision with the conditional, "could I," the poet achieves nondualism paradoxically, representing the poetical character as simultaneously demonic and divine, one who inspires "holy dread."[15] Coleridge thereby underscores the distinction between the poet-figure and the masculinist Kubla of stanza 1. It is the female creativity of the subsequent two stanzas with which the poet identifies, dismantling and reconfiguring patriarchal structure.

Robinson's 1806 "To the Poet Coleridge" has long been held as a tribute to "Kubla Khan." The connection between the poems marks Robinson and Coleridge's ongoing poetic conversation about the relationship between eros and creativity. Robinson's announcement at the beginning of her poem that she will "wander" with Coleridge not only gestures to their relationship as one of equals; as the elder poet, Robinson transforms the traditional relationship between masculine subject and female object on many levels of an equalizing subjectivity, including in this case a reversal of age and experience from the traditional. Further, that together they will "wander"—the etymological root of "err"—suggests the mutual openness the two poets share in following a path not codified by literary tradition. Robinson expands on the subversiveness of their shared poetics in the next line of "To Coleridge": "With thee I'll trace

---

[15] Richardson takes the poetic androgyny further by interpreting the "milk of Paradise" at the end of the poem as the maternal quality of the idealized androgynous figure the poet would become if he could internalize the female as potentially maternal (*Neural Sublime*, 136–7).

the circling bounds / Of thy new paradise extended" (ll. 5–6). She here reads Coleridge's transformation of the "circling bounds" Kubla creates in the first stanza by female nature's violent rupture in the second stanza, the "new paradise" of his recreative vision that reconfigures the fragments of Kubla's pleasure dome in paradoxical union with those of nature.

Robinson pays tribute to the female eroticism that enacts this recreation: "more than vegetating pow'r / throbs grateful to the burning hour / As summer's whisper'd sighs unfold / Her million, million buds of gold" (ll. 28–31). With each iteration of "thy new paradise extended" Robinson deepens the implications of Coleridge's recreative imagination, whose "distant sounds / Of winds, and foamy torrents blended!" (ll. 34–5). By her third iteration of the phrase "new paradise extended," Robinson celebrates the feminine sublime of Coleridge's poem, whose "awful sounds, / Of winds, and foamy torrents blended!" far exceed the power of the emperor, Kubla Khan.

By calling Coleridge's poem a "new creation," Robinson gestures toward what Coleridge would come to call "secondary imagination" in *Biographia Literaria*, a faculty available only to the artist, who "dissolves, diffuses, and dissipates in order to re-create." At this climatic point of her poem, Robinson introduces but transfigures Coleridge's "damsel with a dulcimer," reimagining her as "swift smiting" her instrument. The violent motion suggests even more explicitly the Abyssinian maid's connection to the "sacred river" that Coleridge's second stanza likens to woman wailing for her demon lover. Robinson's description of this female musician's "minstrelsy" echoes her own earlier poem, "The Maniac," and whose witcheries in turn echo earlier poems of Coleridge's such as "The Eolian Harp."[16]

Thus, "To Coleridge" culminates with Robinson reconnecting the energy of Coleridge's powerful, female nature to the Abyssinian maid who in turn reflects the minstrel of Robinson's "The Maniac"; that she now "smites" her

---

[16] See the discussion of "The Eolian Harp" in Chapter 1. Note the distinction between the position of this study regarding the complication of gender for both poets regarding the poetic subject and muse and the positions of others such as Luther, Fulford, and Selzig, who have variously described the relationship between the two poets as traditional embodiments of the gender binary, Coleridge thus taking the traditional role of the poet-subject and Robinson as his muse. For Luther, Robinson is Coleridge's "avatar of the Abyssinian maid" (408), while Fulford argues that Coleridge was "ultimately unsuccessful" in appropriating Robinson's poetics ("Mary Robinson and the Abyssinian Maid," 8).

dulcimer suggests Robinson's embrace of a feminine sublime that goes against the grain of Burke's gendered binary of the sublime and the beautiful. Robinson concludes the poem with a subjectivity that honors the magic Coleridge only offers provisionally at the end of "Kubla Khan," in which he concludes that if only he could "revive her symphony and song" people would "weave a circle round him thrice." Robinson not only refuses Coleridge's failure but builds on his creation by achieving a double subjectivity that hearkens full circle back to "The Maniac."

The Conversation between Robinson and Coleridge in *Walsingham*: Androgyny, Subjectivity, and the Perverse

Robinson's narratives, both fiction and drama, have largely been missing from the discussion of her literary alliance with Coleridge due at least in part to the generic compartmentalizing of both writers' texts. A striking complication of the alignment between Robinson and Coleridge can be found in their monodies dedicated to Thomas Chatterton.

Chatterton was regarded as a forerunner of the Romantic movement not only because of his gothic poetics but because of his demise at the age of seventeen. His apparent suicide was blamed on the scandal created when Horace Walpole, among others, discovered Chatterton to be the author of the poems Chatterton had claimed were written by a fictitious fifteenth-century monk, Thomas Rowley.[17] Chatterton was thus a symbol of impoverished genius for many poets, evidenced by references to Chatterton in Wordsworth's "Resolution and Independence," Keats's Dedication to Chatterton in *Endymion*, and Percy Shelley's reference to Chatterton in stanza 45 of *Adonais*.[18]

---

[17] Though Chatterton's death in 1770 was assumed to be suicide, Halmi et al. note that he may have taken the mixture of water and arsenic to cure himself of a venereal infection (5, n. 1).

[18] In Shelley's elegy to Keats, Chatterton, among others, emerges at a moment of self-doubt: "Far in the Unapparent, Chatterton / Rose pale, his solemn agony had not / Yet faded from him" (ll. 399–401). This spectral cameo significantly appears just before Shelley turns to the traditional elegy's final consolation: "Who mourns for Adonais?" (l. 415). The repression of the anxiety Chatterton represents to Shelley is reminiscent of Chatterton's place in Wordsworth's "Resolution and Independence," in which "the marvelous Boy" is the "sleepless Soul that perished in his pride," Wordsworth's coupling of fear and arrogance in counting himself among the poets who "in our youth begin in gladness; / But thereof come in the end despondency and madness" (ll. 43–4).

Robinson's and Coleridge's monodies have commonalities that distinguish their relationship to Chatterton from that of many of their contemporaries; to describe Robinson's own textual relationship to Chatterton, one must include in the history of her poem its place in *Walsingham*.[19] The difference Robinson achieves simply through giving the same text to her character's subjectivity is the difference between the original monody's kinship with Coleridge's monody as opposed to the relationship of her monody's subjectivity when it is given through the mouthpiece of Walsingham, who shares an ironic entitlement with the coterie of male subjectivities in some of the other tributes to Chatterton.

Cross has written insightfully on the distinction between Coleridge's and Robinson's representations of Chatterton's death in spite of their similar choices of imagery.[20] Yet a return to their similarities points to both a deeper connection between them and their shared distinction from their contemporaries. Not only did Chatterton, Robinson, and Coleridge share Bristol as their birthplace, as Duthrie notes, but they share a complex textual history that blurs lines of influence.[21] The 1796 version of Coleridge's monody appears in his collection *Poems on Various Subjects*, whose Preface is a meditation on the difference between egotism and effusion as an outpouring of subjectivity.[22] Coleridge imagines the descendental journey of Chatterton, the "heart-sick Wanderer," from "heaven-born Genius" to his early demise (ll. 8, 16). Yet as Coleridge's monody probes what that heaven must be, the poem denounces the traditional paradise of canonical poetry, a "land of song-ennobled line" (l. 23). Coleridge thus rejects "the nationalistic poetry of the 18th century" that "pointed with pride at England's care both for liberty and literature" (Halmi et al., 7, n. 3). Chatterton's lineage, Coleridge writes, is that of Spenser's "chill Disappointment" (l. 27). Coleridge's monody thus rejects an idealized England, replacing it here with "the black tide of Death" that

---

[19] Walsingham speaks ll. 3–14 of the monody (Duthrie, 170–1); for Robinson's complete monody, see *Poetry of Mrs. Robinson*, 73–9.

[20] Cross not only connects them through the use of the lyre image but also notes that Coleridge's poem is more politicized than Robinson's (59, 62).

[21] See Duthrie, 170, n. 2. Coleridge revised his "Monody on the Death of Chatterton" for over forty years, his first version a 1790 school exercise in the Graveyard tradition, adapted from Gray, followed by revisions in the 1790s through 1803. See the detailed note on this textual history in Halmi et al. (6, n. 1).

[22] See the discussion of this distinction vis-à-vis Effusion XXXV, or "The Eolian Harp" in Chapter 1 of this study.

rolls "thro' every freezing vein" (l. 91). Coleridge's England is Chatterton's gothic sublime where "screaming sea-gulls soar," an upward movement that parodies the object of mourning's stellification in traditional elegy (l. 103). As the elegist mourning his own failure, Coleridge enters the poem in its final stanzas, blurring the line between "I" and "he," subject and object. As he does in "Dejection," Coleridge brushes away his own dark thoughts: "No more endure to weigh / The shame and anguish of the evil day, / Wisely forgetful!" (ll. 120–1). Given the long textual history of the poem, these lines are laden with irony since Coleridge refuses to forget the "evil day" of Chatterton's suicide. The poem ends with an imagining of Chatterton still alive in "Freedom's UNDIVIDED dale," a modifier that suggests such a union would transcend the binaries of life and death, success and failure, so that his audience would "greet with smiles the young-eyed POESY / All deftly mask'd, as hoar ANTIQUITY" (ll. 129, 132–3). Coleridge gestures toward a new generation of poets for whom Chatterton's inverted plagiarism, "masking" innovation as antiquity, is heroic.

Robinson's monody, first appearing a year after Coleridge's 1790 version and itself undergoing several revisions, opens by having the "sainted spirit" of Chatterton moving upward, in contrast to Coleridge's 1796 poem, on its way to the ironically "bland regions of celestial day" (ll. 3–4). By describing the heaven that her contemporaries imagine for Chatterton as "bland," Robinson implies her rejection of the traditional binary of heaven as eternal rest and hell as eternal torment, a binary she associates with those who hypocritically mourn Chatterton's death. Forcing them to come to terms with the falseness of their elegiac praise, Robinson's monody links Chatterton's "mortal pains" to his "GENIUS" (ll. 8, 10). The following stanza begins a catalogue of negatives interrupted by the stanza Walsingham speaks; this use of litotes underscores the ambivalence underlying the praise: "Not all the graces that to youth belong, / Nor all the energies of sacred song; / No all that FANCY, all that GENIUS gave, / Could snatch thy wounded spirit from the grave" (ll. 15–18). As the poem progresses—past Walsingham's extract—Robinson contemplates the incompatibility between fame and creativity by addressing Chatterton's "borrowed name" of Rowley for his poems: "His timid talents own'd a borrow'd name, / And gain'd by FICTION what was due to FAME" (ll. 57–8). Chatterton's refusal to publish under his own name belies the identification of Robinson's contemporaries with Chatterton.[23] Her praise of him for the "fine raptures of poetic fire" is thus a tribute that stands apart from that of her contemporaries (l. 89).

That the extract of the third stanza from Robinson's monody reappears six years later, in her 1797 *Walsingham*, has implications for the influence of genre on subjectivity, in this case shifting from Robinson's poetic persona to the masculine subjectivity of Walsingham. Robinson reveals her ironic distance from this flawed, eponymous protagonist who reflects the coopting of Chatterton by male poets as a tragic figure who anticipates their own anxieties about fame and poverty.[24] Walsingham has set out to find his way in the world after he has been cast out of his "native haunts" by his aunt who has appropriated his inheritance for his cousin whom Walsingham believes to be the male Sir Sidney (67).

This context for Walsingham's association of Chatterton with Bristol, where he here finds himself, is laden with irony. His newfound sense of impoverishment is far from Robinson's authorial perspective on Chatterton in the monody, as Walsingham projects himself onto the "relentless beings who saw thee exiled, poor and unpatronized, driven to wander, without a friend to guide thee" (170). Walsingham's disingenuousness in projecting Chatterton's suffering onto his own in the context of the novel is underscored by the novel's extract of the third stanza of the monody. That Walsingham begins after the stanzas of the original monody's opening lines describing Chatterton in "POVERTY's cold arms" makes the subsequent lines of horror closer to the egotism that Coleridge ascribes to those who falsely project onto Chatterton their own inconveniences: "To live by mental toil … / Till the last murmur of thy frantic soul, / In proud concealment from its mansion stole, / While ENVY springing from her lurid cave / Snatch'd the young Laurels from thy rugged grave" (170). The implication of these lines in the context of the novel thus changes in the context of the egotism underlying Walsingham's narration.

That *Walsingham* was published in 1799, two years before Robinson met Coleridge, suggests the possibility that either Robinson's novel influenced

---

[23] Cross also speaks to the fiction of Rowley vis-à-vis the connection between Robinson and Coleridge, Robinson having written under the assumed name of Laura Maria in the 1780s (60, 62).
[24] Robinson uses other of her poems in the novel, several of which are discussed in this chapter. For further discussion of the novel, particularly as it relates to Mary Shelley, see Chapter 4.

Coleridge or that Robinson had read Coleridge's lyrical ballads, or both. Regardless of how one identifies influence, however, viewing the novel through the lens of her relationship with Coleridge reveals their mutual engagement regarding the poetics of narrative subjectivity; the psychological depth of the new gothic; and the eroticized revolt against patriarchy. Early in *Walsingham*, the young protagonist's guardians challenge his identity as the rightful heir, catapulting the novel into a complicated plot involving mistaken identities and fights over inheritance, thereby introducing the novel's concern with the larger relationship between gender identity and patriarchy.

Walsingham's rescue of the "ivory cabinet" from the fire that destroys "the old manor house," later unearthed to reveal the evidence of his inheritance, becomes one of the novel's many ironies that speak to Robinson's distance from her novel's protagonist (124). Indeed, the belated discovery that Walsingham's antagonist, Sir Sidney, is a woman is central to the distance between author and narrator in the novel. Sidney's androgyny embodies the mutual concerns for Robinson and Coleridge regarding the tradition of representing eroticism through the heteronormative male narrator. Walsingham, in fact, returns to his "closet," a metaphor of uncanny prescience for the male inability to express sensibility in his heteronormative society, by contrast to the cross-dressing Sidney, a woman able to perform as male (101). One of the most satirical elements of *Walsingham* is the perversity of masculinist aggression as the novel portrays it through Walsingham's pattern of arming himself in self-defense, as he claims, and then acting as the perpetrator of violence himself.

In both Robinson's novel and Coleridge's *Christabel*, patrimony is held in tension with a nondual representation of gender. *Christabel* pits patriarchal dualism against androgynous nondualism through the conflict between Christabel's dead mother, powerless to protect her from the contamination of Geraldine whom the narrator positions as a doppelganger for the mother. Geraldine's androgynous selfhood is a greater threat to patriarchy than a simple reversal of gender would suggest, readers having long speculated about the gender complications of Geraldine, from her androgynous name to the paradoxically rapacious behavior of what appeared to Christabel and her father to be a damsel in distress. Similarly, though Robinson's novel is filled with episodes of cross-dressing, from the dramatic central riddle of the novel, Sidney's lifelong disguise as a man, to a masquerade that includes Amelia's cross-dressing (300), the levels of androgyny in the novel complicate it beyond mere plot device, as Byrne notes: "Sidney is the perfect union of the sexes. S/he quivers with sensibility … but is also fit and strong …. S/he has benefited from a classical education and from vigorous physical exercise.… He is the perfect man because he is really a woman" (332).

As discussed above regarding Robinson's use of her monody on Chatterton in the novel, another element of *Walsingham* that complicates the relationship between gender and genre both in the novel itself and in the novel's relationship to Coleridge is its use of embedded poetry. These poems in the context of the novel give a yet more nuanced view of Robinson's approach to subjectivity, beginning with "The Snow Drop" (59). The textual history of Robinson's "Ode to the Snow-drop," published first in *The Post* and then in the novel as a poem written by Walsingham, is significant not only for what it shows about Robinson herself but about her distance from her protagonist and about her early conversation with Coleridge, who published "Apotheosis, or, the Snow-Drop" in the *Post* as a response to Robinson's poem, either in itself or in its fictional context.

If one attends to the poems' subjectivities, it is striking first to note that Robinson's Snow-drop is neuter throughout the poem. Coleridge's response in "Apotheosis" is that the Snow-drop is nipped in the bud by being born too soon. Robinson's poem itself suggests that its identity is negated by gaudy spring, whose exaggerated femininity is the poem's only reference to gender: Spring "shall all her gems unfold, / And revel 'midst her beds of gold, / When thou art seen no more!" (ll. 27–9). By contrast to spring who is vain and heedless of the Snow-drop, the poet identifies herself only in the last stanza through her empathy for the Snow-drop. Robinson thus performs a poetic move that anticipates Coleridge's in "Kubla Khan," waiting until the final stanza to reveal a poetic subject whose own gender is complicated by the poet's gaze on, not an object, but a fellow subject.

By making the "Snow-Drop" Walsingham's poem early in the novel, however, Robinson only retrospectively emphasizes the distinction between the authorial and the narrative voices. While it is true that Walsingham's "Snow-Drop" suggests his sense of being a victim of circumstance, Robinson's ironic distance from Walsingham is lost when one regards him not only as "a sensitive male character" but as a mouthpiece for Robinson (Cross, "Coleridge and Robinson," 45). That the poem appears early in *Walsingham* gives the reader a false sense of the protagonist's sensitivity. It is only with retrospective irony, from the perspective of Sidney's gender revelation, that Walsingham, the protagonist projecting his subjectivity onto the Snow-drop, comes to embody a histrionic masculinity that is the counterpart to spring's exaggerated femininity in the poem. The irony, therefore, is that Walsingham cannot fathom Sidney as anything but a rival, arming himself for each potential encounter. There have been a number of readings of Coleridge's "Apotheosis" as a response to Robinson's poem in the *Post*; however, if one reads Coleridge's poem as a simultaneous double response to Robinson's poem in the *Post* and to its fictional setting in the novel as Walsingham's poem, Coleridge's play with the Della Cruscan elements can be seen as tinged with the kind of irony recurring in Coleridge's poetry and prose.

One of the problems with treatments of the novel has been taking its narrator at face value as a "child of nature" (Byrne, 331). As in the case of the lines from the Chatterton monody appearing through the subjectivity of Walsingham, Robinson's voice behind Walsingham's narration challenges Walsingham's authority as protagonist. Robinson's satirical representation of Walsingham's masculinist subjectivity is compromised not only through the novel's Della Cruscanism and its gothic elements, but by inclusion of poems from several narrative subjectivities. While readers have been wont to take his voice as authorial in its gravity about his Rousseau-like Romantic heroism and the tragedy of his unrequited love for Isabella, Walsingham's assumptions about her relationship with Sidney make him appear ludicrous from the hindsight of the novel.[25]

Far from merely providing distraction or variety, therefore, the poems in the novel challenge a single narrative subjectivity implicit in the novel's traditional subgenres. The novel's poetry shares Coleridge's concerns with subjectivity in the lyrical ballads' blend of poetry and fiction. Like Coleridge's articulation of a recreative secondary imagination, the novel's poems represent

---

[25] Byrne qualifies Rousseau's influence on *Walsingham* through the novel's influence on Bronte's Heathcliff noting the difference between Walsingham's unrequited love for Isabella in contrast to Heathcliff's for Cathy; Byrne traces to Wollstonecraft Robinson's concerns in the novel about a woman's inheritance (330–2). The differences between Robinson and both Wollstonecraft and Bronte, however, are yet more stark. Whereas Heathcliff is "gypsy-like," Walsingham, as narrator, is so self-conscious about wanting to be a Romantic figure of mystery that he is ludicrous (Byrne, 330).

a splintering of selfhood. Robinson's juxtaposing two poems in the novel, one by Walsingham's landlord, Honest Ned, the other by Walsingham, underscores the centrality of gender in *Walsingham*'s fragmentation of selfhood. Whereas Walsingham's poem appears cliché in its perpetuation of gender binaries, Honest Ned's ballad of "The Doublet of Grey" is a fascinating commentary on the impossible condition of patriarchy (323). Robinson invokes the gothic elements of the Coleridgean lyrical ballad in Honest Ned's poem that tells of a young woman, Madeline, whose parents, "so wealthy, her kindred so proud," forbid her to marry her poor lover, Theodore: "Before they would see her wedded, a shroud / Should be Madeline's bridal array" (VII). Yet Madeline is no passive maiden forced into this binary represented by shroud and wedding gown: when her father murders Theodore, she instead escapes "from the castle of pride," donning a "doublet of grey" (X). Robinson has her heroine perform the symbolic action of dressing in a soldier's uniform and, in the dark, killing "her foe," whom she has heard proclaim that he has come to bury Theodore (XIX). When she discovers that it is her father whom she has murdered, "she bath'd her white bosom with gore" (XXI). Unlike Shakespeare's Juliet, Madeline does not commit suicide because of her lover's death but because of her patricide. That her grief over Theodore's death instead inspires her to dress as a man and wander the heath allows her, however, to perform the taboo murder of her father.

Honest Ned's poem underscores the larger narrative's androgynous underpinnings: that neither Walsingham nor the reader knows until the novel's end that his life-long rival, Sir Sidney, is actually female forces on the reader a reckoning with the assumptions of narrative authority, for Walsingham has been deeply entrenched in the masculinist binaries that Robinson herself subverts in the novel. The means by which the poem contaminates the novel is striking: following Ned's recitation is a gothic description of an approaching storm. Both Walsingham the character and *Walsingham* the novel, on a metanarrative level, are imbued with the eeriness of the ballad. Hearing a bell, Walsingham writes,

> I instantly turned towards the quarter from whence the solemn sound proceeded, and observed, by the grey morning light, the ivy-covered turrets of an ancient village church, just visible above the wood, whose ruined castle

my landlord had so minutely and superstitiously described. One half the mystery of the maid in her grey doublet was now elucidated; and I well knew that a story of supernatural horror requires only a somber outline, which time, and the inventive powers of the human mind, will not fail to fill up with the marvelous and terrific. (330)

Though Walsingham thinks he has a superior power of discernment to the uneducated Ned, both he and the reader are duped by Robinson about the central identity of Sidney which in turn requires a reassessment of all the assumptions Walsingham has made along the way. Even the binary of life and death becomes so muddled in the course of the novel that Walsingham's ratiocinative faculties betray him several times into believing a character dead who then appears alive later.

Epitomizing the divide between Robinson, the author dismantling systematic binaries, and Walsingham, the narrator entrenched in them, is a poem that Walsingham "had written at a very early age, and which, till that hour, had never since recurred to [his] memory" (311). The eight-line poem "Impromptu, on Woman" consists of four lines that are a series of binaries characterizing the gender: "greatest friend or foe"; "source of bliss or evil"; "weal or woe"; "an angel or a devil." The second half of the poem invokes "mother Eve," the first "given, / To make this busy bustling scene / A very Hell or Heaven!" Though Walsingham dismisses the poem as a childish production, it bears noting that the masculine subject is implicit: woman is given [to man, the subject, suggesting a brotherhood between poet and reader] so that by the novel's end, after the revelation of Sidney's female identity, his assumption of fraternity and the role of women in his life must be reevaluated.

Honest Ned's poem thus does not merely expand the theme of cross-dressing but contaminates both protagonist and novel. One can extend the implications of this deeper layer of challenge to gender binaries by revisiting and qualifying Robinson's friendship with Wollstonecraft, commonly seen as an influence on the novel. The novel's satire on patrimony, central to the novel's plot, however, becomes more than a fictionalized *Vindication of the Rights of Woman*. On Sidney's androgyny, studies have segregated the "cross-dressing" Robinson character from the Coleridgean/poetic androgyny of Geraldine. However, Robinson does not merely replicate a Shakespearean scenario nor does she enact a Wollstonecraftian allegory of female education: when the novel is viewed alongside her poetry and its affinity to Coleridge, the larger conflict between creativity and systematic binaries emerges.

Beyond the Wollstonecraft connection, therefore, the androgynous Sidney also speaks to the shared resistance to gender binaries. Larger and more ambivalent notions of identity and subjectivity emerge, such as seen in the representation of Julie, the prostitute who, in spite of her education, is victimized sexually by the nefarious Linbourne in Volume II. Thus, in spite of her Wollstonecraftian education, after the death of her intellectually nurturing father, she is "turned adrift on the merciless world," at which point, she says, "fate threw me into the vortex of dissipation, and I was overwhelmed, before I was aware of the peril that surrounded me" (210).

This theme of androgyny reaches a tipping point when Isabella falls in love with the image of Sir Sidney; this is not merely a Shakespearean plot device but rather resonates with a deeper challenge to epistemological dualism. Thus, Isabella's description of Sidney, whom she describes as "like a constellation," is strikingly nondual (128). In this context, Walsingham's subsequent jealous rage seems cliché, even without the reader's awareness that Sidney is actually female. With the hindsight of Robinson's final disclosure of Sidney's gender, it is ironic to return to Walsingham's initial description of Sidney: "handsome, polite, accomplished[, he] fenced like a professor of the science; painted with the correctness of an artist; was expert at all manly exercises; a delightful poet; and a fascinating companion" (129). Since Walsingham's projection of a love triangle among himself, Isabella, and Sidney drives the plot through the novel's four volumes, neither Walsingham nor the reader can understand until the final pages of the novel the irony of Sidney's assurance to Walsingham, "But do not fear me … . I never will be your rival" (130). When Sidney tells Walsingham, "Resign that which you can no longer possess," Walsingham thinks s/he is referring to Isabella but in fact s/he means the inheritance (132).

Robinson's choice to keep the reader in the dark about Sidney's disguise not only builds the plot's momentum but forces the reader to reevaluate Walsingham's narrative authority in moments when he appears to apply the most hermeneutical of examinations of Sidney to plumb the depths of Sidney's character: "I watched his countenance, and thought it was agitated by the consciousness of duplicity: I could scarcely suppress my rage" (147).

Walsingham here projects his own masculine desire and desire for conquest onto Sidney; the reader can only retrospectively glean the irony of such a moment regarding its repercussions for the patriarchal dualism upon which it is founded. On a metanarrative level, the reader can detect the male narrator is an ironic disguise of the female writer just as Sir Sidney's disguise allows the woman to claim her inheritance. Ultimately, Robinson, Coleridge, and, as Chapter 4 will argue, Mary Shelley form a lineage neither patriarchal or matriarchal, but androgynous in its dismantling of these binaries.[26]

Honest Ned's poem, "The Doublet of Grey," shares many levels of resonance with Coleridge's poetics, not only the concern with androgyny, but the deeper psychological questions of motive behind immoral acts, the intended subject of Coleridge's fragmentary *Magnum Opus*. Related is the subject of the perverse, a seemingly motiveless act otherwise considered evil. Shortly after Honest Ned recites his ballad, Walsingham speculates on the impulse of a "cool-blooded wretch who, calmly, thinkingly prepares the means of annihilating a fellow-creature—who waits with his intellects clear, his reason predominant over the violence of his passions, to destroy a being" (334). The notion that perversity instigates the greatest evil is closely aligned with masculinist ideology and its roots in dualism. Thus, Walsingham concludes Volume III with the recognition that his "perverse nature" has led him to the conflict that has driven him through the novel in his misbegotten erotic unions and their unhappy endings for, he says, if not for his perversity, "I should at that moment have proudly claimed the name of husband from the unhappy and neglected Amelia" (370).

A mysterious mariner who appears in the novel not only echoes both Coleridge's *Ancient Mariner* and Robinson's own "The Haunted Beach," but reveals the way both writers problematize subjectivity vis-à-vis the notion of evil. Early in Volume IV of *Walsingham*, a character named "old Griffith" appears, mirroring Coleridge's Mariner, who subverts the

---

[26] Among the satirical scenes of the novel are those in which characters opine about literature. One such scene involves a conversation about Charlotte Smith's poetry, one criticizing it for compromising the pleasure of the reader with genuine pathos: "[T]he pleasure experienced by her readers must be greatly diminished, by the reflection that so cultivated a mind should feel the pressure of real sorrows, amidst the rich and beautiful effusions of imagination" (238).

pious moral that "he prayeth best, who loveth best / All things both great and small" (ll. 647–8). As discussed in Chapter 1, instead of rejoining his community, the Wedding Guest turns "from the bridegroom's door. / He went like one that hath been stunned, and is of sense forlorn" (ll. 654–5).[27] The lack of redemption in *The Ancient Mariner*, in spite of the ostensibly pious message of the poem, takes on cosmic irony that reflects Coleridge's fascination with the perverse. Rather than redeem his auditor, the Mariner contaminates him with his sad wisdom that keeps him from the community represented by the wedding. In Robinson's novel, Griffith too needs to tell his tale to end suffering and, as with Coleridge's Mariner, telling his tale does not seem to help; however, unlike the story of Coleridge's Mariner, Griffith's is about his grief over his lost love, "little Peggy Gwynn" (385). Gender in this sequence, from Griffith's tale to Walsingham's response, bears study: Griffith refers to his once manly leg as a "flipper" (385). Not only emasculated by his wound, he has become dehumanized as a grotesque sea creature. He thus stands in contrast to Walsingham, whose narrative subjectivity is firmly masculinist as he contemplates which woman he will choose in the course of the novel.

By contrast to Coleridge's Wedding Guest, who resists the mesmerizing hold of the storyteller, Walsingham at first urges Griffith, the "honest soul," to tell his story: "It will relieve thy full heart, and, perhaps, enable it to bear an accumulation of sorrow without breaking it" (384). However, Walsingham grows uncomfortable even as the mariner begins: "I felt a strong desire to bid him depart; something of sympathy began to excite emotions which it had long been the labour of my mind to overcome" (385). From the perspective of Coleridge's Mariner, there is irony to Walsingham's resistance since it is not the strangeness of the mariner that disturbs him but rather the familiarity of something that hovers at the edge of consciousness.[28] Walsingham's discomfort seems to tap into a level of communication unnarrated in the story, since Griffith compares Peggy Gwynn's beauty and innocence to Walsingham's,

---

[27] This is the 1798 version, the only one Robinson would have known.
[28] Freud, citing Schelling, calls this the *unheimlich*, literally "unhomely" as that which is defamiliarized or, as it is translated, the uncanny. Freud describes it as ambivalent in containing what in a binary system is its opposite, *heimlich*, or homely (226). See Chapter 3 for discussion of Life-in-Death as a figure of the *unheimlich*.

drawing attention to the oddness of the comparison with an abrupt pause: "The girl was as fresh as a daisy, and had a heart as tender as—your honour's" (385).

Yet Walsingham identifies his discomfort with his own likeness to the position of Griffith, not Peggy: "Every vein in my heart throbbed in unison with old Griffith's as he advanced his story" (385). Griffith's story tells of his own kidnapping by a press-gang; his loss of a leg by a cannonball in a sea battle; a hurricane; and finally growing "old and helpless ... wandering about the world" (387). All the while it is Walsingham who induces Griffith to tell his story, plying him with wine as inducement for him to continue (386). The story, however, appears to end relatively happily with the erotic union of Griffith and Peggy, who "found no alteration in [him], except the want of a leg" (387). However, after four years of marriage, Peggy dies, leaving Griffith with their babies. He elaborates on the expenses of Peggy's funeral and raising the daughter, Judy, who eventually leaves him to become a companion to a wealthy woman, never returning.

Griffith's story resonates with echoes of and contrasts not only to Coleridge's Mariner but to Robinson's own "Haunted Beach"; like the fisherman of "The Haunted Beach," in the final stage of his life, Griffith lives in a "hovel, on the sandy beach, without a friend in the world to comfort me" (389). He says, "I used to sit and make my fishing-nets, and hear the salt waves dashing against the rocks or rolling on the sands, even to the very threshold of my little hovel" that is ultimately destroyed by winter storms, leaving him again to wander (389). Robinson has a different use for Griffith here than she has for the fisherman in "The Haunted Beach," of course: the novel is satirical, and Griffith is both pathetic and comical in the twists and turns of his story, especially by contrast to the gravity of Coleridge's Mariner and her poem's fisherman. Further, Griffith's purpose in the novel is to advance Walsingham's evolution, and so, unlike Coleridge's Wedding Guest, who goes off alone, a wiser man, Walsingham fills in the final pause with "reflection" about "those beings who, in the full enjoyment of every luxury, complain of Heaven's injustice, and hourly wish for death" (389). Indeed, Walsingham then writes a poem, "The Exile," inspired by Griffith's story. Walsingham inverts Griffith's gender binary, erasing the idealized women of Griffith's story to replace wife and daughter with a ravenous and menacing "she-wolf," mentioned twice in the poem (391–2).

As discussed earlier in this chapter, Robinson represents Walsingham as masculinist, her irony toward him detectable in her authorial voice behind his narration. Yet Walsingham is aware of his "egotism" that takes Robinson's novel beyond neoclassical satire (70). At times, Walsingham moves beyond the dualistic, Wordsworthian epistemology to behold a "liquid" nature rather than a universe of discrete objects (75). Robinson's tone toward her protagonist is ironic; as the novel comes to its climax with the revelation of Sidney as female, the novel realigns itself away from Walsingham's masculinist perspective to one of empathy for women's struggle with patriarchy. Yet the disguised Sidney is not just a plot device nor an opportunity for Wollstonecraftian polemic; a deeper sense of dismantling binaries can be seen in the novel particularly through the embedded poetry.

In the final volume of the novel, what had appeared earlier as satire on both Della Cruscan sensibility and gothic hyperbole shifts into a more pronounced indictment of a Wordsworthian poetics. Robinson shares with Coleridge a critique of memory that projects "a variety of hopes and fears" onto the "floods, which had been formed by mountain torrents in many parts of the country," as Walsingham muses upon his return to his childhood home, the manor house (435). The terror is literalized when, "wrapt in reflection," Walsingham is pushed and falls "headlong down the side of the mountain" (436). In spite of the moment functioning to move the plot forward, the language is increasingly Wordsworthian and thus ironic in its use of the gothic. Thus, Walsingham contemplates "the retrospect of my past life" and, as he does, discovers an old sword lying at the threshold of his door. True to his character throughout, he takes the opportunity to arm himself, thus descending from the lofty poeticizing to the bathetic, all the while remarking to his reader, Rosanna, "If any thing could reconcile my heart in sighing an eternal farewell to my native scenes, it would be the gloomy desolation in which I then beheld them" (439).

This reflection is followed by his decision to take the concealed sword into his aunt's chamber, further complicating the plot that is being hatched upon him by Mrs. Blagden and her nephew. In Walsingham's character, therefore, Robinson increasingly combines Wordsworthian nostalgia with gothic dread that yields the perverse; in so doing, Robinson dismantles the Wordsworthian subject. His predilection to reflection lapses into nostalgia that seems to satirize such elegiac poems of reflection and description as Wordsworth's "Intimations Ode," nowhere more obvious than in his final poem, "My Native Home":

> And oh! When Youth's extatic hour,
>> And Passion's glowing noon are past;
> Should age behold the tempest low'r,
>> And Sorrow blow it keenest blast. (443)

The irony is that Walsingham's emotionalism has been associated with violence throughout the novel, provoking aggression in others when he perversely arms himself, fleeing yet becoming aggressor in episode after episode.

The novel's nostalgia is undercut most dramatically following Walsingham's disbelief over the discovery of Sidney being a woman. While Walsingham despairs, "From my infancy I have been the dupe of false hopes and imaginary evils: I have alternately trusted the world, and been deceived by my credulity," Hanbury remarks that Walsingham is the "most persecuted of mortals" (470). The irony is pointed. Robinson shares with Coleridge a "willing suspension of disbelief," a quality that neither Wordsworth nor Walsingham can muster. Robinson's authorial voice behind Walsingham demands of her reader this willing suspension of disbelief for the same reason that Coleridge came to identify it as the recreative power of secondary imagination.

There is a connection, then, between the polarizing of scholarship on the relationship between Coleridge and Robinson—the divide being between the biographical and the poetic—and the polarizing within Coleridge scholarship between the poetic and religiophilosophical. Just as Coleridge's engagement with Robinson underscores the rigor of her approach to poetic voice, so too does Robinson's engagement with Coleridge underscore the way gender and sexuality function beyond the biographical in his poetics.[29] Robinson's reader, in turn, can glean the refusal to indulge in either nostalgia or the simplistic

---

[29] Anya Taylor has argued forcefully for Coleridge's sensitivity to the feminine in her book; this study wishes to take the argument further in the direction of the epistemological implications of his empathic writings on female sexuality.

binaries that the dense fabric of the novel dispels even as the characters embrace them.

Coleridge after Robinson: The Paradox of Mourning Fellowship Founded on Nondualism

Coleridge's 1800 "A Stranger Minstrel" celebrates Robinson's writing as he mourns her death in precisely the terms they had shared, namely the dismantling of binaries, not only those found in the Wordsworthian poetics of description and reflection but the larger binary systems of western thought. He begins the poem lying "Midway the ascent" of Mount Skiddaw, a position itself that refuses connection to the phallic peak nor the valley below (l. 2). During the repose, his "sweet mood of sad and humorous thought" mirrors his physical position with the nondual emotion that simultaneously embodies laughter and tears (l. 9). Suddenly "a form within me rose, within me wrought / With such strong magic" (l. 10). Coleridge does not identify the "form" nor where it is, but one senses it is her nondual spirit freed of the physical body that separates them. By contrast, Skiddaw speaks with "sullen majesty," a masculine presence that nevertheless corrects the poet who wishes "SHE were here," demanding her biographical selfhood in the specific location he inhabits (l. 23). Skiddaw instead responds, "She dwells belike in scenes more fair / And scorns a mount so bleak and bare" (ll. 32-3). Paradoxically, the mountain recognizes that she is free from the binaries that have constrained her in life. Skiddaw ends the poem with echoes of her poems, from "haunted beach" to "maniac," recognizing that Robinson inhabits him and so frees him of his masculinist symbolism:

> I too, methinks, might merit
>
> The presence of her spirit!
>
> To me too might belong
>
> The honour of her song and witching melody!
>
> Which most resembles me,
>
> Soft, vaporous, and sublime (ll. 61-6)

The vaporous sublimity of Robinson's witchery permeates both poet and landscape in spite of Coleridge's wish for her physical presence, the elegy thus ending with the poet still longing: "I would, I would, that she were here!" Coleridge expresses the paradox of nondual vision for the living poet, namely, that in spite of the permeable creative spirit, the human longing for the "other" remains.

Yet Robinson herself anticipates the paradox of such mourning in her 1793 "Stanzas to a Friend, Who Desired to Have my Portrait," a poem built around intensifying ironies as she moves from the ludicrousness of a portrait to her own "living portrait" in poetry. She begins the poem by asking her friend why one would desire a portrait. She then responds with an image whose complex epistemological implications take the rest of the poem to unravel. Robinson asks whether the purpose is "[t]o keep a shade on Mem'ry's eye" (l. 2). Robinson shares with Coleridge a suspicion of memory as a lesser faculty than imagination. To keep a shade on memory would on the surface mean not to allow memory to see, the implication being that once she has died, the portrait freezes her at a specific point in time and dims earlier memories. But shade can also suggest "spirit" or "ghost," in which case the desire to freeze her in time is undermined by her "shade" that cannot be contained in the "frame" she goes on to develop in the next lines. Her response, therefore, a rhetorical question, is paradoxical: "What bliss can REASON prove / To gaze upon a senseless frame?" (ll. 3–4). The "senseless frame" plays upon the picture's frame and her physical being. Robinson here upsets the binary of reason and emotion, "Reason," traditionally opposed to such emotions as "bliss," especially because such an emotion cannot be "proven." Through the viewer's gaze, she not only "looks eternally the same," but she is denied a voice: her "lips" will "NEVER move" (ll. 5–6).

Robinson gradually unravels the earlier "shade on Mem'ry's eye" by first suggesting that behind the friend's request for her portrait is a desire to remember her as smiling and gentle since "those lips no anger can betray"; the portrait thus excludes from the frame all emotions not traditionally acceptable for women including "reproach" and "disdain" (ll. 8, 11, 12). She speculates more deeply on the friend's concern that "FORM may quickly fade," remedied by the PAINTER'S skill" that keeps her perpetually "blooming" (ll. 13, 16, 17). Robinson thus responds with vehement rejection of memory as the friend would have it, substituting her own portrait, "The PICTURE of MY MIND!" (l. 24).

The rest of Robinson's poem is a powerful self-portrait that begins with the epistemological statement, "'Tis difficult ourselves to know" that she attributes to a "BARD" who "was conscious grown; / And when he scrutiniz'd HIS HEART," discovered ugly emotions such as envy that "lurk'd in ev'ry part" (ll. 26–9). Such a poetic consciousness rivals the inferior faculty of memory, a courageous exploration of the deepest consciousness where one "Scarce" recognizes it as "HIS OWN!" (l. 30). Robinson thus proceeds through a sequence of stanzas that note the many facets of her paradoxical nature, replacing the painter's brush with her pencil that can be called recreative in its breaking down the objectified representation of her "self" and replacing it with a complex interplay of "the brightest tints" and "darkest shades" (ll. 112–13).

This sequence of texts by Robinson and Coleridge, in their poems, essays, and fiction complicates the subject/object duality that has dominated discussion of male and female poets, as both Robinson and Coleridge dismantle the systematic binaries of gender, genre, and epistemology in order to explore the recreative. That such a process is both individual and shared adds another complicating dimension to the canonical/noncanonical binary.

3

Secondary Imagination, Contamination, and Androgyny: Rethinking Coleridgean Fragmentation from "Kubla Khan" and *Christabel* to *Magnum Opus*

As Chapter 2 has discussed, the poetics of androgyny and contamination common to Coleridge and Robinson exposes their representations of flaws in the materialist foundation of their late Enlightenment world. Their shared dismantling of systematic binaries, taken together with the foundation in Chapter 1 of Coleridge's early ambivalence toward philosophical dualism he inherited as a male writer, provides a foundation for turning to Coleridge's literary fragments in this chapter.[1] The polarization between gender and philosophy in Coleridge studies detailed in Chapter 1 has been an obstacle for exploring the androgynous epistemology that undergirds Coleridge's poetry and prose. This chapter thus returns to Coleridge by adding a third dimension, textual fragmentation, along with androgyny and contamination, to describe the paradoxical trajectory toward his *Magnum Opus*.

As seen in *Biographia Literaria*, Coleridge's frustration with philosophical precedents, including both the materialism of his earliest influences and the transcendentalism that overturned it, is integrally connected to his alienation from the masculinist poetics that continue to tie him to Romantic canonicity.

---

[1] As the Introduction to this study has argued, that such systematic binaries are foundational to a masculinist epistemology should not create its own essentializing binary of male and female writers. William Blake most consistently embraces the nondual, including its implications for the gender binary. His figure of Oothoon in *Visions of the Daughters of Albion* in particular reflects the plight of the visionary woman in a patriarchal society. See the Introduction to my *Guide to the Cosmology of William Blake* for a fuller discussion.

Shifting focus to the interplay between Robinson's and Coleridge's nonbinary response to categorical imperatives centralizes their representations of the relationship between gender and creativity, a commonality that Chapter 4 links as well to Mary Shelley. Along with the incoherence of *Biographia Literaria*, the fragmentary state of *Magnum Opus* is often explained by what appears the inability of Coleridge "the philosopher" to emerge from his sources. Fragmentation has thus been connected to charges of plagiarism, thereby reducing his prose works to failure. However, the paradoxical nature of the recreative act Coleridge calls secondary imagination can serve as a lens both to view the fragments of *Magnum Opus* as well as to look retrospectively at those earlier fragments discussed in Chapter 1.

To address the fragmentation of the longer prose works, this chapter first revisits "Kubla Khan." Discussed first in Chapter 1 as working against Wordsworth's systematic binaries, then in Chapter 2 in conversation with Robinson's poetry regarding subjectivity and gender, this chapter adds new focus on the poem's incoherence vis-à-vis its subversion of categorical imperatives. "Kubla Khan" does not move toward completeness according to neoclassical standards. Instead, the poem builds fragment upon fragment, a metatextual commentary on the recreative act of nature in stanza 2. Coleridge's insertion of the passage from "The Picture, or the Lover's Resolution" at the end of his Preface to "Kubla Khan" is a poetic interruption to the prose introduction that the reader assumes will explain the meaning of the poem. The extract from "The Picture" instead creates a moment of incoherence mirroring the knock at the door, the visitor's interruption of the poet's vision. Yet paradoxically it is through the interruption rather than the fictional editor's attempt at explanation that the reader gains access to the poem that follows. The insertion of the stanza from "The Picture" occurs just after the fictitious editor has described the poet's "mortification" upon discovering only a fragment of his vision remains following the equally fictitious visitor from Porlock interrupting his recording the "whole" of the vision (181). The intrusion of the lines, "all the charm/Is broken—all that phantom-world so fair / Vanishes," gestures toward the means by which "Kubla Khan," the poem itself that follows, dismantles the aesthetic binaries of wholeness and fragmentation connected, respectively, to success and failure. Thus, the line, the "thousand circlets ... each mis-shape the other," is itself the paradoxical vision.

Coleridge thus subverts his editor-persona: the reader does not see the promised reintegration of the "poor youth's" reflection for, according to secondary imagination, the misshaping of the image into a thousand circlets is itself the artistic vision. The second stanza of the poem itself tells of a powerfully feminized nature who, paradoxically savage, holy, and enchanted, fragments and recreates Kubla's pleasure dome into "a miracle of rare device" (l. 35). By the third stanza, the poet mourns his fragile vision of the Abyssinian maid as merely conditional, "Could I revive within me / Her symphony and song," implying that he will not achieve the poetical character he nevertheless envisions at the end of the poem. Like nature in stanza 2, he is both demonic and divine (ll. 42–3). As the interrupted Preface has shown, the rupturing of binaries foundational to traditional precepts of artistic success would be equated with failure. In the context of the poem, however, the nonbinary poetics, simultaneously demonic and divine, achieves secondary imagination. From Kubla's perspective, the feminized nature that explodes his pleasure dome is evil. From the editor's perspective, the poet is a tragic failure. For the poet, however, the wailing that is simultaneously erotic and mournful, "holy and inchanted [sic]," is the symphony and song of the damsel that he can only hope to "revive," perhaps the most nonbinary of paradoxes since the representation of artistic failure is itself the achievement of the poem (ll. 14, 42).

Christabel: Subverting Masculinist Subjectivity

During his transformative German tour, Coleridge immersed himself in the transcendental writings of Schelling, Kant, and Schlegel, whose powerful influence speaks to the impulse that, as I have argued above, had been present though repressed even in Coleridge's earliest poetry, namely the nondualism that challenged the foundation of associationism and that would in turn be the key to his literary relationships with women writers.[2] The textual history

---

[2] Though McFarland's 1969 study of Coleridge's relationship to German Romantic writers was published roughly twenty years before the emergence of gender studies and the recovery of romantic women writers' texts that transformed the field of Romanticism, its influence continues to be felt through more recent though equally hermetic studies that treat the philosophical tradition that influenced Coleridge. Thus, McFarland underscores that Coleridge "did not, like Goethe, stifle his metaphysical interests the better to breathe in the green world of things, and he did not, like the transcendental systematists, distort the texture of experience to achieve a completed network

of *Christabel* can be seen as a map to trace the journey of Coleridge's gendered revolt against dualism. In his 1816 Preface to the poem, written the year before *Biographia Literaria*, Coleridge himself speaks of *Christabel*'s failure, the culmination of its textual history that holds a key to its willful incoherence.³ Begun in 1798 (Part One), revised in 1800 (Part Two), published in 1816, *Christabel*'s section titles correspond to the phases of Coleridge's work on it, suggesting the sea change Coleridge experienced epistemologically between Part I and Part II, when he visited Germany after his early immersion in Wordsworthian poetics that Coleridge himself shaped through associationist philosophy.⁴

Coleridge's March 1801 letter to Thomas Poole not only connects the effect of his "most intense study" of Kant and other German philosophers to his having "overthrown the doctrine of Association, as taught by Hartley" but the letter's imagery itself suggests the integral relationship between his divorce from Wordsworth's poetics of association with the fragmented composition of *Christabel*: "Poverty was staring me in the face, yet I dared behold my Image miniatured in the pupil of her hollow eye, so steadily did I look her in the Face!—for it seemed to me a Suicide of my very soul to divert my attention from Truths so important, which came to me almost as a Revelation / Likewise, I cannot express … the loathing, which I … felt, when I attempted to write, merely for the Bookseller, without any sense of the moral utility of what I was writing.—I shall therefore …, immediately publish my CHRISTABEL" (Halmi et al., 627). Coleridge genders the situation as outside the philosophical system of cause and effect: beholding Poverty personified female, he discovers his "Image miniatured in the pupil of her hollow eye," an intersubjectivity between himself and feminized Poverty. The contrast between Coleridge's

---

of abstraction," thereby debunking the older dismissal of Coleridge as merely adapting German romanticism (*Coleridge and the Pantheist Tradition*, 110). However, this study challenges the limitations posed by these parameters in their masculinist exclusivity. Even as recently as van Woudenberg's 2018 study of Coleridge's "cosmopolitan intellectualism," the focus on Coleridge's intellectual engagement at Gottingen University continues to be exclusively patriarchal.

3   The importance of *Christabel* to *Biographia Literaria* is central to this chapter because it links this gendering to Coleridge's contention not only against associationism but because of the German philosophy with which he wrestles in *Biographia Literaria*.

4   It is often said that Wordsworth was Coleridge's most important poetic creation as he encouraged the Wordsworthian poetics of memory that Coleridge then denounced most explicitly in *Biographia Literaria* chapter XIV. The early influence was so deep and personal to Coleridge that he named his two sons after its central proponents, Hartley and Berkeley.

nondual state of penury and the mercenary world of interdependent writers, readers, and booksellers suggests the source of tension between Coleridge and Wordsworth, not only in the latter's refusal to include *Christabel* in the ostensibly collaborative *Lyrical Ballads*, but also in his blaming *Rime of the Ancient* Mariner for poor sales of the volume.[5]

As discussed in Chapter 1, the plasticity of Coleridge's larger poetic consciousness is the artist's recreative gift that evolves into the secondary imagination of *Biographia Literaria*. Due to Coleridge's paradoxical play between the plagiarisms preceding chapter XIII and attributing his original hierarchy of mental faculties to a "judicious friend" in chapter XIII, his revolutionary concept of the recreative has remained elusive. In fact, the definition of secondary imagination and the denunciation of memory as a faculty he calls, disparagingly, "Fancy" signal a dramatic turn in the subsequent chapter XIV regarding the way he characterizes Wordsworthian poetics. Not until chapter XIV of his 1817 *Biographia Literaria* does Coleridge articulate the poetic foundation of his bitterness and frustration with Wordsworth. Coleridge can only do so following the literal and figurative center of the book, chapter XIII, in which he defines secondary imagination as the recreative faculty that he sets above Fancy, that faculty merely rearranging memories, Coleridge thereby dismissing in a single statement the associationism with which he had grappled for decades. Thus, chapter XIV contrasts his own poetics as a "willing suspension of disbelief" to Wordsworth's "language of *real* life" (Engell and Bate II, 6, 8). Behind the contrasting terms Coleridge uses is a distinction between his own poetics as transgressing the bounds between binaries and Wordsworth's separation between his poetic subjectivity and its objectification of the world of phenomena.

With irony, then, Coleridge uses the language of contamination to describe the effects of wealth on creativity in a 1797 letter to Poole; Coleridge claims that his veins are "uncontaminated with one drop of Gentility" (Halmi et al., 613). In his poetry, however, Coleridge often gives the language of contamination

---

[5] See Halmi et al., 54. Dorothy Wordsworth was much more taken with the poem than her brother. In *Grasmere Journal* of 1800, on August 31 she records, "Coleridge read us a part of *Christabel*. Talked much about the mountains, etc. etc" (39). On 4 October she writes, "[e]xceedingly delighted with the second part of *Christabel*," and the following morning, "Coleridge read a 2nd time *Christabel*; we had increasing pleasure" (45).

to his masculinist narrator and other patriarchal figures in their response to any threat to their world of gender binaries. Coleridge's sexually ambiguous figures swerve from masculinist binaries that demean all that is not "self"; in *Christabel*, his prudish male narrator takes unreliability to a new level, balking at what is going on between Christabel and Geraldine when they are alone in Christabel's bedroom; the literal and symbolic patriarch, Sir Leoline, represents the inflexible and wrongheaded repressiveness by patriarchy of female eros, nondualism, and creative energy. Geraldine subverts this repressiveness, spreading her contamination of the dualistic realm. Even the bard, Bracy, misinterprets his own dream of "a bright green snake / Coil'd around [the dove's] wings and neck" (*Christabel*, qtd. in Halmi, et al., 537–8). The unreliable narrator has led the reader to the hermeneutical goal of identifying Geraldine with evil and therefore with the snake, and Christabel with innocence and therefore the dove. However, while the Bard's interpretation is incorrect from a traditional perspective, the poem, reflecting Coleridge's larger challenges to dualism, subverts the equation of Geraldine's contamination of the patriarchal abode with evil and Christabel's virginal objectification as good. McGavran observes that Coleridge appends as the Conclusion to Part II the verse letter he had written to Southey on his baby, Hartley, thus putting at stake patriarchy's "fault lines" in the poem (5).

From the poem's first critical reception, *Christabel* inspired shock and repulsion in terms that betray its threat to tradition. It was seen as particularly disturbing because it was not fully understood: a "something disgusting at the bottom of his subject," as William Hazlitt wrote in first reviewing the poem for the *Examiner* in 1816, "which is but ill glossed over by a veil of Della Cruscan sentiment and fine writing—like moon-beams playing on a charnel-house, or flowers strewed on a dead body" (Jackson et al., *Critical Heritage*, 1:207). A second attack appeared in *The Edinburgh Review* in September of that year: "Some Genius in a pamphlet ... has pronounced poor *Christabel* 'the most obscene poem in the English Lange [sic]'" (*Collected Letters*, 4:917–18). Regardless of who authored the review, it is significant that Coleridge assumed it was also Hazlett, whose *Examiner* statement first unwittingly captures the poem's exploration of a psychological nondualism that juxtaposes the gothic horror and the sentimental through the reference to Della Cruscanism. With its own figurative language, the review represents the ironic interplay of the human with nature by bringing together the multiply clashing images of "moon-beams playing on a charnel-house" and "flowers strewed on a dead body."

Though the reviewers could not pinpoint why the poem so disturbed them, Coleridge's early claim that Geraldine was witch or vampire begs the question of why she was so disturbing rather than offers a definitive explanation. Criticism thereafter, explaining Coleridge's contradictions in *Christabel* as an attempt to defend himself against charges of indecency, has gone so far as to suggest that *Christabel* would have been improved with glosses such as those in the 1834 revision of the original 1798 *Rime of the Ancient Mariner*. This suggestion not only misses Coleridge's irony in adding those glosses to *Mariner* as a means to create a most unreliable marginal "narrator" in the form of a fictitious and imposing editor, but, more to the present point, *Christabel* is precisely about moral ambiguity with repercussions for the multiple valences of epistemology, creativity, and eroticism.

Geraldine has continued to be equated with evil in many scholarly iterations. Harold Bloom, for instance, remarks that "it is Christabel who actively introduces evil into the castle by lifting the vampire over" (*Visionary Company*, 214). For Bloom, Geraldine represents the chaos traditionally known as evil resulting from the repression of imagination: "The work of Imagination in *Christabel* is to transform the crudity of evil into something beautiful" (*Visionary Company*, 213). In spite of the masculinist position Bloom here assumes for Coleridge, his observation that, for Coleridge, evil is the result of driving imagination underground resonates as a reading that does not take "evil" at face value but rather finds irony in Coleridge's ability to divide himself from his narrator and enter the very evil the narrator decries. Nevertheless, contemporary scholarship has largely perpetuated the vampire/lamia interpretation of Geraldine, including what has been reduced to Geraldine's "sexual initiation" of Christabel, "creating another femme fatale much as vampires kissed their victims into fellowship" (Hoeveler, 184).

Sexually, the androgynous Geraldine embodies the "witchery" of an imagination that defies patriarchal binaries and their attendant taboos represented by Sir Leoline and his manor. Into this bastion of patriarchy Christabel carries Geraldine, introducing contamination into its rigidly defined world. Coleridgean witchery—whether that of Geraldine here; Nature bursting forth in the second stanza of *Kubla Khan* and destroying Kubla's pleasure dome; or the animating breeze that plays the Eolian Harp—wreaks havoc with a patriarchy founded on the conventional dualism that induces Sarah to bid Coleridge "walk humbly" with his God.

Viewed in the context of the range of androgynous figures Coleridge creates to represent the dismantling of binaries, Geraldine thus can be seen to embody the elasticity that recurs as one of the most revolutionary forms of nondualism. Coleridge connects Geraldine's ambiguous sexual identity to the poem's play with epistemological binaries. Her contamination of the character Christabel may thus be described as metasexual as her contamination of the poem *Christabel* is metatextual. Geraldine thus spreads both sexual and textual chaos through the patriarchal world of stark binaries represented by Sir Leoline's ancestral home.

This paternalistic dualism also induces the prudish narrator of *Christabel* to pray for protection from the unnamable moment of contamination by Geraldine of both the character Christabel and the poem *Christabel*. Though readers have projected an authorial voice that assumes Coleridge "needed to be lord of his own utterance" (Fulford, "Mary Robinson," 10), it is the androgynous Geraldine who speaks the lines from which the phrase is drawn: "In the touch of this bosom there worketh a spell, / Which is lord of thy utterance, Christabel!" (169, ll. 255–6).

Geraldine's words here speak to a more complex gendering in the poem, a form of androgyny suggested by the tension between the masculine power in "lord" of thy utterance created by "the touch of this bosom"; she thereby contaminates not only Christabel, whose name suggests that she is pure martyr or victim, but the full structure of patriarchy represented by the Baron and his castle. Coleridge's 1824 annotation might explain the scholarly predilection for reading these lines as Coleridge's denunciation of Geraldine as "wicked" and "evil": "As soon as the wicked Bosom, with the mysterious sign of Evil stamped thereby, touches Christabel, she is deprived of the power of disclosing what has occurred" (169, n. 4). Certainly this is the view of the narrator and of the patriarchal presence represented by Leoline, but the larger consciousness of the poem undermines the statement's denunciation of Geraldine's power; to use Coleridge's annotations as a means to argue for authorial intention dismisses the ways he not only decomposes selfhood in his poetics but often treats the assumption of authorial intention with irony.[6]

Complicating this notion of Coleridge's decomposition in *Christabel* is its echoing of Robinson's 1791 "Ode to Beauty," at once celebration and elegy to the fragility of beauty, "phantom of an hour," and the cruelty of the world (*Poems*, 1). This poem's contemplation of the female persona as simultaneously subject and object, natural and "witching," culminates with Beauty represented as a fragile bud, though previously "Scorch'd by the burning eye of day," transplanted "Beneath an aged oak's wide spreading shade" (ll. 4, 62, 55). The oak tree proleptically echoes that in *Christabel*, where Christabel prays for the safety of her lover, only to manifest as Geraldine. Bringing Robinson's ode into conversation with *Christabel* gestures to a yet more radical nondualism of *Christabel*, in which age and youth, self and other, defy the abuses of systematic binaries. The connection between the two works would suggest, then, that Coleridge decomposes not only the double identification of the female but complicates it further through the masculinist context of his poem.

For Coleridge's concern with masculinist objectification of the female, the problem of hermeneutics is itself the message of the poem: through Geraldine, Coleridge dismantles the male subjectivity central to the ballad genre. The bard Bracy doubly misinterprets his dream of the dove strangled by the snake: on one level, the imagery of the poem has anticipated a "correct" interpretation from a traditional narrative point of view. Christabel, not Geraldine, is the dove, Geraldine the snake. Yet just as Geraldine's eyes are described as reptilian, so are Christabel's: the contamination has drawn out an element of Christabel's selfhood that has been repressed as her doubly martyred name suggests.

As Christabel is left without a voice to warn her father that Geraldine is contaminating their world, her status as pure victim comes to a climax. The poem collapses into the coda called Conclusion to Part the Second that appears as a disconnected fragment, having nothing explicit to do with the plot of the lyrical ballad:

---

[6] See Chapter 1 for the term "decomposition" as Ernest Jones uses it in its literary context. That Coleridge's poetics operates on a principle similar to Shakespeare's takes on added significance for the discussion, at the end of this chapter, of Coleridge's lecture on *Othello*.

> And what, if in a world of sin
>
> (O sorrow and shame should this be true!)
>
> Such giddiness of heart and brain
>
> Comes seldom save from rage and pain,
>
> So talks as it's most used to do.
>
> (Christabel, qtd. in Halmi, et al., 179, ll. 661–5)

That *Christabel's* profoundly unreliable narrator cannot sustain control over the story he is trying to tell in turn suggests the metanarrative message in which Geraldine represents that witchery that breaks apart a conventionally told story, perhaps the one that Wordsworth would have included in *The Lyrical Ballads* rather than the *Christabel* on whose incoherence Coleridge insists and for which Wordsworth jettisoned it in the second edition.

In his Preface to *Christabel*, Coleridge describes having seen the whole with a "liveliness of vision"; his problem from a conventional point of view is in translating vision into the discursive linearity of narrative form. Coleridge's son, Hartley, in later characterizing *Christabel* as a "narrative fragment" understood the metatextual level of the poem that he referred to as "the fondling of his [father's] genius"; this observation plays on the creation of upheaval by the poem that tells a story about the upheaval created by the contaminating power of secondary imagination. Coleridge describes his struggle in producing the poem using terms of a maternal poetic identity: "Every line has been produced by me with labor-pangs" (*Notebooks of STC*, 4, 5032).

That Goethe's 1797 *The Bride of Corinth* may have inspired *Christabel* has led to arguments reinforcing the very gender binary that the poem subverts. As in the case of so many other of Coleridge's "borrowings" from sources, his changes to his sources reveal how radically he departs from them. Yet criticism largely projects the source onto Coleridge's echo of it. Describing Goethe's "daring ballad" as the "first literary depiction of a female vampire who was not monstrous but beautiful and irresistible," for instance, Lore Metzger claims that "vampiric Geraldine probably owes her beautiful looks and seductive demeanor to Goethe's 'bride'" (7).[7] Rather than merely imitate

---

[7] Metzger notes that Coleridge borrows from Bishop Thomas Percy's 1765 *Reliques of Ancient English Poetry* "only the material for an opening tableau: Christabel in the Castle woods late at night praying for her distant lover's well-being" (13). The textual history appears yet more complicated regarding

Goethe, however, Coleridge subverts him by complicating the relationship between the unreliable male narrator and the underlying subjectivity of the ballad. Coleridge not only splits the maternal role between the spirit of Christabel's dead mother and Geraldine but scrambles the gender relations of a male poet to his text by identifying not as father but mother.[8] Coleridge thus keeps the unreliable male narrator but, unlike Goethe, makes his presence felt throughout, Goethe equalizing his characters through their long speeches to each other. Coleridge problematizes the patriarchal abode of Leoline in his poem, a structure that comes to represent Coleridge's most radical departure from Goethe, namely Coleridge's transformation of the protagonist from the naïve young man in Goethe's poem. The eponymous "Bride" would therefore become Geraldine in Coleridge's poem; Goethe's mother figure skulks about the doorway to keep the young woman from her son by contrast to the ghostly presence of Christabel's mother who is inadequate to "protect" her from the ambiguously gendered Geraldine.

A figure emerging from the dismantling power of secondary imagination, Geraldine exposes the illusion underlying the patriarchal world that results in a series of failures in the poem: the inability of the virginal Christabel to tell her own story because it defies narrative decency; the inability of the bard Bracy to understand his vision so that he reduces it to the conventional story of a virgin in distress, thereby collapsing Christabel and Geraldine into the passive victimization of the female. The most hermeneutically controversial moment in the poem is Geraldine's disrobing in Part I, itself signaling the distance between Coleridge's demand for a "willing suspension of disbelief" and the narrator who, abashed, cedes control over the ballad to the reader's imagination: "Her silken robe, and inner vest, / Dropt to her feet, and full in view, / Behold! Her bosom and half her side — / A sight to dream of, not to tell" (ll. 244–7). The "sight to dream of" suggests either the wishfulness of the male narrator as voyeur or the repression of the taboo sight, or both: the reader is given the moment from the male narrator's perspective as well as the poem's authorial perspective as nondual.

---

the relationship of gender, child–parent relationships, and victimization: Percy's source was, in turn, a treatise by Phlegon of Tralles of which only a fragment remains.

[8] See McFarland on the distinction between Goethe and Coleridge regarding the mother.

The narrator is not the only male figure to fail in the poem; Christabel's father fails his daughter. His name, Leoline, gestures to his embodiment of patriarchy that demands primogeniture and points to one of several reasons for his resentment of Christabel, whose mother died giving birth to her, thereby not only depriving Leoline of his wife but of the possibility of siring a son to carry on his noble line. His home is contaminated, from the perspective of a patriarchal literary tradition represented by the narrator and Leoline, who thus pushes away his own voiceless daughter. By contrast to Christabel, Leoline regards Geraldine sentimentally as the beautiful daughter of an estranged friend; thus, for him Geraldine is a means to ending his feud with her father. In this way, there is a split between Leoline's interpretation of Geraldine and that of the narrator, who has told the reader about the spell Geraldine has cast on Christabel. However, there is also a split between both men and the authorial voice, whose secondary imagination creates Geraldine as the contaminating agent who dismantles patriarchy. The metatextual overturning of patriarchy represented by Leoline not only subverts the ironically conventional narrator's control over the text but defies the new literary culture Coleridge himself had formed that lauds the Wordsworthian poetics that rejected *Christabel*.

Coleridge's ultimate defiance of the systematic binaries underlying Wordsworth's definition of poetry in his Preface to *Lyrical Ballads* is Coleridge's Conclusion to Part II, an appendage of a verse letter he had written to Southey on his baby, Hartley; by recontextualizing it as a coda to *Christabel*, as McGavran states, Coleridge puts at stake no less than the "fault lines" in patriarchy (5).[9] What may have been no more than doggerel as a letter becomes sinister in the context of *Christabel*, suggesting the perverse suppression of transgressive desire by patriarchal domination. The couplets, as the poem itself states, "force together / Thoughts so all unlike each other," thereby creating in the singsong quality of the short rhyming lines a haunting sense of the father's predatory "pleasures" that "flow in so thick and fast / Upon his heart, that he at last / Must needs express his love's excess / With words of unmeant bitterness" (ll. 654–5; 650–3). Yoking apparently antithetical ideas and emotions is the epitome of the willing suspension of disbelief in an imagination beyond the discursive mind's mutually impermeable binaries.

---

[9] Regarding this textual history, see Halmi et al., 179, n. 6.

Dejection's Layering Fragments of Selfhood

Dejection is the most textually androgynous of Coleridge's poems, whose drafts betray a shapeshifting, desired reader. The many layers of revision speak to a union desired (to Sara Hutchinson) set against unions that constrict (to Sarah Fricker, to materialist philosophy, and ultimately to the Wordsworthian poetics of memory), and, bitterly, to Wordsworth's own successful unions, literally to Mary Hutchinson, and, figuratively, to a new literary public that has lauded Wordsworth for a poetics that has both abandoned Coleridge and from which Coleridge has turned away.[10]

Coleridge's epigraph to this 1802 poem, a passage from the Ballad of Sir Patrick Spence, imbues with irony the cause-and-effect relationship of the folkloric omen that the "the new Moon, / With the old Moon in her arms" signals the coming of a "deadly storm" (l. 155). In this image, all three elements—gender, creativity, and epistemology—work together to complicate Coleridge's poetics. The new moon embracing the old moon both hearkens back to and complicates the bedroom scene in *Christabel* in which Geraldine "holds the maiden in her arms" (l. 287).[11]

The biographical emphasis of *Dejection* that has dominated discussion of the poem points to Coleridge's use of opium as "necessary to deaden his feelings about his unhappy marriage, his love for Sara Hutchinson, his lack of achievement" (Hayter, 208), Coleridge's layering of addressees in the poem wreaks havoc with traditional readings of the conversation poem, however. The poem's textual history suggests a temporal linearity that lies at the foundation of readings of the poems such as that of Alan Richardson, who writes that, in switching the addressee first from Sara Hutchinson to Wordsworth, the line "we receive but what we give" (Dejection, qtd. in Halmi et al., 55) moves from "almost pedagogical" to "agonistic"; when the addressee shifts from Wordsworth back to Sara—now as the less personal "Lady"—the shift, Richardson writes, "saps the address of the familiar tone that characterizes the

---

[10] See Halmi et al. for more on the textual history of the poem (155, n. 1).
[11] The roles of new moon and old moon appear reversed regarding who is in the arms of whom; if one takes the traditional reading that Geraldine is a witch or hag under her disguise of a beautiful young woman, then she would be translated as the old moon in this poem; however, the very echo of the earlier poem in this imagery suggests that Coleridge continues to challenge the implicit binaries of youth and age, the beauty and the hag.

earlier versions" (Richardson, *Neural Sublime*, 69). However, if one regards the palimpsest as a text that does not privilege one version nor cancel the others, the auditors fuse into one nondual figure so that the poem's multiple revisions appear simultaneously; the poem thus reveals Coleridge's nonlinear and more prismatic ideal of secondary imagination, in which fragments of self are reflected in the addressees. Coleridge's creative process thus sets the subject–object dualism of a masculinist poetics against nondualism. Extending Richard Berkeley's critique of McFarland's claim to finding it "necessary to lump all 'pantheist' thinkers into the 'It is' camp," this reading underscores that, as an ambivalent nondualist, Coleridge demonstrates repeatedly his resistance to projecting power outside himself (3).[12]

Coleridge's nondualism is thus idiosyncratic in its ambivalence: it is characterized by self-deprecation and a tendency to close out the visionary that unfolds at the center of many of his texts, as "The Eolian Harp" demonstrates. While Coleridge berates himself for his failure to realize his vision of the uncanny that permeates both dark and light, night and day, his albeit ambivalent nondualism contrasts with the insistently dogmatic dualism of Wordsworth. In chapter XIV of *Biographia Literaria*, immediately following this definition of imagination, Coleridge describes *Christabel* and *Rime of the Ancient Mariner* as poems of the supernatural, of dream and his failure to capture "witchery by daylight" (qtd. in Halmi et al., 160). Typical of his ambivalent expression of the polarities of defiance and self-deprecation, Coleridge here in chapter XIV for the first time defends his poetics against Wordsworth's censorship in omitting *Christabel* from the second edition of the *Lyrical Ballads*. Thus, having created his own hierarchy of imaginative levels in chapter XIII, Coleridge now defines the poet "in *ideal* perfection," as one who "diffuses a tone, and spirit of unity that blends, and ... fuses, each by each, by that synthetic and magical power, to which we have exclusively appropriated the name of imagination reveals itself in the balance or reconciliation of opposite or discordant qualities" (Engell and Bate II, 15).

---

[12] By contrast to Berkeley's emphasis on Coleridge's engagement with German idealism, this study puts greater emphasis on Coleridge's struggle to move past that influence.

Written fifteen years before *Biographia Literaria*, "Dejection" marks the textual beginning of Coleridge's emergence from Wordsworth's dominant voice. It is well-established that "Dejection" answers the rhetorical questions that end the first four stanzas of "The Intimations Ode," the original ending of the poem: "Whither is fled the visionary gleam / Where is it now, the glory and the dream?" Simultaneously, Coleridge refers to his own poetic powers waning and to his criticism of Wordsworth:

My genial spirits fail....

It were a vain endeavor,

Though I should gaze for ever

On that green light that lingers in the west:

I may not hope from outward forms to win

The passion and the life, whose fountains are within. (ll. 39–46)

Auditor-as-Wordsworth fuses with subject-as-Coleridge, yet Wordsworth's poetics of rainbows and roses appears cliché to Wordsworth in the opening stanzas of the "Intimations Ode," culminating in his casting out his former poetic vision: "there hath past away a glory from the earth" (18). Coleridge, by contrast, knows that the jaundiced "yellow green light" he sees in the sky is a projection of his own state of "genial" failure (ll. 30, 39). The response is paradoxical, for Wordsworth had said the world "did seem" appareled in celestial light before but now, he says, "I know" a glory has past away (ll. 3, 16). According to Coleridge, Wordsworth's claim to know is delusion, for it is founded on that fundamental binary of self and other.

When the next stanza shifts to "O Lady," Coleridge is still speaking to Wordsworth but the poem-as-palimpsest state of the text adds another layer of irony. He despairs to Sara Hutchinson that "in our life alone does nature live: / Ours her wedding-garment, ours her shroud!" (ll. 48–9). Theirs cannot be an erotic relationship of self and other, husband and wife. Underscoring the conflict among his wishfulness for their union, his jaundiced projection of selfhood onto the western sky, and the intersubjectivity of Sarah's relationship to nature, he wishes for her a "fair luminous mist, / This beautiful, and beauty-making power" (ll. 62–3).

After addressing Sara in stanzas 4 and 5, Coleridge returns to a subjectivity that appears not only to speak to Wordsworth and Sara in the terms the earlier stanzas have used but he is now in the realm of pure subjectivity: "There was a time when, though my path was rough, / This joy within me dallied with distress" (ll. 76–7). Coleridge recognizes ambivalence as the truest emotion; in this case, it emerges from the same perverse that he represents in the coda to *Christabel*. Thus, fifteen years before *Biographia Literaria*, Coleridge's prolepsis of "the willing suspension of disbelief" here is striking for, he says, "each visitation / Suspends what nature gave me at my birth, / My shaping spirit of Imagination" (ll. 84–6). Coleridge works with the same materials that he does in *Biographia Literaria* to assert his poetics of secondary imagination over mere fancy, for Coleridge's is a "shaping spirit" in spite of the failure of his "genial spirits" (l. 39).

The paradox of this nondual relationship between success and failure echoes through Coleridge's writings: "Dejection" is, after all, an "Ode" just as, at the end of "Kubla Khan," the poet can only conditionally harness the energy of the Abyssinian maid to embody the demonic and divine. Both iterations of failure underscore, proleptically, the importance of the clause following his definition of secondary imagination as the will to recreate: "or where this process is rendered impossible, yet still at all events it struggles to idealize and to unify" (488). While "Kubla Khan" and *Christabel* both embody the relationship between female eros and the recreative process of secondary imagination, by contrast to the ambiguous nature of Geraldine's power in *Christabel*, "Kubla Khan" overtly represents nature as a nondual, female erotic energy.

Dismantling Dualistic Systems of Morality in Order to Recreate: German Philosophy, *Biographia Literaria*, and the "Positive Negation" of *Magnum Opus*

By 1811, Coleridge's nondualism emerges more explicitly as a state he refers to as "positive negation"; he plumbs the psyche in "notebook fragments" that become two published poems, "Limbo" and "Ne Plus Ultra," in 1834.[13] Through

---

[13] Coleridge's *Notebook Fragments* of 1811 [three fragments of which were published in Coleridge's lifetime (*CN*, 3: 4073–4): "Limbo" (35–59, 91–4) and "Ne Plus Ultra" (73–83) in 1834 (*Poetical Works*). *The Friend*, ll. 3034, "satire on materialists" (Friend [*CC* I: 494]) later titled "Moles" in *Poetical Works* (1834), qtd. in Halmi et al., 233, n. 1.

them, Coleridge returns to a feminized limbo or purgatory reminiscent of the female figure "Life-in-Death," the grotesque parody of the female object of Petrarchan love in *Rime of the Ancient Mariner*, who wins over Death the soul of the eternally tormented Mariner:

> Her lips were red, her looks were free,
> Her locks were yellow as gold:
> Her skin was as white as leprosy,
> The Night-mare Life-in-Death was she,
> Who thicks man's blood with cold. (ll. 190–4)

Though this description is often labeled as misogynistic on Coleridge's part, in the context of Coleridge's swerve from the male poetic tradition toward an androgynous poetics, one can better understand Life-in-Death as the intersection of epistemological and gender nonbinaries. She embodies the ambivalence that underlies Freud's *unheimlich*: like the beautiful Geraldine, whose serpentine eyes roll round and who contaminates Christabel, Life-in-Death's "looks were free"; like Geraldine, her features resemble the feminine ideal of sentimental fiction, but in this context she parodies the passive and cold object of the Petrarchan lover's desire: her coldness, unlike that of the necessarily sexual unresponsiveness of the Petrarchan female, "thicks man's blood."[14] Far from passive and objectified, with her skin white "as leprosy" she like Geraldine is a figure who actively spreads contagion rather than inspires redemption.

Though from the masculinist perspective of Coleridge's male characters, narrators, and fictional editors, the feminine is a devouring eros, in other contexts Coleridge represents feminine nondual power more directly, without the mediation of a tale-teller or unreliable narrator. The "Lampads seven" of "Ne Plus Ultra" are perhaps Coleridge's most personal representation of a feminine, nondual energy. They refer to the Shekinah of *Kabbalah*, an "[a]ll-compassionate," nondual spirit in nature (Halmi et al., 236, n. 4). In his *Lectures on the History of Philosophy*, Coleridge writes of *Kabbalah* that there is "no essential distinction between God and his creation" and that the

---

[14] As noted in Chapter 2, in discussing the uncanny or *unheimlich*, Freud cites Schelling (226). See Chapter 4 for a discussion of Life-in-Death vis-à-vis Shelley's *The Last Man*.

Shekinah is "a concentration of all the seven spirits of the manifestation, a doctrine which must have been very early indeed in the Church because we find a clear reference to it in the beginning of Apocalypse" (*Lectures* 1818–19 [*CW*], I: 435–6, qtd. in Halmi et al., 236, n. 4).

Underscoring the centrality of Coleridge's resistance to patriarchal, dualistic systems, Coleridge at this late stage thus delves back to the precursor of the Old Testament to find nondualism written outside the strictures of the Judeo-Christian tradition. She is a precursor of the androgynous figure of the animating breeze in "The Eolian Harp," inspiring the poet who is nevertheless chastened by his ironically dubbed new bride, "Meek Daughter in the Family of Christ." The epithet becomes yet more ironic when one considers that Coleridge identifies the last of the Lampads as "the Messiah or the Shekinah"; the most striking representation of androgyny in Coleridge's corpus, Shekinah as the Messiah suggests that this female nondual manifestation evolves into Jesus in the New Testament (Halmi et al., 236, n. 4).

That Coleridge's source for his study of *Kabbalah* was likely Spinoza, who was opposed to Cartesian dualism, further suggests the tension of nondualism behind Coleridge's challenge to the deistic materialism of the British Enlightenment whose patriarchal God is separate from the universe that He controls.[15] Yet because scholarship on Coleridge's relationship to German sources has tended to isolate chapter XII of *Biographia Literaria* rather than contextualize it, the plagiarism argument has persisted as though Coleridge himself does not move past these sources. One such study, for instance, claims that "Schelling provided Coleridge with a model of imagination, the self, and the philosophical system, which lent themselves much more readily to the development of a truly all-encompassing and palatable philosophical perspective"; that Coleridge "purloined [words] directly from Leibniz" leads

---

[15] McFarland notes, "Exactly when Coleridge began to read Spinoza is not known, and in view of his youthful saturation in the Neoplatonists is not very important" (161). Coleridge's nondualism suggests that it is important precisely because Spinoza would have given Coleridge an alternate path toward a religiophilosophical paradigm that defies materialist binaries. Yet Spinoza's departure from previous Epicureans also lies in his belief in the unity of Nature: substance (that which stands beneath) is the basis of the universe; Spinoza's *Deus sive Natura*, "God or Nature," is a monist philosophy. Spinoza's writings on ethics form a yet more critical distinction from Coleridge. As a determinist, Spinoza claimed that everything happens through necessity, including human behavior. Coleridge, by contrast, engaged with human behavior that evades this systematization, especially the state labeled evil that Coleridge deconstructs in his fragmentary *Magnum Opus*.

to that study's larger argument that "for Coleridge, just as for Descartes, Kant, Fichte, and Hardenberg, the unity and successful completion of such a philosophical meta-system is directly predicated upon the unity of subjectivity" (Schutz, 217–18).[16] Yet even in its epigraph, "A Chapter of requests and premonitions concerning the perusal or omission of the chapter that follows," chapter XII gestures ahead to chapter XIII in which Coleridge throws off the yoke of German influence (Engell and Bate, 232). The enigmatically paired terms "requests and premonitions" can be seen as ironic in the suggestion that the German philosophers may anticipate but do not proleptically echo the theory Coleridge expounds in chapter XIII. Chapter XII is also one of "requests" that Coleridge clarifies by the third paragraph of the chapter: "In lieu of the various requests which the anxiety of authorship addresses to the unknown reader, I advance but this one; that he will either pass over the following chapter altogether, or read the whole connectedly. The fairest part of the most beautiful body will appear deformed and monstrous, if dissevered from its place in the Organic Whole" (Engell and Bate, 234–5). Though Engell and Bate suggest that Coleridge must be referring to this chapter rather than chapter XIII, I would suggest that the relationship between the two is critical to his anxiety here (234, n. 1). If one reads the statement as ironic, then this "request" to the reader to skip chapter XIII would suggest that a reader who looks for wholeness from the perspective of any of the philosophical systems he is jettisoning by chapter XIII will take offense at the aesthetic he puts forward. In fact, Coleridge's metaphor in his claim here that the dismantling of wholeness "will appear deformed and monstrous" suggests Mary Shelley's grotesque parody of secondary imagination through Frankenstein's creation.[17] Thus, while the consensus has been that Coleridge is referring to plagiarism here, it would appear that what he is far more anxious about is owning what is original in chapter XIII, particularly his definition of secondary imagination.

In order to discuss the relationship between chapters XII and XIV, in which Coleridge proceeds to dismantle such unity, it is necessary to return to the

---

[16] Schelling's notion of the uncanny is perhaps the closest element of his philosophical system to Coleridge's poetics. However, as the Introduction notes, by gendering the idea of the uncanny with its focus on "abjection," twentieth-century feminist psychoanalysis suggests an important means to qualify Schelling's influence on Coleridge.

[17] See Chapter 4 for a fuller discussion of this connection between Coleridge and Shelley.

discussion in Chapter 1 of this study of how the plagiarism of the German writers in XII functions vis-à-vis the fictional letter from a "friend" that interrupts Coleridge's treatment of the German writers. Coleridge's rejection of German transcendental philosophy is a critical step before he can articulate his theory of imagination—albeit without acknowledging it as his. Coleridge precedes with a "very judicious letter" from an imaginary friend his hierarchy of primary and secondary imagination that together eclipse memory-based thought as fancy. It is ironic, for the letter is the inverse of plagiarism (488). The consequence of the letter is to interrupt the "purloined" philosophizing that preceded it with "complete conviction" about the layering of imagination, whose artistic faculty is preeminent: the secondary imagination "dissolves, diffuses, dissipates, in order to re-create" (488). The disclaimer that follows this statement is Coleridgean self-effacement at its most misleading: "or where this process is rendered impossible, yet still at all events it struggles to idealize and to unify" (488). That Coleridge suggests his own failure to "idealize and unify" does not mean that he is incapable of systematic philosophy according to German sources. Instead, he gestures not to a system but to a poetics of fragmentation that represents a selfhood splintered and recreated such that unity loses any valence from the systematic binaries that form the bulwark of Western philosophy in all its permutations.

Through the internal logic of *Biographia Literaria*'s trajectory towards chapter XIV, Coleridge clears the way for his most overt diatribe against Wordsworth there; underscoring his remove from German philosophy by the end of chapter XIII, he dismantles that which had liberated him from Wordsworth before he can recreate imagination and thus liberate himself in his own terms from Wordsworth. The essence of chapter XIV is contained in the phrase "willing suspension of disbelief" to distinguish his poetics from Wordsworth's. Coleridge's parenthetical aside contains the most damning criticism of Wordsworth's Preface to the second edition of *Lyrical Ballads* in which, Coleridge writes, "he was understood to ... reject as vicious and indefensible all phrases and forms of style that were not included in what he (unfortunately, I think, adopting an equivocal expression) called the language of *real* life" (491).

Though *Magnum Opus* never came to fruition as a religiophilosophical system, then, Coleridge endows his corpus with multiple permutations of an androgynous power that confronts patriarchy's projection of evil onto it. Coleridge repeatedly struggles with systematic literary and religiophilosophical positions that he represents both poetically and decries in prose as multiple subjectivities laying claim to a universal or absolute moral compass.[18] Elinor Shaffer's discussion of the "Opus Magnum" in her 1968 essay on "Iago's Malignity" takes up Coleridge's position on the debated relationship between selfhood and morality.[19] Schaffer describes the "controversy between, on the one hand, the sceptics, notably Hume, who claimed that the self is a kind of fiction ... and, on the other hand, Kant and, more extravagantly, the idealists, who suggested various versions of a fundamental self that could not be reduced to the flow of sense impressions" (196–7). Though working within the religiophilosophical paradigm that has dominated the discussion of Coleridge's writings on evil, Schaffer's discussion of the problem of "self-love" for Coleridge suggests that his notion of recreation undoes traditional systematizing. Thus, Schaffer writes, "'Self-love,' in separating the self from God, annihilates the self: for it is reduced to the disconnected and ephemeral passage of sense perceptions"; from this point, Schaffer continues, "the self has no direct access to itself, but recognizes itself only in and through the 'contents' of consciousness" (197). This point can be extended to Coleridge's meditation on his poetic self vis-à-vis the various traditions pressuring his conformity to emerge. The separation of self from God is the very essence of tradition, of systematization, as it emerges at his moments of revelation about the necessity of secondary imagination, beyond the primary, in its recreative rupture and the ideal of its rebuilding from the perspective of selfhood having no access to itself.

It is striking that, in spite of the scholarly attention paid to "Opus Maximum" upon its 2002 publication, there is no connection made between this deepest of Coleridge's religiophilosophical writings and gender beyond the splitting

---

[18] Extant are Coleridge's Notebooks, written in the 1820s, the last decade of his life, to which scholars refer with various titles, including, most recently, his "Opus Maximum," in the *Collected Works* XV; see McFarland, Evans, and Beer for further textual details.

[19] Editors and scholars of the fragments refer to the work by various versions of the title. Schaffer refers to the Notebooks as "Opus Magnum." As she writes, "These Notebooks, unlike most of Coleridge's notebooks, are not made up of isolated jottings, but represent an attempt to compose a complete, connected treatment of his ideas, in short, the philosophical *magnum opus* he had promised under a variety of titles throughout his life" (196).

of Coleridge's persona between a masculinity grappling with the relationship between father and son and his poetic expression of masculine failure in erotic relationships.[20] Beer, for instance, notes the prevalence of the "father-son relationship" in *Opus Maximum* against which he sets the "philosophy of love" that had been "undermined by the failure of his love for Sara Hutchinson" whereas, set in conversation with the androgynous subjectivity of Coleridge's poetics, a different dimension emerges (291–2). McFarland's "Prologomena" to the *Collected Works*, Volume XV, reduces Coleridge's unrealized *Magnum Opus* to a "conservative venture" because of its anti-Enlightenment stance. McFarland cites Coleridge's 1796 statement of a need "to rescue this enlightened age from general Irreligion" (xliii). However, reducing Coleridge's notion of "Irreligion" to one pole in a liberal/conservative binary fails to represent the nuanced political and epistemological concerns involved in the shifting tides of the late Enlightenment.[21]

Though Coleridge's prose may claim to look for systematic religiophilosophy, his is a decomposed poetic creativity.[22] The problem of interpretation cannot be located in a single genre of Coleridge's corpus, but rather in looking at the network of relationships among texts—both his own and those with whom he was in conversation. Thus complicating these questions of evil and subjectivity, *Anima Poetae*, a collection of Coleridge's notebook fragments edited by Hartley Coleridge, contains a section dated October 27, 1803, called "The Origin of Evil." In it, Coleridge speculates not only on the connection between "malignity" and the notion of the "I," but adds the third dimension of "creatibility"; in characteristic fashion, Coleridge claims to digress from the topic of evil with the notion of imagination and creation whereas he connects the three concerns throughout his works:

> There is no *all* in creation. It is composed of infinites, and the imagination, bewildered by heaping infinites on infinites and wearying of demanding increase of number to a number which it conceives already infinite,

---

[20] *CW*, Vol. XV.
[21] Indeed, McFarland himself notes the similarity to Blake "who was forever trying to cast off Bacon, Locke, and Newton from Albion's covering" (lix).
[22] See the earlier reference to Ernest Jones's term for Shakespeare's projection of selfhood into multiple characters in his plays. It was Coleridge who first located Shakespeare's "genius" in his ability to do so.

deserted by images and mocked by words, whose sole substance is the inward sense of difficulty that accompanies all our notions of infinity ..., turns with delight to distinct images and clear ideas, contemplates a world ... where an infinity of kinds subsist each in a multitude of individuals apportionate to its kind in conformity to laws existing in the divine nature. (32)

This "digression" ends with a dream he had of his infant, Hartley, being christened. In the dream, when Hartley is asked who redeemed him he was to say, "God the Son," but, Coleridge writes, Hartley instead "went on humming and hawing ... (like a boy who knows a thing and will not make the effort to recollect) so as to irritate me greatly"; Coleridge then explains that he woke, discovering that the sound he mistook for Hartley, was the ticking of his watch (33–4). As is so often the case in Coleridge's prose, juxtapositions suggest more than the words themselves claim, and so when he says, "To return to the question of evil" one suspects that there is a level of logic that escapes discursive coherence. Indeed, he interrupts the sentence just begun with an aside: "—woe to the man to whom [evil] is an interesting question, though many a mind over-wearied by it may shun it with dread" (34). Though for Coleridge evil is hardly uninteresting, he paradoxically represents this shunning with dread throughout his career (34).

Coleridge denounces assumptions of selfhood as defined by various religiophilosophical systems. Through these systems, Coleridge writes, feelings are "alienated and estranged from their rightful objects" (qtd. in Shaffer, 198). For Coleridge, by contrast to these systems, the perverse camouflages itself as that hegemonic claim to morality. Coleridge plays with subjectivity so that, in spite of the presence of orthodox views in both poetry and prose, the idea of multiple orthodoxies is inherently ironic. It results in a universe in which the illicit trafficks with the moral, the masculine with the feminine, the notion of the real with the unreal.

The fragmentation of *Magnum Opus* likewise represents Coleridge's rejection of systematic binaries—in this case, good and evil—from which the poet-figure of "Kubla Khan" is liberated by the representation of a poetics at once holy and demonic. In an 1830 notebook entry, Coleridge wrote that supernatural poetry should be "true *to Nature*—i.e. where the Poet of his free will and judgement does what the believing Narrator of a Supernatural Incident, Apparition or Charm does from ignorance & weakness of mind,—i.e. mistake a Subjective product (A saw the Ghost of Z) for an objective fact = the Ghost of Z was there to be seen" (*CN*, 5, 6301). That the "believing Narrator" mistakes a "Subjective product … for an objective fact" is what Coleridge saw as the central flaw in the materialist tradition. This tension between the subjectivity of narrator and author is the point of intersection with Robinson and, as Chapter 4 discusses, links Robinson and Coleridge to Mary Shelley.

Coleridge's texts variously represent dualism in which he often embeds startling moments of liberation from binaries within a framework of pious self-denigration. In the case of those systems of philosophy and theology that had been foundational, Coleridge goes deeper than his sources to a repressed feminine principle of creativity that he often represents as an androgynous subjectivity at odds with an ideology that centralizes an oppressive patriarchal figure.[23] A more flexible paradigm of Coleridge as poet, philosopher, and literary critic emerges once the discussion is released from the totalizing materialism embedded in Western philosophical systems.

Coleridge's resistance to the systematic binaries underlying the materialism of the British Enlightenment is important to understanding the phrase he wrote in his copy of Shakespeare's plays, "the motive-hunting of motiveless Malignity"; written as he prepared lectures in 1818, Coleridge's remark addresses Iago's line to Roderigo, "Go to, farewell. Put money enough in your purse" after which he soliloquizes, "Thus do I ever make my fool my purse" (*Lectures on Shakespeare*, 164). The common thread among disparate readings of the line has been the attempt to place it within a moral code of either orthodox Christianity, materialist philosophy, or German idealism. However, the phrase resists all of these. The larger context of the line helps to show that it reverberates with Coleridge's many iterations of the nonbinary:

---

[23] As discussed earlier in this chapter, exemplifying Coleridge's fascination with nondual traditions are his writings on the Shekinah, the female principle of the *Kabbalah*, that had been repressed in the Old Testament. See Wheeler for a discussion of the influence by Orientalism on "Kubla Khan." In the epilogue to *British Women Writers and the Asiatic Society of Bengal*, I gesture ahead to this study by including Coleridge among the male writers who appear to have had an affinity to the nondualism of Sanskrit texts (128).

The triumph! Again, put money after the effect has been fully produced. The last speech: the motive-hunting of motiveless malignity—how awful! In itself fiendish—whilst yet he was allowed to bear the divine image, too fiendish for his own steady view,—a being next to devil,—only not quite devil,—and this Shakespeare has attempted and executed, without disgust, without Scandal! (*Lectures*, 165)

As Elinor Shaffer has observed, for Coleridge, "Iago is Othello's objectified self" (201). Shakespeare's achievement from Coleridge's perspective is the artist's gift of secondary imagination, taking apart the structures that appear to be real and to reconfigure them, thereby challenging the most foundational beliefs of his audience.

Shakespeare is indeed the consummate Coleridgean tale-teller, whose plays, free from the rigid mores of a single-minded belief structure founded on systematic binaries, elude the moral tags of "disgust" and "Scandal." The power of *Othello* for Coleridge is therefore not that Iago has contaminated Othello but that the play has contaminated the audience's desire for a tidy moral, much as the Mariner must "teach" the Wedding Guest, from Anna Barbauld's view, the pious lesson to pray well, love all God's creatures, and to "walk together to the kirk / With a goodly company" (*Rime*, qtd. in Halmi, et al., ll. 603–4). They do not return together to his community, however. The Mariner had conjured an image of the church in which "each to his great Father bends, / Old men, and babes, and loving friends, / And youths and maidens gay!" (ll. 607–9). The promise of a "goodly company" that consists of a society entrenched in the binaries of gender (youths and maidens), generation (Old men and babes), and creation (the patriarchal God of the Judeo-Christian tradition as creator to whom the pious, as the created, bend). Instead, the Mariner is simply "gone": a declarative statement followed by a caesura followed by "and now" (l. 620).

The Mariner has disrupted the time/space continuum so that his departure may be immediate, though the context suggests either that ages could have gone by or that he may not have been "real," thus requiring a willing suspension of disbelief. The ambiguity is important to the final lines, for the Wedding Guest turns "away from the bridegroom's door ... like one that hath been stunned"; he is "of sense forlorn: A sadder and a wiser man" (ll. 621–5). The wisdom of the Mariner's tale is not the pious lesson that he could take back to the assembled "goodly company" in the church. Instead, it is the message that Coleridge could not bring to fulfillment in his *Magnum Opus*: Life-in-Death disassembles the very pretense of piety by defying mutually insulated binaries.

4

The Plague of Storytelling: Mary Shelley through the Lens of Robinson and Coleridge

This final chapter addresses the long-held assumptions about Shelley's literary relationships, exploring her engagement with Robinson and Coleridge not only as it contrasts her filial relationships with Wollstonecraft and Godwin but also as it underscores her resistance to the masculinist poetics of Wordsworth and Percy Shelley. Wollstonecraft's posthumous textual influence on her daughter cannot account for the radical subversiveness of her daughter's fiction, namely its disruption of the traditional binaries of morality, gender, and narrative that Wollstonecraft herself merely inverts for polemical purposes but does not dismantle and therefore destabilize. Mary Poovey, in 1984, was among the first to point out Wollstonecraft's inversion of the gender binary: "The root of the wrongs of women, according to Wollstonecraft, is the general acceptance of the idea that women are *essentially* sexual beings .... Wollstonecraft's response to [Rousseau's] sexual characterization of women is simply to reverse the charge: not *women*, she argues, but *men* are dominated by their sexual desires" (71). Two years after Poovey's study, Margaret Homans projected Wollstonecraft's dualism into her reading of *Frankenstein*: "Married to one romantic poet and living near another, Mary Shelley, at the time she was writing *Frankenstein* experienced with great intensity the self-contradictory demand that daughters embody both the mother whose death makes language possible by making it necessary and the figurative substitutes for that mother who constitute the prototype of the signifying chain" (100).[1]

---

[1] For other examples of those who, in the 1980s, built arguments about Wollstonecraft on this inverted dualism, see Kaplan's study as well as that of Gilbert and Gubar.

Studies of Robinson's intertextual relationship with Mary Shelley have largely substituted Robinson for Wollstonecraft in the paradigm of the mother–daughter theme.[2] One can trace a parallel critical problem with the father–daughter relationship between Godwin and Shelley that has been the focus of criticism particularly on *Mathilda*, since the tendency has been to read the novella biographically. A projection of the father–daughter relationship has been the focus of reading Coleridgean imagery in Shelley's fiction, specifically *Frankenstein*'s references to the albatross, discussed vis-à-vis the biographical curiosity that the nine-year-old Shelley had heard Coleridge recite *Rime of the Ancient Mariner*.[3] Further, there has been little distinction made among Shelley's many references to the canonical male poets, particularly in *Frankenstein*. This critical tendency has collapsed Shelley's relationship to the verse of Coleridge, Wordsworth, and Percy into the claim that she denounces a common masculine poetics.

By exploring the mutual concerns among Coleridge, Robinson, and Mary Shelley that bridge *Frankenstein*, *Mathilda*, and *The Last Man*, it becomes possible to escape both the reductiveness of the canonical/noncanonical binary as well as the linear notion of influence that reinforces gender binaries, especially problematic when biographically based.[4] The notion of writing as recreative is, for all three writers, a process of contamination that subverts the very binaries under which criticism has continued operating. Nevertheless, notable exceptions to Romanticism's continued division of two generations

---

[2] As discussed in more detail later in this chapter, the scant critical attention to Robinson's influence on Shelley has hinged on the "layers of first person narratives" suggested, for instance, by the common name Perdita, Robinson's stage name, and that of the character, Perdita, in Shelley's *The Last Man* (Young, 84). See Byrne, who first made the association, as well as Young and McWhir. The last section of this chapter details the importance of Perdita beyond being merely a biographical nod to Robinson. Kristeva's concept of abjection, noted in the Introduction to this study, is a useful means of connecting gender to the uncanny. Rather than psychoanalyze Shelley's biographical relationships, the concept of abjection grounds Shelley's relationship with Robinson and Coleridge in a literature of the uncanny in which the feminine has a central role.

[3] See Halmi et al., 12, n. 7.

[4] Regarding my choice of Shelley texts, it may be worth noting that *The Last Man* is a more radical subversion of traditional narrative than *Valperga*, written two years earlier. Stuart Curran's point is well-taken that, compared to Scott's objectification of female characters in his use of the historical novel genre, Shelley refuses women to be "thrust into erotic competition …; while one woman succors the other, the men betray them both and one another" (xviii). Castruccio, Curran notes, "is reduced to being a means to an end, and a mere one at that, for he is a slave to his own craving for power, lacking any existence independent from its maintenance" (xvii). Yet the revolutionary qualities of *Valperga* pale by comparison to those of *The Last Man*; through the lens of the latter's relationship with both Robinson and Coleridge, its importance on epistemological, social, and narrative levels emerges as a multilayered denunciation of patriarchy.

have helped pioneer nonbinary approaches to literary engagement, beginning with Barbara Johnson's 1987 study of *The Last Man*; Johnson underscores that in the novel not only is Percy "entombed," but "a certain male fantasy of Romantic universality" is as well (33).[5]

The Introduction to this study describes a triangulated literary fellowship among Robinson, Coleridge, and Mary Shelley, represented by tale-tellers who promise their audience a moral lesson by which to live while hoping for their own redemption in the act of telling their tales, an intention against which each writer works. Completing the triangle, this chapter takes up Shelley's aesthetic, epistemological, and social commonalities with Coleridge and Robinson revolving around the recreative act as a nonbinary impulse. Coleridge's publication of *Biographia Literaria* a year after Shelley wrote *Frankenstein* collapses the rigid distinctions of generational divides that have been the bases of discussing literary influence. That Frankenstein forms the creature from recycled body parts put together in his pseudoscientific laboratory is a grotesque parody not only of God's creation, readily seen through the novel's overt references to *Paradise Lost* but, viewed through the lens of Coleridge's definition of secondary imagination, Frankenstein's utopian attempt to recreate human history without death parodies the artist's work to dismantle and reconfigure traditional epistemes that Coleridge calls secondary imagination in *Biographia Literaria* XIII. Of their shared impulse to explore the consequences of tearing down and reassembling, Shelley's is an act with disastrous consequences, Coleridge's an unrealizable ideal.

Just as Chapter 2 of this study has sought to redescribe Coleridge through his connection with Robinson and their shared interest in dismantling masculinist subjectivity, this chapter extends the discussion of Coleridge and Robinson's shared challenge to systematic binaries while offering a qualification to Wollstonecraft's influence on Shelley's fiction. Wollstonecraft and Robinson themselves had an ambivalent friendship, Wollstonecraft reviewing Robinson's works critically at times, enthusiastically at others; however, because the

---

[5] Stephen Goldsmith's 1993 study traces Shelley's subversion of the nineteenth century's fashionable "Last Man" poems in her "counterapocalyptic" novel of the same name, arguing that Shelley parodies the "masculine theme" (267). William Keach's 1998 study of Dante's influence on both Mary and Percy through the Matilda of the *Purgatorio*, discussed later in this chapter, is a useful departure from the more typically biographically based treatments of *Mathilda*. It offers a provocative means of discussing the literary relationship between Mary and Percy through her novel and his *The Cenci*.

assumption has been that Wollstonecraft was uncomfortable about Robinson's friendship with Godwin before his marriage to Wollstonecraft, suggested by the abrupt end of that friendship, the biographical element has eclipsed the more nuanced literary implications of their textual relationship.

Among those scholars who have argued for a more rigorous, intellectual relationship between Wollstonecraft and Robinson, Sharon Setzer emphasizes their epistemological differences: "Robinson announces that she will not follow Wollstonecraft in criticizing 'the doctrines of certain philosophical sensualists,' most notably Rousseau"; instead, Setzer observes, Robinson "seems to be pleading her own case more than the general injustice of mental subordination" (31). This observation of Robinson's intellectual freedom from the sensibility/reason binary is central to redefining Robinson's epistemology founded on paradox and the artistic impulse to dismantle and reassemble the constitutive parts of an assumed whole.

Like the tales of Coleridge and Robinson, Shelley's fiction is recreative, most obviously as it manifests through Frankenstein's metatextual reassembly of body parts. Yet with increasing urgency across Shelley's fiction, the intention of each taleteller to redeem both himself and his auditor gives way to the tale's subversive contamination of the auditor. Bringing together the dismantling of gender binaries that Robinson and Coleridge link to traditional morality, Shelley realizes perhaps most fully of the three the nondualism that Robinson shares with Coleridge and that Coleridge sought to develop in the unwritten *Magnum Opus*.

Contamination spreads from *Frankenstein*, whose layered stories subvert Victor's ostensible goal to teach Walton a moral lesson, through *Mathilda*, in which the line between incest and literary legacy is blurred, to *The Last Man*, whose own literalizing contamination manifests through the vengeance against humanity of a feminized plague even as the narrative dismantles the heteronormative relationships to which the narrator clings as the foundation of human society.

Undercutting Masculine Subjectivity: *Walsingham* and *Frankenstein*

Walsingham is a lynchpin connecting Robinson epistemologically and artistically to Coleridge and Shelley while revealing Shelley's ambivalence toward Wollstonecraft's inverted binaries. The androgynous climax of Robinson's novel revolves around the belated discovery, for both Walsingham and the reader, that the presumed antagonist in the novel's love triangle, Sir Sidney, is actually a woman who has withheld her identity to gain both her inheritance and the right of a woman to receive a "masculine education" (Byrne, 332).[6] *Walsingham* thus gained critical attention with the rise of feminist criticism because it shares with Wollstonecraft's *Vindication of the Rights of Woman* the concerns of women's education and patrimony. Yet Robinson's departure from Wollstonecraft in the novel is significant both in itself and in its repercussions for Shelley's literary inheritance. Byrne suggests the influence came about through "her parents' friendship with Robinson," further connecting *Frankenstein* to *Walsingham* through the books the creature reads: "*Walsingham* is given a Rousseauistic education and his favorite books are *La Nouvelle Heloise* and *The Sorrows of Young Werther*," anticipating Shelley's "account of the natural education of Frankenstein's creature" (331–2).

The relationship between Robinson's *Walsingham* and Shelley's *Frankenstein* evinces a more complex equation than that usually drawn between Wollstonecraft's and Shelley's writing. Feminist criticism has been divided on where it positions Shelley in terms of the representation of women in the novel, many claiming that she reinforces male writers' objectification of the feminine. However, by coming to the novel's representation of gender through the nondual androgyny of Coleridge and Robinson, this chapter suggests a more radical departure from patriarchal tradition: not merely an inversion of the binary but a departure from systematic dualism. Walsingham claims, "Good frequently originates in evil, and the persecutions of fate bring with them the weariness of an existence which, if perpetually happy, would shrink from annihilation" (187). The statement is ironic in the context of the novel. Walsingham proves to be an unreliable narrator since he blunders

---

[6] Cross's monograph on Robinson and gender represents a significant step toward liberating Romanticism from the binary system that has limited it. Citing the anonymous review of the novel in the 1798 *Analytical Review*, Cross claims that Walsingham knows the truth of Sidney's sex from the fourth letter to Rosanna Harland. The critical difference between this assertion and the standard interpretation—that Walsingham either does not know or represses this information until the end of the novel, the interpretation with which this study concurs—does not detract from the importance of Cross's shrewd observation that Walsingham "misinterprets" the behavior of Sidney and Isabella, "reading signs of female agency, education and friendship as a form of contamination" (130, 136, n. 62). This study extends Cross's concern with contamination by connecting it to that of Coleridge and Shelley.

through his story because he does not know what lies beneath appearances. However, the statement resonates with both Robinson's and Coleridge's larger concern with the subversion of the moral binary and, as this chapter argues, that Shelley shares with them.

That Frankenstein's narrative is surrounded by an epistolary frame consisting of letters by an English sea captain, Robert Walton, on an increasingly dangerous journey to the North Pole, has been a point of comparison made between the novel and Robinson's *Walsingham*. Though *Walsingham* is an extended epistle written by Walsingham to a woman, Rosanna, the epistolary genre is less the point of interest in the comparison, the epistolary novel popular especially among women in the eighteenth century. The letters are significant to the comparison because in both cases they function to destabilize the central authority of the protagonist. *Walsingham*'s epistolary opening gives way to narrative as does Shelley's, though Shelley complicates narrative structure further through the use of embedded narratives, a device whose layered points of view intensify the subversion of Victor's claim to an authoritative subjectivity.

Walton's letters that frame *Frankenstein* thus share with Robinson's letters the purpose of beginning her novel by destabilizing its eponymous hero. Walton writes exclusively to his sister, Margaret Saville; though Margaret's letters to him are not included, one of the novel's many representations of the silencing of women's voices, her rationality can be gleaned through Walton's attempts to dispel her concern about his safety, reassurances taking on greater irony as the journey becomes more perilous. Walton rescues the drowning Victor Frankenstein from the icy waters of the Northwest Passage off Russia. Frankenstein, recognizing Promethean aspirations similar to his own in Walton's quest to find the "secret of the magnet," tells his story about the tragic consequences of creating life out of dead matter, presumably to warn Walton of overstepping one's human limitations (8). However, the end-frame—Walton's resumption of his narration after the dying Frankenstein concludes his story—exposes the double irony of Frankenstein's moral imperative: Walton decides to continue his quest despite the crew's threats of mutiny, Frankenstein chastising them for betraying their captain.

In the case of *Walsingham*, three earlier letters precede the narrative proper, functioning to throw Walsingham's authority as protagonist into question: the first two letters are written to Walsingham's father, the first by Walsingham himself. Walsingham tells his father he cannot bear his misfortunes as his father has counseled he should. Though Walsingham portrays himself as "the child of sorrows, the victim of deception," he acknowledges that he has made errors because of his "too vivid imagination; the miseries of sensibility," a double view of the "evil power" that he claims "attends the actions of some men, so undefineable, so like the potent hand of destiny"; this synecdoche speaks ironically to Walsingham's fatalism while functioning as a metanarrative gesture to remind the reader of Robinson's authorial voice behind Walsingham's (42–3). In this way, all the obstacles that he faces in the course of the novel appear to be self-created, so "like" the "potent hand of destiny." The second letter, by Jemima Harland, underscores the irony of both Walsingham's claim of being persecuted and his father's claim that he is "the victim of deception" for, she notes, "is it possible that a mind so cultivated should turn from that reason and that philosophy which present their united powers of resistance. It cannot be" (44). A simple-minded character, Jemima is later seen exclusively from Walsingham's point of view as an antagonist. Her clumsy either/or binary here, that if Walsingham is educated he should be reasonable, is no more validated in the novel than is Walsingham's inability to resolve the conflict between his awareness of his overweening sensibility and his state of despair.

By the novel's end, four volumes later, Walsingham discovers that the underlying source of his erotic suffering has been the gender deception by his cousin, Sir Sidney, who turns out to be a woman. The novel therefore can be read retrospectively through the assumptions behind Sidney's deception that have led Walsingham to make a series of misjudgments. An earlier moment of retrospective irony with significance for *Frankenstein* occurs when Walsingham overhears Sidney speaking to Isabella, the woman Walsingham loves but whom he thinks Sidney is seducing. Walsingham, we only learn later, misconstrues the entire conversation. Thus, Sidney tells Isabella, "What a sacrifice you have made, for a being lost and wretched as I am! How shall I repay your goodness? My mother's cruel and ambitious spirit will prevent my marrying" (161). Walsingham, with his hand on his pistol, states that he "scarcely could refrain from committing an act of violence" (161). Sidney continues to Isabella,

> We will return to Switzerland; you shall be my dear and inseparable associate: I will, by every kind and affectionate assiduity, teach you to forget the ill-fated Walsingham. I have opened my heart to you, Isabella; you have explored its innermost recesses. You must, by your pity and forgiveness, alleviate my sorrows. We will wander amidst Alpine scenery, we will imbibe the refreshing breezes of morning, and scatter with our footsteps the soft dews of summer twilight. (161)

Through Walsingham's narrative point of view, the reader pursues the false hermeneutics regarding the relationship between Sidney and Isabella, namely, a heteronormative assumption that one man—the apparent antagonist—has taken the object of the protagonist's love from him.

Walsingham's hyperbolic, armed reactions to events through the course of the novel appear increasingly ridiculous, much as are those of Frankenstein at the end of Shelley's novel. Walsingham and Frankenstein as male subjects differ in their erotic relationships with women, Walsingham with desire for Isabella, Frankenstein with avoidance of Elizabeth in a repulsion that is magnified by his destruction of the female creature; Isabella and Elizabeth further suggest a variation on the subject/object binary, connected immediately through their names, Isabella as the Spanish name for Elizabeth. The likenesses in the egotism of the two male protagonists are striking in spite of the attraction/repulsion binary the two men represent, Elizabeth marked by both Frankenstein's parents as his intended but from whom he flees throughout the novel. The climactic scene of Elizabeth's murder borders on Robinson-like satire: there is an increasing distance between the reader's awareness of the creature's intention to exact a bride for a bride and Frankenstein's obliviousness to the harm into which he has placed Elizabeth until it is too late. The creature's multiple warnings to Frankenstein, "I will be with you on your wedding night," are a threat against Elizabeth, of course, in a classic *quid pro quo*: if Frankenstein fails to produce a bride for him, Frankenstein will pay with his own bride. Frankenstein, however, only hears these words as a threat against his own life: "That then was the period fixed for the fulfilment of my destiny. In that hour I should die.... [W]hen I thought of Elizabeth,—of her tears and endless sorrow, when she should find her lover so barbarously snatched from her,—tears, the first I had shed for many months, streamed from my eyes" (121). Abandoning Elizabeth, therefore, Frankenstein arrives with his pistol "hidden in [his] bosom" and, after hearing the "shrill scream," the return of the repressed comes too late: "Every where I turn I see the same figure—her bloodless arms and relaxed form flung by the murderer on its bridal bier. Could I behold this, and live?" (140–1). The creature escapes before Frankenstein can fire his pistol.

At the heart of Shelley's commonality with Coleridge and Robinson regarding the nature of evil is Victor's inability to see that the creature is not interested in killing him, thriving instead on their agonistic relationship. The creature's threat against Elizabeth had come after Victor has ambivalently agreed to create a companion for him. When the creature comes upon Victor tearing apart the unfinished female, the gruesomeness of the moment is the novel's most rending—literally and metatextually—in terms of the subjectivity it grants the creature. As he describes his arrested creation of the female, Victor compromises his control over his narrative, even as the reader observes Victor's brutal dismemberment from his point of view:

> As I looked on him, his countenance expressed the utmost extent of malice and treachery. I thought with a sensation of madness on my promise of creating another like to him, and, trembling with passion, tore to pieces the thing on which I was engaged. The wretch saw me destroy the creature on whose future existence he depended for happiness, and, with a howl of devilish despair and revenge, withdrew. (*Frankenstein*, 119)

Frankenstein's combined thickheadedness, egotism, and brutality bring together the darkness and irony of both Coleridge and Robinson as their novels explore the dire results of patriarchy's imposition of categorical imperatives founded on systematic binaries.

Contamination and the Subversion of the Moral Tale: *Frankenstein* and *Rime of the Ancient Mariner*

Besides their common use of letter writing, *Walsingham* and *Frankenstein* share the device of embedded poetry. Like the letters, the extracts undermine the central voice of the male protagonist.[7] For Shelley, the embedded poetry creates ironic distance between Frankenstein's narration and her authorial perspective. Both novels use a range of poetic voices to counter the monovocal narration of the male protagonist. In the case of *Frankenstein*, the Coleridge references function differently from those passages of Wordsworth and Percy Shelley. While the references to Coleridge underscore his representation of narrative contamination, those of Wordsworth and Percy are ironic commentary that betray Victor's egotism.

Though the earliest reviews of the anonymous 1818 edition of *Frankenstein* condemned its violence, the novel has been celebrated since the twentieth century for revolutionizing the gothic tradition through its psychological depth. However, there has been little attention to Shelley's commonality with Coleridge beyond *Frankenstein*'s references to *Rime*.[8] Yet *Rime*'s resistance to the dualism of good and evil reverberates through *Frankenstein*. Coleridge's lyrical ballad and Shelley's novel both experiment with narrative structure through their common destabilized authority of a single masculine subjectivity.

Frankenstein's first direct reference to *Rime* is in Walton's letter reassuring his sister not to be "alarmed for his safety" for, he says, "I shall kill no albatross" (12). Walton's reference to the Mariner is an odd way to assuage Margaret's worries, since the narrative of the Mariner revolves around the consequences of his motiveless malevolence. Walton's Prometheanism in seeking the "secret of the magnet" could not be further from the apparent randomness of the Mariner's shooting of the albatross. Indeed, Walton tells Margaret, "Do not suppose that … I am wavering in my resolutions. Those are as fixed as fate" (11). Implicit in connecting his quest to the Mariner's shooting of the albatross is not his own potential danger, Margaret's worry, but the danger into which he is bringing his crew. In fact, the end frame confirms that Margaret was right to worry, even if not for the crew, confirming that Walton has brought them into grave danger, "encompassed by peril" (153).

---

[7] See Chapter 2 for discussion of Robinson's embedded poems in relationship to Coleridge.
[8] Notable exceptions include Anya Taylor and James Holt McGavran; the latter's study is an important exception, connecting the two works through contamination. McGavran suggests that Coleridge's text represents a repressed homosexuality, whereas this study resists the biographical, instead focusing on the multiple ways systematic binaries and subjectivity are at odds in all these texts (54–5).

Upon Walton's rescuing Frankenstein, the irony of Walton's allusion to *Rime* intensifies with his claim, "I have found a man who, before his spirit had been broken by misery, I should have been happy to have possessed as the brother of my heart" (16). By connecting Walton and Frankenstein through the Mariner references, the novel undermines Walton's utopian claim for the benign surface of such brotherhood. As discussed in Chapter 1, Coleridge's Mariner rejects the pious lesson his tale is meant to perform, namely, that "He prayeth well who loveth well / Both man and bird and beast" (645–6). By not only telling his tale, but concluding with this moral tag, the Mariner suggests that he himself will be redeemed by telling the story. Yet instead of being redeemed and offering the Wedding Guest redemption, the Mariner has infected him with knowledge of the perverse that undermines the piety keeping society intact.

Although the Mariner tells him, "[Tis] sweeter than the Marriage-feast …, / To walk together to the Kirk / With a goodly company," the reader does not know whether the Wedding Guest ever arrives at the wedding ceremony in the church (*Rime of the Ancient Mariner*, ll. 633–6). In fact, how much time passes during the telling of the tale becomes irrelevant, the hypnotic effect of the Mariner's tale suggesting he has suspended the Wedding Guest in a dimension outside of the time-space continuum. The text instead reveals that he "went, like one that hath been stunn'd" after he "[t]urn'd from the bridegroom's door" (*Rime of the Ancient Mariner*, ll. 643–54). Though the Mariner has assured him that the homosocial bond that story-teller and auditor have forged is far "sweeter" than the "Marriage-feast," the Mariner's influence over his auditor functions as influenza, isolating the Wedding Guest rather than fulfilling the promise of "goodly company" (*Rime of the Ancient Mariner*, 636). This outcome subverts the Mariner's moral platitude that precedes it: "He prayeth best who loveth best / All things both great and small; / For the dear God who loveth us, / He made and loveth all" (*Rime of the Ancient Mariner*, ll. 614–17).

However, the poem has already subverted this glib moral, as Shelley appears to have understood, for she has Frankenstein quote directly from the section of *Rime* after the ghosts of the dead crew take over the ship:

Like one who, on a lonely road,

Doth walk in fear and dread,

And, having once turn'd round, walks on,

And turns no more his head;
Because he knows a frightful fiend

Doth close behind him tread.

(*Frankenstein*, 37; *Rime*, ll. 446–56)

The Mariner's double valence of conventional piety followed by diabolical subversion is nowhere more apparent than the section just before this passage, in which the Mariner tells the Wedding Guest, "Never sadder tale was told / To a man of woman born: Sadder and wiser thou wedding-guest! / Thou'lt rise to morrow morn" (*Rime of the Ancient Mariner*, 366–9). The knowledge that makes him "sadder and wiser" is that the platitudes are false promises of salvation.

Shelley literalizes Coleridge's lines describing the anxiety produced by being followed by a "frightful fiend." Frankenstein's use of Coleridge's words to describe his anxiety about the creature serves to emphasize Frankenstein's narcissism since his assumption from the beginning is that the creature wants to harm him, a fear that grows increasingly narcissistic as he misinterprets the creature's warnings about his murder of Elizabeth on their wedding night. That Shelley alludes to *Rime* in this way, particularly, suggests even more about her commonality with Coleridge: rather than having the Mariner's auditor either literally miss the wedding or feel apart from the heteronormative wedding as in the case of Coleridge's poem, Shelley undermines the traditional male protagonist's heteronormative erotic desire for his intended. She replaces it not only with a pattern of male homosocial bonding, but with Percy Shelley's creation of the epipsyche, a feminized doppelganger that is the product of his egocentrism.

Shelley introduces the masculinist desire for a homosocial bond from the beginning of the novel through Walton's letters describing the limitations of his crew members: yes, they are men, but they are not the aristocratic embodiments of knowledge and sentiment he is seeking and finds in the frozen waters, whose "constant and deep grief fills me with sympathy and compassion. He must have been a noble creature in his better days, being even now in wreck so attractive and amiable…. I have found a man who, before his spirit had been broken by misery, I should have been happy to have possessed as the brother of my heart" (*Frankenstein*, 16). The deeper layers of connection between Coleridge and Shelley go beyond the homosocial worlds of *Rime* and *Frankenstein*, however. Returning to Walton's reassurance of the concerned Margaret that "I shall kill no albatross, therefore do not be alarmed for my safety," Walton assumes that the Mariner's killing of the albatross is the cause of danger (12). Through this logic, if indeed Walton has erred in his judgment and he has metaphorically killed an albatross, then he too would need to redeem himself by telling the now-dead Frankenstein's story. However, the common message between Coleridge and Shelley is that storytelling not only fails to redeem but infects its listener. One does not need to go back to Coleridge's poem to discover this truth in the novel. Frankenstein had told Walton that he would tell his tale so that Walton would not make the same mistake he did, namely overreaching his human limitations. That the novel concludes with the dying Frankenstein urging the crew not to mutiny against Walton in spite of the dangers but to press ahead on Walton's ill-fated quest underscores the irony of this claim to redemptive storytelling.

Deeper narrative layers further complicate the notion of masculinist overreaching suggested by the subtitle, "The Modern Prometheus." Within the novel itself is a dissonance between Victor's perspective of the creature's first acts of murderous revenge and the creature's finely honed sensibility, moral outrage, and intellectual grasp of Frankenstein's cruelty. Describing his anguish at Frankenstein's rejection, the creature contrasts Victor to God in Milton's *Paradise Lost*: "I ought to be thy Adam; but I am rather the fallen angel" (68). Following his abuse by disgusted strangers, the creature says, he took refuge outside the De Lacey cottage where he was vicariously educated, eavesdropping on the lessons by Felix De Lacey to his Arab lover, Safie. Like the creature, Safie proves an adept student of European and English literature. Though a brief subplot, Safie's story of fleeing religious, political, and paternal persecution in Turkey is the structural center of the novel. Through Safie, Shelley both deepens and literally centralizes the novel's concerns with gender and otherness through the only female character whose voice—albeit one the reader never hears directly—is mediated through the creature who gives Frankenstein Safie's letters. These letters thus not only authenticate her story, but also connect Safie, at the novel's center to that other voiceless letter writer, Walton's sister, Margaret, at the novel's circumference. Through this narrative tension, Shelley balances the intervening narratives of men who pursue nature to "her hiding places" and who barter women in their negotiating male friendship (*Frankenstein*, 29, 33).

Two such transactions begin Victor's narrative in Volume I: his father, Alfonse, marries his mother, Caroline Beaufort, as a promise to her father, Alfonse's dying friend; Victor's adopted sister, Elizabeth, daughter of another friend of Alfonse, is likewise tendered in an exchange of masculine friendship. Having imbibed the antiquated teachings of alchemy against his father's wishes and, after his mother dies of scarlet fever contracted from nursing Elizabeth through the disease, Victor becomes obsessed with reversing death; at the university in Ingolstadt, Victor sequesters himself in his "workshop of filthy creation," becoming gaunt and restless (*Frankenstein*, 34). The night the creature awakens, Victor dreams he embraces Elizabeth who turns into his dead mother. The dream, conflating dead mother, would-be lover, and the awakening creature, contributes to the novel's deepening of the gothic: repulsed by the hideous creature, Victor not only rejects it, but represses the memory until the creature forces his attention through a series of murders beginning with Victor's brother, William, whose death is blamed on the ironically named Justine, William's caretaker. Elizabeth's eloquent defense of Justine during her trial backfires: Justine is executed while Victor, acknowledging his guilt to Walton, remains silent.

Deepening *Frankenstein*'s psychological, aesthetic, and sociopolitical elements, Victor's return to Geneva after William's death parodies the masculinist projection of selfhood through Percy Shelley's "epipsyche," the feminine ideal, or "soul out of my soul." Victor apostrophizes the "wandering spirits" of the alps immediately after which the creature appears, seeming to materialize out of the "sublime" landscape (67). Just before this moment, Shelley has Victor quote from Percy Shelley's "Mutability," in which "one wandering thought pollutes the day" (66). That the "wandering thoughts" turn to "wandering spirits" in Victor's apostrophe is significant, since just after this moment the creature appears out of that sublime landscape, a juxtaposition suggesting the connection between the "figure of a man" moving with "superhuman speed" out of a landscape whose sublimity suggests Frankenstein's profound repression of his guilt (67). That Victor had recreated human flesh as an ideal transcending death is thus a grotesque literalizing of Percy's epipsyche.

The events leading to Victor's aborted recreation of the female are laden with references to Percy in Victor's behavior, including his passing "whole days on the lake alone in a little boat, watching the clouds, and listening to the rippling of the waves" (*Frankenstein*, 107). Victor's escapism from the burden of his guilt is reminiscent of Percy's predilection for nautical escape, both in life and in his poetic self-portraiture, especially *Alastor*, the poem of Percy's with which *Frankenstein* is in most direct conversation. Shelley's use of poetic extracts by William Wordsworth when Victor and Henry Clerval travel through the Lake District reveal a yet deeper layer of the novel's recreation of the patriarchal privilege that Victor represents. Thus burdened by the task at hand, Victor regards the "scenery of external nature" through the eyes of Clerval (110). Victor quotes from "Tintern Abbey" to portray Clerval's freedom from "remoter charm, / By thought supplied, or any interest / Unborrowed from the eye" (*Frankenstein*, 112). In the context of this journey, in which Victor is moving toward his dreaded recreation of the female, the Wordsworthian passage, in which he describes his childhood experience as "an appetite; a feeling, and a love" appears ironic when Frankenstein applies it to Clerval, who seems closer to Dorothy at the end of "Tintern Abbey," in whom the poet beholds in her "what I was once … /Knowing that Nature never did betray / the heart that loved her" (ll. 120–1). Victor has feminized Clerval throughout the first two volumes, describing him as his nurse and the one he turns to rather than Elizabeth when he despairs. Through Victor's feminizing of Clerval, Shelley gestures to the objectified and infantilizing feminine that Wordsworth and Percy represent in their poetry.

By connecting Victor's rhapsodic diction to the poetics of Percy through direct quotation and biographical elements such as his solitary boat rides, Shelley represents her indictment of masculinist narcissism that simultaneously idealizes and degrades the feminine. Victor's references to Wordsworth's and Percy's poetry reveal his likeness to them in the dualistic selfhood they project onto nature, that very epistemology that Coleridge's "Dejection" criticizes in Wordsworth. Taken together with Victor's recreative misgivings, the allusions to Percy are damning on a level deeper than biography: they reflect the failure of Percy's attempts to redeem himself through a poetics that recreates the idealized self as epipsyche, in Mary's rendering a grotesque and misbegotten image of the male subject.

Yet Mary's textual conversation with Coleridge complicates that with Wordsworth and Percy. The androgynous Life-in-Death who wins the soul of the Mariner, cursing him to a nightmarish nonbinary state that is neither wholly life nor death, is kin to Frankenstein's creature, whose beauty, at which Victor had marveled before the creature awakens, suggests that of a heroine of sentimental fiction; when the creature is jolted into new life, his yellow, speculative eyes create a grotesque contrast to the "luxuriances" of the features Victor had selected in his charnel house and graveyard sprees, including "lustrous black, and flowing" hair and "teeth of a pearly whiteness" (*Frankenstein*, 35). Like Life-in-Death, whose "lips were red, her looks were free, / Her locks were yellow as gold: / Her skin was as white as leprosy," the creature's androgyny is linked to his state of living death (*Rime of the Ancient Mariner*, 1834, ll. 190–2).[9] His promise of suicide at the end of the novel thus resonates with Coleridgean irony, especially in the context of Walton's contamination by Frankenstein, going not back to England as his sister had urged him, but to what may be his own death and that of his crew in what the novel has promised to be an ill-fated quest.

Daughters, Fathers, and Recreated Mothers: *Mathilda* and *Christabel*

Rime of the Ancient Mariner thus leaves its mark throughout *Frankenstein*, from Walton's and then Victor's direct references to the perverse undermining of the categorical imperative with the storyteller's contamination of his audience. Though *Christabel* and *Mathilda* also share a subversion of linear narrative, Coleridge's text is filtered through an unreliable narrator, whereas Shelley's consists of letters by its female subject. Yet taken together, their treatment of the perverse in the father/daughter relationships of their respective tales complicates the relationship of moral and gender binaries.[10] *Mathilda* has no Geraldine-like doppelganger for the mother of the eponymous female

---

[9] In the earlier version of *Rime*, Coleridge does not call her Life-in-Death but rather refers to her as "far liker Death than he" (1798, l. 189). This change is significant since the paradox of life-in-death is not only a concept that begins appearing in the so-called canonical "second generation" with such works as Percy Shelley's bitterly ironic *Triumph of Life*; it also suggests Coleridge's bringing to the surface the nondualism of the state that wins the soul of the Mariner.

[10] See Anya Taylor on the influence of Coleridge's eroticism on Mary Shelley.

protagonist. Instead, Mathilda's relationship to her unnamed father is filtered through her own ambivalence whose implications for its challenge to the moral binary take a different turn from Coleridge's.[11]

Coleridge's narrative in *Christabel* moves obliquely, each part recurring to the previous one as a retelling that highlights the poem's ironic subversion of its unreliable narrator's attempts at coherent storytelling. By the "Conclusion to Part the Second," a coda whose title gives a misleading impression of coherence, Coleridge swerves from plot resolution by calling attention not to the destructive power of Geraldine but to the perverse "wrong that does no harm" of an unnamed father toward his child, not only unassigned a gender but who appears nonhuman, "a limber elf … A fairy thing" (ll. 643–5).[12] The child appears connected to both the fairy world of "The Eolian Harp," forbidden by the chastising glare of the narrator's new wife in that poem, and the taboo of an erotic desire of father for daughter. In one of Coleridge's clearest articulations of the perverse, the father's "pleasures flow in so thick and fast … that he at last/Must needs express his love's excess / With words of unmeant bitterness" (ll. 650–3).

Whereas Geraldine's contamination seeps into the patriarchal world of Sir Leoline slowly and insidiously, even to the point of stripping both narrator and father of their authority in the poem, *Mathilda* begins with the eponymous heroine in the subject position as she directly equates her tale with contamination: "I thought indeed that there was a sacred horror in my tale that rendered it unfit for utterance, and now about to die I pollute its mystic terrors" (41). That the tale is taboo connects it to Christabel's narrator who, upon telling of Geraldine's disrobing in Christabel's bedroom, writes "A sight to dream of, not to tell!" (l. 247). Yet, giving voice to the victimized daughter, Shelley adds further irony to the notion of uttering the taboo as contamination.[13]

---

[11] See both Hoeveler and Richardson for discussions of Romantic era writing on incest. Richardson observes that, while Coleridge links sibling incest aversion to the associationism of Jeremy Bentham, it does not explain the "great religious Horror attached to Incest" (qtd. in Richardson, *Neural Sublime*, 112). This point can be extended to link Coleridge's retreat from materialist philosophy/psychology toward a deeper construct of consciousness that takes him beyond the duality of good and evil.

[12] See Chapter 3 on the textual history of the Conclusion to Part the Second in the context of Coleridge's letter about Hartley as an infant.

[13] There are many important intersections with Percy's *The Cenci* that are beyond the parameters of this study, though one relevant comparison here is Percy's Cenci literally and metaphorically

Unlike the tale-tellers discussed previously, Mathilda only asks sympathy of her auditor, Woodville: "I record no crimes; my faults may easily be pardoned; for they proceeded not from evil motive but from want of judgement" (42). Indeed, the evil in the story is that of the father whose implicit sexual abuse and ultimate suicide appear to make Mathilda pure victim.

However, *Mathilda*'s connections to *Christabel* suggest greater complexity to her character than has been discussed previously, largely because scholarship on the novella has focused on the biographical. For instance, that Mathilda writes, "Fifteen months after their marriage I was born, and my mother died a few days after my birth" has typically suggested the comparison to Wollstonecraft's death after giving birth to Mary (47). Yet even this biographical detail is complicated by the connection to *Christabel*, whose mother also died giving birth to her. This echo connects the two tales through the father's resentment of his daughter for the death of his wife, Coleridge subverting the patriarchal view through the narrative voice that objectifies Christabel, Shelley casting the victim in the subject position.

Mathilda plays with this notion of victim as subject, thereby calling attention to its narrative irony. Mathilda's "favourite vision" as a child, for instance, was that, "disguised like a boy I would seek my father through the world" (51). Instead of her reunion with her father replicating this cross-dressing fantasy, however, it is a complex interplay of subjectivity in which Mathilda appears to objectify herself in a sexualized vision as she appears to her father: "As I came, dressed in white, covered only by my tartan *rachan*, my hair streaming on my shoulders, and shooting across with greater speed that it could be supposed I could give to my boat, my father has often told me that I looked more like a spirit than a human maid" (53). Her father's etherealizing her echoes Percy Shelley's objectifying women as variants of the "epipsyche." Mathilda's father represents the narcissism of such projection, idealizing his daughter as the "soul out of his soul." His suicide is not only his self-inflicted punishment for breaking the incest taboo but an act of violence against Mathilda as well.

Thus, the ambivalence of Mathilda's father toward her as epipsyche nevertheless responsible for the death of his wife complicates Shelley's

---

wishing to infect Beatrice, her own violent retribution suggesting Percy's representation of his central belief that violence begets violence. That Percy maintains a didactic position regarding treatment of the evil of incest. That Mathilda's father is struck by the grown Mathilda's likeness to his wife is a perversion of the simple cause-and-effect relationship between the death of his wife and his resentment of Mathilda. In a grotesque parody of Frankenstein's ambivalence toward his ultimate destruction of the female creation, Mathilda feels she has been "recreated" with her father's return, her life now seeming to be "a various river flowing through a fertile and lovely lan[d]scape, ever changing and ever beautiful" (55). However, she discovers that this recreation is a delusion. This likeness to Coleridge's secondary imagination suggests that Mathilda recreates her own selfhood just as her imagination recreates the familiar landscape, a reflection ending with the abrupt transition from "divine happiness" to grief (55).

With an allusion to *Paradise Lost* that echoes the creature's ironic references to Milton's Creator/creature relationship in *Frankenstein*, Mathilda writes, "I lament ... those few short months of Paradisaical bliss; I disobeyed no command, I ate no apple, and yet I was ruthlessly driven from it. Alas! My companion did, and I was precipitated in his fall. But I wander from my relation—let woe come at its appointed time; I may at this stage of my story still talk of happiness" (55). This moment, dense with Miltonic allusion, is nevertheless a radical departure from both Milton and the Miltonic in *Frankenstein*, bringing the incest taboo to the surface. As the companion tale to *Frankenstein*, *Mathilda* takes on the problem directly. By likening Mathilda to Eve in the context of her father's incestuous desire for her, Shelley implicitly denounces Milton's representation of God the Father-as-Creator in relation to his female creation.[14]

Refusing to name her father, Mathilda refers to him as her "companion," suggesting that she sees herself as complicit in her father's incestuous desire. The unresolved question of whether the sin is his desire for Mathilda or his withholding of familial love underlies her discomfort and sense of self-condemnation. Mathilda plays on the relationship between narrative and the family romance when she says, "I wander from my relation," the term "relation"

---

moral pollution reveals one of the striking differences between him and the Mary/Robinson/Coleridge connection of using contamination ironically to subvert such moral binaries.

[14] See Gilbert and Gubar's discussion of the implications of Eve's absence in *Frankenstein*.

a pun: as "tale," it calls attention to the significance of this moment even as it claims to be a digression from the narrative; as "family" it suggest that she is the one who refused her father by wandering from him (55). However, he is the one who abandoned her, thereby bringing into play another pun: to "wander" is also the etymology of error, so that to wander from her relation could imply not merely digressing from the narrative but, in her self-blame for her father's sin, erring morally as connected to erring in her telling her tale because it cannot redeem her. In this way, the perverse psychology of Mathilda's sense of guilt connects Shelley's novella to Coleridge's concern with the nature of evil in *Christabel*.

While Mathilda is split between her doubt about her innocence and her self-representation as victim, like Christabel, she is aware that her father has cast her as Eve or, closer to Coleridge's maternal doppelganger, Geraldine. Thus, Mathilda's father thereafter avoids her: "[H]e, my beloved father, shunned me, and either treated me with harshness or a more heart-breaking coldness" (57). While Leoline shuns his daughter, "cursed" by the contaminating Geraldine, he can act on his attraction to Geraldine, whose father is Leoline's rival, Lord Roland. The conclusion to Part II brings the perverseness of this paternal desire to the surface through its cryptic allusion to the psychology of desire unacted upon as evil. The child

> Makes such a vision to the sight
> As fills a father's eyes with light;
> And pleasures flow in so thick and fast
> Upon his heart, that he at last
> Must needs express his love's excess
> With words of unmeant bitterness. (ll. 648–53)

Describing the novella's concern with parents giving "their children death, not life," Michelle Faubert underscores the notion of contamination: "Mathilda's father apparently infects his daughter with the desire for death" (12–13). That the suicide of Mathilda's father contaminates her takes Coleridge's scrambling of the system of moral binaries into yet darker territory. Thus, Mathilda writes, "This is my curse, a daughter's curse: go, and return pure to thy child, who will never love aught but thee" (71). The taboo of incest has repercussions for the metanarrative of infection for both writers: just as Mathilda thinks but does not write these words, they express what Coleridge does not of the tongue-tied Christabel whose eyes roll in her head but cannot speak as her father embraces the infectious Geraldine.

Mathilda's dream of her father reveals her ambivalence. Like the rich interpretability of Victor's dream of Elizabeth just after the creature awakens, Mathilda's dream is triggered by her hearing her father's dreaded / desired footsteps outside her room: "But why approach my chamber? Was not that sacred? I felt almost ready to faint while he had stood there, but I had not betrayed my wakefulness by the slightest motion, although I had heard my own heart beat with violent fear" (71). "Fear" is perhaps a disingenuous term, as the dream suggests, for it is a byproduct of a welter of emotions rather than simply primal fear for one's safety:

> I thought that I had risen and went to seek my father to inform him of my determination to separate myself from him. I sought him in the house, in the park, and then in the fields and the woods, but I could not find him. At length I saw him at some distance, seated under a tree, and when he perceived me he waved his hand several times, beckoning me to approach; there was something unearthly in his mien that awed and chilled me, but I drew near. When a short distance from him I saw that he was deadlily pale, clothed in flowing garments of white. Suddenly he started up and fled from me; I pursued him: we sped over the fields, and by the skirts of woods, and on the banks of rivers; he flew fast and I followed. We came, at last, methought, to the brow of a huge cliff that over hung the sea which, troubled by the winds, dashed against its base, at a distance. I heard the roar of the waters: he held his course right on towards the brink and I became breathless with fear lest he should plunge down the dreadful precipice; I tried to augment my speed, but my knees failed beneath me, yet I had must reached him; just caught a part of his flowing robe, when he leapt down and I awoke with a violent scream. (72)

The dream is prophetic, as Shelley makes sure the reader notes by later connecting Mathilda's approach to the "fatal waters" directly to her dream: "The sound is the same as that which I heard in my dream" (81). Yet this is not mere gothic machinery, for it signals Mathilda's processing of the earlier events and her complicated emotions regarding her bond to her father. Most striking, her father is wearing "flowing garments of white," just as she was when he first returned. Her father's feminization puts her in the position of erotic desire, while the speed with which she pursues him in the dream suggests the speed of her boat as she rushes toward him. Looking at Mathilda's dream retrospectively, Shelley's complication of the gender and generational binary of father and daughter suggests both desire for and fear of her father's escape from her, ultimately through suicide.

Shelley further complicates Mathilda's dream in its echo of the final chase scene in *Frankenstein*, in which case Mathilda takes Frankenstein's role and the father takes the creature's role, suggesting irony in their both being unnamed. While *Frankenstein* ends with the creature's promise of self-immolation, suicide as a "sacrifice" (161), the suicide of Mathilda's father is a cruel gesture of contamination upon his living antagonist as object of desire. Shelley underscores the theme of contamination when Mathilda, awakening from the dream, contemplates writing a note to her father, whose name she "dared not utter" when the servant answers her bell, and so she orders breakfast instead (72). The servant, however, returns with a letter from her father that begins, "I have betrayed your confidence; I have endeavoured to pollute your mind" (73). That Mathilda preempts her own attempt at speaking the unspeakable with the father's confession suggests that *Mathilda*'s narrative contamination is as complex as Coleridge's: though there is no Geraldine poisoning a male narrator's story of *Christabel*, Shelley lays the burden of guilt with the father's "endeavor" to pollute Mathilda's mind, closer to the innuendo of incest in *Christabel*'s "Conclusion to Part the Second," in which the child

> Makes such a vision to the sight
> As fills a father's eyes with light
> And pleasures flow in so thick and fast
> Upon his heart, that he at last
> Must needs express his love's excess
> With words of unmeant bitterness. (ll. 649–53)[15]

---

[15] See the earlier references to the source of this final section of *Christabel* as his letter describing his infant son, Hartley. In the context of *Christabel*, it resonates with a far more complex set of implications regarding Coleridge's notion of the perverse.

Shelley leaves the reader with no doubt of the perversity of her father's overlaying of "love's excess" and "bitterness," his letter describing his "devilish levity" in endeavouring to "steal away her loveliness to place in its stead the foul deformity of sin" (73). He then redescribes the same scene of Mathilda rushing out to meet him when he returned: "You appeared as the deity of a lovely region, the ministering Angel of a Paradise to which of all human kind you admitted only me. I dared hardly consider you as my daughter; your beauty, artlessness and untaught wisdom seemed to belong to a higher order of beings" (74–5). Returning to the moment itself underscores the way that Mathilda had originally described herself in that scene from her father's point of view. When we see it here, spoken in his own voice, it is laden with double objectification: his statement, "I dared hardly consider you as my daughter," suggests sexual desire that is projected as reverence for femininity that Wollstonecraft decried. Though Mathilda has commonalities with both Christabel and Geraldine, they are the projections of the father onto the daughter in Shelley's tale.

Complicating the subjectivity of this pivotal moment in the novella, in which Mathilda describes herself from her father's perspective, her father's reference to Dante echoes Mathilda's in an earlier passage, "Ond' era pinta tutta la mia via ["Whose painted forms had all her path besprent" (50, n. 1).[16] Giving her female protagonist the same name as Dante's Matilda, Shelley suggests a departure from her wrestling with Milton in *Frankenstein*. There, Victor himself as Creator gave his Eve more than a second thought, brutally dismembering his half-finished female creation. Dante's Matilda first appears in the *Purgatorio*. *Mathilda*'s reference to Dante through the phrase, "Whose painted forms had all her path besprent," is yet more significant when the fuller context of Dante's passage is taken into account. Matilda, who is not named at this stage of the *Purgatorio*, is custodian of Dante's memory, helping him both to forget his obstacles and to remember his artistic purpose. Dante's Matilda embodies virginal modesty: "A woman all alone, who walked along / Singing, and picking flower after flower, / For her whole path was painted with their colors" (Canto XXVIII, ll. 40–2). Yet Shelley's choice of the single line alluding

---

[16] See Keach's intertextual comparison of Percy's *The Cenci* and Mary's *Mathilda* to Dante's figure of Matilda in *The Divine Comedy*.

to the artist's creation at this early phase of Mathilda's narrative announces her artistic sensibility, offering her Mathilda the subjectivity Dante's never fully realizes.

However, when Shelley recurs to Dante's Matilda through the subjectivity of Mathilda's father in his letter, he co-opts Mathilda/Matilda's voice. It is a ludicrous attempt at self-justification, in spite of his beginning the letter by confessing to her that he has "endeavoured to pollute [her] mind" (73). The passage, from Dante's *Paradiso* rather than the *Purgatorio* of the earlier passage, literalizes her father's appropriating Mathilda's vision: "E quasi mi perdei con gli occhi chini" ["I seemed unconscious, with mine eyes bent low" (75, n. 1)].[17] The letter's subsequent self-denunciation echoes *Christabel*'s Conclusion to Part II:

> Was my love blamable? If it was I was ignorant of it; I desired only that which I possessed, and if I enjoyed from your looks, and words, and most innocent caresses a rapture usually excluded from the feelings of a parent towards his child, yet no uneasiness, no wish, no casual idea awoke me to a sense of guilt. (75)

The father's use of litotes when questioning the relationship of love and guilt heightens his manipulation of Mathilda; one hears the wishful casualness of his guilt in his claim that "no wish, no casual idea" awakened a sense of guilt.

Narrative Contamination and Gender in *The Last Man*: Plague as "Queen of the World"

While female subjectivities are brutally silenced in the patriarchal world of *Frankenstein*, Mathilda's inability to inoculate herself against her father's contamination is an even darker representation of a daughter's failure to realize her potential for recreating her subjectivity, wrested from her by her father's demand that she stand in for her mother, his dead wife. *Mathilda* is thus kin

---

[17] See Keach on the translation of "chini"; the implications for Shelley's interrogation of Orientalism have rich potential when considered with Neff's argument: Frankenstein's creation is the construction of an ur-human from India, the type of being that was being discussed throughout the salons of late eighteenth-century Europe (qtd. in Halmi et al., 345).

to Coleridge's narratives in imagining the radically contrasting failures of both patriarchy and matriarchy.

Mathilda bridges Shelley's two larger representations of human history in Frankenstein's perverse attempt to begin human history anew without death and Shelley's imagined end of human history in her 1826 novel, *The Last Man*. Whereas *Frankenstein* treats the relationship between evil and contamination through metanarrative, as described earlier in this chapter, *The Last Man* literalizes this relationship through the plague as both physical and moral disease, seen for instance when the teller of this tale, Lionel Verney, rides through "unpeopled London" while his child lies "dead at home" (266). Lionel notes that "the seeds of mortal disease had taken root in my bosom," the difference between "mortal" and "moral" disease collapsing in the "bosom" of a man who holds himself responsible for the deaths of his sister, Perdita, and his wife, Idris, both of whom leave behind children he fails (266).

Though on the surface, Lionel has little in common with Frankenstein or Mathilda's father as powerful male figures, Shelley's trajectory can be traced through the relationship between gender and narrative contamination among the three novels. As with both *Frankenstein* and *Mathilda*, early criticism focused on the biographical significance of the novel, written after the death of Percy, while later scholars have explored the political message of its dystopian plot.[18] Some of these later studies, noting the novel's metanarrative, connect Shelley's indictment of Enlightenment humanism with the plague in its leveling all social strata. Young-Ok An observes, for instance, that the novel complicates the "ultimate binarism—life or death" by suggesting that the plague is not "conterminous" with death though the characters "continually misread" the signs of the plague (588, 589, 585).[19] Steven Goldsmith adds another dimension to the symbolism of the plague by observing that it "replaces the human with narrative" (311). This study extends these more recent approaches by looking at the novel through the lens of Shelley's relationship with both Coleridge's and Robinson's dismantling of the materialist underpinnings of narration,

---

[18] See Young-Ok An for a useful list of such citations (582–3, n. 3).
[19] An also adds nuance to discussion of the novel's female characters, noting that Perdita and Evadne are atypical while Idris undergoes transformation, an observation this study explores in more detail (592).

extending their concerns by exploring the temporal binary of futurity and history.

Shelley's introduction to *The Last Man* frames her tale with an allusion to Coleridge's 1817 collection, *Sibylline Leaves*, written a year before Shelley and her "companion," who has been assumed to be Percy, visited the Sibyl's cave. By announcing the connection to Coleridge's poetry at the outset, Shelley's introduction is, as Mary Poovey has said, her "most elaborate strategy of indirection" (*The Last Man*, 157).[20] To extricate the novel and its introduction from the gender binary foundational to previous studies, one can trace in both the elements of Coleridge's and Robinson's reflections on the recreative.

The echoes of "Kubla Khan," though not included in Coleridge's *Sibylline Leaves*, are unmistakable, especially through Shelley's odd use of the word "damsel" to describe the Sibyl. As Goldsmith notes, the "Cumean Sibyl possessed none of the noble and sentimental innocence implied by the term *damsel*"; Shelley's primary source for this introduction, Book 6 of the *Aeneid*, describes the Sibyl as "mad, monstrous and frenetic, rendering the phrase 'Cumaean damsel' incongruous to the point of absurdity" (277). In the context of the introduction's Coleridgean title, the word damsel connects the Sibyl to the damsel of the poet's vision in the third stanza of "Kubla Khan," though Coleridge's damsel may too find its origin in *The Aeneid*. As discussed in Chapter 3, Coleridge's damsel gives voice to the powerfully recreative, female energy of nature in the second stanza of "Kubla Khan." As female subjectivities framing that of Lionel's narrative voice in the novel, both Shelley and the Sibyl orient the narrative told by Lionel, the sole survivor of the plague. The Sibyl, and behind her, Shelley, give voice to the recreative feminine energy; like that of nature subsuming Kubla's patriarchal power in "Kubla Khan," she inhabits a "cavern with a dome-like roof" (*The Last Man*, 2). Though the Coleridgean persona of "Kubla Khan" can only hope to harness the energy of the "damsel"

---

[20] Goldsmith notes how little attention the introduction has garnered, other than the studies of Poovey and of Gilbert and Gubar (277, n. 24). In 1985, Toril Moi objected to Gilbert and Gubar's interpretation deriving from "patriarchal aesthetic values of New Criticism"; in the twenty-first century we are in a position to reflect on relationships across genders that are not relegated to one or the other side of the binary created in the earlier work that challenged the Modernist paradigm of the canon (67). At odds with the argument of this study, Gilbert and Gubar see the Sibyl's cave as a "female space" in a matriarchy that makes Shelley herself "figuratively the daughter of the vanished Sibyl, the primordial prophetess who mythically conceived all women artists" (96–7).

as a means to be that wild-eyed prophet, Shelley allows the Sibyl to cast doubt on the authority of Lionel's narration in the novel. In Shelley's imagining of the Sibyl's cave it is the place of discovery of the ancient language that the writer deciphers: "This was certainly the Sibyl's Cave; not indeed exactly as Virgil describes it; but the whole of this land had been so convulsed by earthquake and volcano, that the change was not wonderful" (*The Last Man*, 3). The voice behind Lionel is the Sibyl herself, and behind the Sibyl, Shelley. Not only is the cave she happens upon "not exactly as Virgil describes it," but, in her fictional "adaptation and translation" of the Sibylline leaves, Shelley recreates it to reflect the novel's transmission itself as plague, the message a fulfillment of Coleridge's unrealized *Magnum Opus*: evil as, in Shelley's words, "narration of misery and woeful change" (*The Last Man*, 5).

Completing the triangulated relationship among the three writers, Shelley's novel not only makes reference to Robinson through the character, Perdita, Robinson's stage name, but also suggests a deeper affinity to Robinson's subjectivity as a poet, fiction writer, and actress whose identity became conflated in popular culture with the name's literal translation, "the lost one" of the Shakespearean play, *The Winter's Tale*. The conflation of Robinson's character on stage and her personae in fiction and poetry is a source of irony for Shelley. Robinson's rendering of Perdita on stage recalls the Sibyl of the introduction as well as a composite of the Abyssinian maid and the poet-narrator of "Kubla Khan." Like Frankenstein, when Lionel approaches Perdita after the death of her husband, he "stood fearful to advance, to speak, to look. In the midst of the hall was Perdita; she sat on the marble pavement, her head fallen on her bosom, her hair disheveled, her fingers twined busily one with the other" (*The Last Man*, 159). Here, through the lens of her brother, Lionel, Perdita is described as a tableau, a deranged figure of grief. Lionel's reaction to Perdita's pleading with him to release her recalls Victor's vacillation with the creature's pleading to make him a female companion, Lionel saying, "At first these agonizing plaints filled me with intolerable compassion. But soon I endeavoured to extract patience for her from the ideas she suggested" (*The Last Man*, 159). Like Frankenstein, Lionel is deluded in premature self-congratulation. Here, Lionel is proud when, having "accomplished" everything "with speed under my direction," he plans to leave for England and, forcing Perdita to come, to restore all to "the tranquility of our family circle at Windsor" (*The Last Man*,

166). He rightly blames himself for Perdita's subsequent suicide after he drugs her when she will not yield to his demand that she leave Greece. Perdita's name takes on deepening irony when Lionel refers not to her but to her husband, Raymond, as the "lost one," Perdita thus doubly lost as a Sibyl or Abyssinian maid manque (*The Last Man*, 159).

Lionel's narrative in *The Last Man* consists of a series of tales that parallels the spread of disease. The novel represents ironically the idealism of the male characters, in particular, Raymond, whose utopianism echoes Godwin and Percy. Like Percy, Raymond undercuts his idealistic claim, "I have much to do before England becomes a Paradise," with his infidelity to his wife, Perdita (*The Last Man*, 84). By representing Raymond's infidelity as a "cureless evil," the novel gestures to the inexorable evil associated with the plague that destroys the world (*The Last Man*, 112). *The Last Man* thus realizes Coleridge's *Magnum Opus* in its own terms. The first suggestion of the plague associated with moral disease is the unraveling of the relationship between Raymond and Perdita, who must learn to negotiate her society's inequities as Raymond embodies them. Thus, when Raymond betrays Perdita, he "forgot that each word he spoke was false. He personated his assumption of innocence even to self-deception.... A more intense feeling of the reality of fiction possessed Raymond" (*The Last Man*, 96).

Shelley comes closest to creating a Coleridgean female character who undermines patriarchy with Evadne, Raymond's lover. She is both androgynous, disguising herself as a soldier, and the first person to bring the plague close to home for Lionel. She thus does not simply die of the plague, but rather embodies it. Through Evadne, Shelley juxtaposes death with the spread of contamination: "The dress of this person was that of a soldier, but the bared neck and arms, and the continued shrieks discovered a female thus disguised.... With wild and terrific exclamations did the lost, dying Evadne ... recognize the language of her lover" (*The Last Man*, 142). When she cries out, "Many living deaths have I borne for thee, O Raymond, and now I expire.... By my death I purchase thee—lo! The instruments of war, fire, the plague are my servitors" (*The Last Man*, 142), Evadne's closest literary kin is Life-in-Death herself who, "casting dice" with Death, wins the soul of the Ancient Mariner (*The Ancient Mariner*, 1834, l. 196).

By contrast to Evadne, Perdita, Lionel's sister, and Idris, Lionel's wife, are long-suffering wives. Victimized, passive, and "lost," they recall the female characters in *Frankenstein*. Just as Victor's remorse is belated as he gets news of each character's death, from Justine and William to Clerval and Elizabeth, Lionel resembles Victor through his "regret and remorse" for his responsibility in the deaths of Perdita and then Idris (*The Last Man*, 169). The pattern of Lionel's objectification of the female gestures back to the importance of Frankenstein's dream that, coinciding with the awakening of his creature, exposes Victor's repulsion toward the repressed, tripartite female: Elizabeth, in the imagined present of the dream, is both his dead mother and, yet deeper in the field of the unconscious, the female creature he will destroy in the novel's future. The creature, the grotesque epipsyche, links Elizabeth to his own imagined female when he threatens and then carries out retribution with his murder of Elizabeth for Frankenstein's destruction of his female. The dream thus resonates throughout the novel, looking both to Victor's personal history and ahead to the potential history that began his quest for a deathless state and that he thereafter negates. Frankenstein's imaginative failure to understand the dream thus belies the redemptive claim of his early obsession to recreate a deathless Adam: his vision of a human history free of death does not include a female, notwithstanding his begrudging promise to his creature who reminds him that there is more to the Biblical story than the first Father and Son relationship. The end of the claimed utopian fantasy of a deathless human race is realized with Frankenstein's destruction of the female mid-creation, for fear of their deathless race.

Percy's epipsyche returns through Lionel's vision of his wife, Idris, as a female paragon. She is the "personification of all that was divine in woman, she who walked the earth like a poet's dream, as a carved goddess endued with sense, or pictured saint stepping from the canvas—she, the most worthy, chose me, and gave me herself—a priceless gift" (205). It is difficult not to hear Shelley's irony in Lionel's hyperbolic praise; that Lionel echoes the poet of *Alastor* in his pursuit of such a goddess as epipsyche suggests that his fate will be a death not unlike that of Percy's poet-figure. Indeed, the novel ends with another echo of *Alastor*. Alone in the world after humanity has been eradicated by the plague, Lionel sets out in his "tiny bark" with neither history nor futurity but rather a "monotonous present"; it is "restless despair and fierce desire of change" that lead him on (367). Lionel, kin to both Victor and his creature, is forced to outlive those he has ignored in his self-absorption. Lionel's fascinated horror at the dying Idris's physical deterioration gestures back to the connection among Frankenstein's dream of Elizabeth turning into his dead mother, his destruction of the female creature, and Elizabeth's death:

> Her hollow eyes and worn countenance had a ghastly appearance; her cheek-bones, her open fair brow, the projection of the mouth, stood fearfully prominent; you might tell each bone in the thin anatomy of her frame. Her hand hung powerless; each joint lay bare, so that the light penetrated through and through. It was strange that life could exist in what was wasted and worn into a very type of death. (*The Last Man*, 271)

Whereas Idris does die along with everyone else except for Lionel, echoing Coleridge's Mariner, Lionel is cursed by Life-in-Death. History unspools in the novel, in which linearity is blurred for Lionel as he contemplates the death of Idris. Lionel appears to be the fulfillment of Victor's wish for a deathless man, the only one who contracts and then recovers from the plague: "I felt that my death must be voluntary. Yet what more natural than famine, as I watched in this chamber of mortality, placed in a world of the dead, beside the lost hope of my life?" (*The Last Man*, 281). If Idris is the epipsyche, soul out of his soul, her death equates to his life-in-death.

Lionel's name echoes the regal paternity of Leoline, infected by Geraldine's androgynous energy. In Shelley's created universe, however, Lionel is the only person to survive the plague, thus perhaps closer to Coleridge's Mariner who is cursed with Life-in-Death. When Lionel sentimentally imagines his "upright, manly" son, Alfred, advancing to take his own place in his fantasy of patriarchal lineage as a natural process, the irony is clear: contagion will destroy all, Lionel left solitary (*The Last Man*, 180). Discussing Shelley's novel vis-à-vis the "Last Man" poems of the period, such as Byron's "Darkness," Goldsmith asks, "What happens when Shelley enters this manly genre and writes from the position of that which is already excluded?" (274).[21] In Shelley's rendering through Lionel's narration, the curse of the wanderer is

---

[21] Goldsmith notes studies since the late 1970s locating Shelley's novel as part of a "Last Man" trend (267, n. 11).

most fully realized: like that of Coleridge's Mariner, evil is perverse, Shelley's male protagonists destroying others out of thoughtlessness. From Elizabeth to Perdita, who dies because Lionel refuses to grant her wish to stay in Greece, women are the victims of a patriarchy that naively believes it can force its will on those around him. Lionel believes he can wall off contagion after escaping the plague in Greece; returning to England after Perdita drowns herself, he convinces himself that he and his domestic circle are immune to the "physical evils of distant countries" until he discovers, "our island had become the refuge of thousands" (177, 184). Like Life-in-Death's winning of the Mariner's soul, Lionel's is a life-in-death.

Following Perdita's suicide earlier, Lionel describes the "strange story" of the "parched-looking" ship that appears in Portsmouth with a man who dies, presumably of the plague, on the beach (*The Last Man*, 170). That he bears the plague from America is an ironic reversal of the spread of human migration west. His grotesqueness creates another layer of irony in his echo of Frankenstein's creature. He is a vision of humanity's annihilation, the dark truth set against Frankenstein's deluded belief that he can create deathless life: "His skin, nearly black, his matted hair and bristly beard, were signs of a long protracted misery" (*The Last Man*, 170).

As noted earlier, the novel's connection to Robinson through the character of Perdita goes beyond Shelley's allusion to Robinson's stage name. Robinson too explores the relationship between the so-called sane and those who, labeled mad, challenge systematic binaries. As Chapter 2 has discussed, for instance, the subjectivity of Robinson's "The Maniac" deepens from the poem's opening distance between narrator and Maniac, the former describing the latter through the gothic trappings of madness, to the narrowing of the divide between them, in which the struggle with the binaries of Enlightenment reason suggests that the narrator's discomfort with the grotesqueness of the Maniac leading her to a poet-figure whose art reflects one whose "sense [is] unchain'd"; in turn, it leads the narrator to celebrate a mental state liberated from the binaries imposed by Enlightenment reason (41). As the poem shifts from the narrator's horror to one of empathy, the narrator makes a pact with the Maniac that she will provide a voice for him that does not objectify him but rather provides the double vision in which subject reflects subject, both horrifying and familiar.

The novel thus shares and extends the recreative in Coleridge and Robinson and in Shelley's own *Frankenstein* and *Mathilda*. Of the works among the three writers, *The Last Man* represents the relationship between narrative and contamination most allegorically. The plague that Shelley imagines in *The Last Man* germinates in the contaminating tales of both Coleridge and Robinson and of Shelley's earlier novels. The plague vanquishes patriarchy, appearing in the novel as both monarchy and the Judeo-Christian tradition that Raymond embodies. The failure of Shelley's characters to read and thereby immunize themselves against the plague underscores her recreation of a world antithetical to Percy's and Godwin's utopianism.[22] *The Last Man* expands the literalized recreation of the ironic literalizing of recreation in *Frankenstein* as it literalizes the contamination that Geraldine brings to the patriarchal world of Sir Leoline in *Christabel*.

Through the lens of *Frankenstein*, *The Last Man* dismantles and recreates the earlier novel's universe. The fate of the last man, Lionel Verney, is an ironic realization of the most hopeful future the creature of *Frankenstein* could imagine, namely the utopian life that the creature had promised Frankenstein he and his companion would live, apart from a society that abhorred him. Without a companion, and ultimately without Victor to hate, the creature chooses to immolate himself in a final scene that Walton, as the framing tale-teller, will record. Lionel, alone, has the story of the plague to tell but no one to hear it.

Rather than submerge the feminine as she does in *Frankenstein*, whose women are silenced, whose female nature is violated, and whose female creation is destroyed by her creator in a grotesque parody of the recreative act, Shelley represents the force that brings down patriarchal history in *The Last Man* as the plague gendered female. The plague is most overtly identified as such with Lionel's bitter reflection of "those times when men walked the earth fearless, before Plague had become Queen of the World" (273). In so

---

[22] Speaking to Mary's antipathy to Percy's utopianism, Mary thought *The Cenci*, Percy's darkest work, to be his greatest. Underscoring this conflict between Percy and Mary is Percy's decision to add a fourth act to *Prometheus Unbound* following what he described as the "sad reality" in his Preface to *The Cenci* as a means of reinforcing the idealism of that play (140). See Reiman and Freistat on Mary's part in the textual history of *The Cenci* (138–9).

personifying the plague, Shelley pays homage to Coleridge's Life-in-Death who condemns the Mariner to the endless spread of a tale that destabilizes the pieties of categorical imperatives. By the end of *The Last Man*, Shelley has collapsed even the implicit binary of tale-teller and auditor, Coleridge's Mariner and Wedding Guest. Though stunned like the Wedding Guest at the end of *Rime of the Ancient Mariner*, Lionel, unlike the Mariner, is cursed to tell his tale to no one.

Coda

Mary Shelley's twenty-first-century plague in *The Last Man* is only a half-century later than the COVID-19 pandemic. A new generation that attempts to find footing in the uncanny narrative of a contaminated planet may find cold comfort in a return not only to this first dystopian novel but also to that triangular literary fellowship among Coleridge, Robinson, and Shelley that produced tale-tellers and other unreliable subjectivities spreading disease even while promising catharsis.

As levels of contamination become mutually infectious, the line between the metaphorical and literal becomes untraceable. Contaminating narratives within texts gesture to literary influence as metatextual influenza. One might trace the origin of this disease to Coleridge's beautiful, leprous Life-in-Death, who may well be the progenitor of the mutated gene that wins the soul of the Mariner who, in turn, spawns infectious tale-tellers and their recreators. Thus, for instance, Robinson's Walsingham compels another mariner, the disfigured Griffith, to tell his sad tale. Unlike the Wedding Guest, who struggles to escape the hypnotic effect of Coleridge's Mariner, Walsingham encourages Griffith to tell him the story of how his arm was reduced to a "flipper" to help ease Griffith's mind. As Griffith finishes, Walsingham discovers his own disease hovering at the edge of consciousness, perhaps reminiscent of the Wedding Guest walking away a sadder and wiser man.

In a parody of tale-telling as self-consolation that follows, Walsingham is compelled to write a poem he calls "The Exile." In Walsingham's poem, the masculinity of his exiled persona is underscored from the first line where he stands on a "rock of dreadful height," cast out of his home and community in favor of what he thinks is his masculine rival, Sir Sidney. While Walsingham had understood Griffith's disfigured arm to be the cause of his sorrow,

Walsingham disfigures Griffith's anticlimactically heteronormative story of his relationship with his wife and daughter; in "The Exile," set against Walsingham's masculine persona atop a high peak, the feminine is transfigured to a landscape of cataracts, yawning gulfs, and a predatory "she-wolf" prowling nearby. As Robinson's novel, *Walsingham*, thus unfolds, gender is at the heart of Walsingham's sublimated disease: under the surface of his narrative, his poetry tells us that his is not the ostensible story of male antagonists vying for the love of a woman, but one that has dismantled the gender binaries of the sentimental novel.

Like Walsingham's androgynous cousin Sidney and Coleridge's dismantled, reassembled sentimental heroines, Life-in-Death and Christabel, Victor Frankenstein's creature is uncanny in his grotesque beauty. The female companion of Victor's creature, in turn, is a more diseased embodiment of Victor's contaminating and disfiguring recreative urges: odious to Victor from her partial creation to dismemberment, she is a grotesque parody of Percy Shelley's feminine ideal, the epipsyche.

Whereas Mary Shelley dares to imagine the end of human history in *The Last Man* with one last tale-teller writing for no one, our pandemic offers us the opportunity to discover our own voice—the authorial—behind the multiplying subjectivities demanding priority that crowd our collective imagination. The nature of the uncanny, *unheimlich*, may ease our global anxiety: returning home—however temporarily—we forge new or renewed awareness of our own authorial home to which we may continue returning, perhaps sadder and wiser, from tales of woe in a perpetual process of recreation.

Selected Bibliography

Primary Works

Burke, Edmund. "A Philosophical Enquiry into the Origin of Our Ideas of the Sublime and the Beautiful." 1757. http://find.galegroup.com/ecco/retrieve.do?scale=0.33&sort=Author&docLevel=FASCIMILE&prodId=ECCO&tabID=T001&resultListType=RESULT_LIST&qrySerId=Locale%28en%2C%2C%29%3AFQE%3D%28BN%2CNone%2C7%29T042257%24&retrieveFormat=MULTIPAGE_DOCUMENT&inPS=true&userGroupName=miami_richter&do cId=CW3320735814&currentPosition=1&workId=0357900100&relevancePageBatch=C W120735813&contentSet=ECCOArticles&callistoContentSet=ECCOArticles&resultList Type=RESULT_LIST&reformatPage=N&retrieveFormat=MULTIPAGE_DOCUMENT &scale=0.33&pageIndex=3&orientation=&showLOI=&quickSearchTerm=&stwFuzzy=&doDirectDocNumSearch=false (accessed August 1, 2020).

Byron, George Gordon, Lord. *Byron's Poetry and Prose*. Ed. Alice Levine. New York: Norton, 2010.

Coleridge, Ernest Hartley, ed. *Anima Poetae: From the Unpublished Note-books of Samuel Taylor Coleridge*. New York: Houghton, Mifflin and Co., 1895.

Coleridge, Samuel Taylor. *Biographia Literaria*. Ed. James Engell and W. Jackson Bate. Princeton, NJ: Princeton University Press, 1983.

Coleridge, Samuel Taylor. *Collected Letters*. Ed. E. L. Griggs. 6 vols. New York: Oxford University Press, 1956–71.

Coleridge, Samuel Taylor. *Coleridge's Notebooks: A Selection*. Ed. Seamus Perry. New York: Oxford University Press, 2002.

Coleridge, Samuel Taylor. *Collected Works*. Ed. Thomas McFarland. vols 1–16. Princeton, NJ: Princeton University Press, 1969.

Coleridge, Samuel Taylor. *Confessions of an Inquiring Spirit*. Stanford: Stanford University Press, 1957.

Coleridge, Samuel Taylor. *Lectures on Shakespeare (1811–1819)*. Ed. Adam Roberts. Edinburgh: Edinburgh University Press, 2016.

Coleridge, Samuel Taylor. *The Notebooks of Samuel Taylor Coleridge*. Ed. Kathleen Coburn. 5 vols. London: Princeton University Press, 1957–2002.

Coleridge, Samuel Taylor. Marginalia to *Othello*. 1807. https://www.bl.uk/collection-items/coleridges-annotated-copy-of-shakespeare (accessed August 1, 2020).

Coleridge, Samuel Taylor. *Opus Maximum*. Ed. Thomas McFarland. *Collected Works*. Vol. XV. Princeton, NJ: Princeton University Press, 2002.

Coleridge, Samuel Taylor. *Specimens of the Table Talk*. 3rd Edition. Ed. Coleridge, Henry Nelson. London: John Murray, 1851.

Dante Alighieri. *The Purgatorio*. https://www.gutenberg.org/files/8795/8795-h/8795-h.htm (accessed August 5, 2020).

Erdman, David, ed. *The Complete Poetry and Prose of William Blake*. New York: Doubleday, 1988.

Goethe, J. W. *The Bride of Corinth* ["Die Braut von Korinth"]. Trans. William Edmondstoune Aytoun and Tehodore Martin. New York: Delisser & Procter, 1859.

Halmi, Nicholas, et al., eds. *Coleridge's Poetry and Prose*. New York: Norton, 2004.

Jackson, H. J., ed. *Coleridge: The Critical Heritage*. 2 vols. London, 1970–91.

Jones, Ernest. *Hamlet and Oedipus*. New York: Norton, 1949, 1976.

Kant, Immanuel. *Groundwork of the Metaphysics of Morals*. Trans. Mary Gregor, Mary and Jens Timmermann. Ebooks Corporation. Cambridge: Cambridge University Press, 2012.

Keats, John. *Keats's Poetry and Prose*. Ed. Jeffrey N. Cox. New York: Norton, 2009.

Poe, Edgar Allan. "The Imp of the Perverse." *The Raven: Tales and Poems*. New York: Penguin, 2013, 233–9.

Robinson, Mary. *A Letter to the Women of England and The Natural Daughter*. Ed. Sharon M. Setzer. Orchard Park, NY: Broadview Press, 2003.

Robinson, Mary. *Memoirs*. http://www.archive.org/stream/memoirsoflatemrs02robiuoft/memoirsoflatemrs02robiuoftdjvu.txt (accessed August 5, 2020).

Robinson, Mary. *Poems by Mrs. M. Robinson*. London: J. Bell, 1791. http://digital.library.upenn.edu/women/robinson/1791/1791.html (accessed August 5, 2020).

Robinson, Mary. *Selected Poems*. Ed. Judith Pascoe. Orchard Park, NY: Broadview, 2000.

Robinson, Mary. *Walsingham; or, The Pupil of Nature*. Ed. Julie A. Shaffer. Orchard Park, NY: Broadview, 2003.

Schiller, Friedrich von, "On the Sublime." Trans. Julius A. Elias. New York: Ungar Publishing Co., 1966.

Shelley, Mary. *Frankenstein*. 2nd Edition. Ed. Paul Hunter. New York: Norton, 2012.

Shelley, Mary. *The Last Man*. Ed. Anne McWhir. Orchard Park, NY: Broadview Press, 1996.

Shelley, Mary. *Mathilda*. Ed. Michelle Faubert. Orchard Park, NY: Broadview Press, 2017.

Shelley, Mary. *Valperga, or, The Life and Adventures of Castruccio, Prince of Lucca*. Ed. Stuart Curran. New York: Oxford University Press, 1997.

Shelley, Percy. *Shelley's Poetry and Prose*. Ed. Donald H. Reiman and Neil Fraistat. New York: Norton, 2002.

Smith, Charlotte. *The Poems of Charlotte Smith*. Ed. Stuart Curran. New York: Oxford University Press, 1993.

Swedenborg, Emanuel. *Heaven and Its Wonders and Hell*. https://swedenborg.com/wp-content/uploads/2013/03/swedenborg_foundation_heaven_and_hell.pdf (accessed August 1, 2020).

Wollstonecraft, Mary. *Vindication of the Rights of Woman*. Ed. Deirdre Lynch. New York: Norton, 2009.

Wordsworth, Dorothy. *The Grasmere and Alfoxden Journals*. New York: Oxford University Press, 2002.

Wordsworth, William. *Selected Poems and Prefaces*. Ed. Jack Stillinger. New York: Riverside Editions, 1965.

Criticism and Biography

Abrams, M. H. *The Mirror and the Lamp: Romantic Theory and the Critical Tradition*. New York: Oxford University Press, 1953.

Airey, Jennifer L. "'Abused, Neglected,—Unhonoured,—Unrewarded': The Economics of Authorial Labor in the Writings of Mary Robinson." *ABO: Interactive Journal for Women in the Arts, 1640–1830*, 6, 1, 1–13.

An, Young-Ok. "'Read Your Fall': The Signs of Plague in *The Last Man*." *Studies in Romanticism* 44, 4 (2005): 581–604.

Armstrong, Isabel. "The Gush of the Feminine: How Can We Read Women's Poetry of the Romantic Period?" In *Romantic Women Writers: Voices and Countervoices*. Ed. Paula Feldman and Theresa M. Kelley. Hanover. New Hampshire: University Press of New England, 1995, 14–32.

Arnold, Matthew. *Essays in Criticism: Second Series*. 1888. Cambridge: Chadwyck-Healey, 1999. https://miami-primo.hosted.exlibrisgroup.com/permalink/f/1k369cc/TN_hathitrust_suva_x000197105 (accessed August 1, 2020).

Barbeau, Jeffrey W., ed. *Coleridge's Assertion of Religion: Essays on the Opus Maximum*. Dudley, MA: Peeters, 2006.

Beavers, Katy. "The Legacy of the Ancient Mariner: Mary Shelley's Interpretation of 'The Wanderer.'" *Coleridge Bulletin* 43 (Summer 2014): 55–63.

Beer, John. "Coleridge's Magnum Opus and His Opus Maximum." In *Coleridge's Assertion of Religion: Essays on the Opus Maximum*. Ed. Jeffrey W. Barbeau. Dudley, MA: Peeters, 2006, 281–92.

Berkeley, Richard. *Coleridge and the Crisis of Reason*. New York: Palgrave Macmillan, 2007.

Bloom, Harold. *The Anxiety of Influence: A Theory of Poetry*. New York: Oxford University Press, 1973.

Bloom, Harold. *The Visionary Company: A Reading of English Romantic Poetry*. Ithaca, NY: Cornell University Press, 1961, 1971.

Butler, Marilyn. *Romantics, Rebels and Reactionaries*. New York: Oxford University Press, 1981.

Byrne, Paula. *Perdita: The Literary, Theatrical, Scandalous Life of Mary Robinson*. New York: Random House, 2004.

Carlson, Julie. "Gender." In *The Cambridge Companion to Coleridge*. Ed. Lucy Newlyn. Cambridge, England: Cambridge University Press, 2002, 203–16.

Carr, Julie and Jeffrey C., Robinson, eds. *Active Romanticism: The Radical Impulse in Nineteenth-Century and Contemporary Poetic Practice*. Tuscaloosa: University of Alabama Press, 2015.

Coburn, Kathleen. *Experience into Thought: Perspectives in the Coleridge Notebooks*. Toronto: University of Toronto Press, 1979.

Colmer, John. Review of McFarland, *Coleridge and the Pantheist Tradition*. *Yearbook of English Studies* I (1971), 287–8.

Cooke, Katharine. *Coleridge*. Boston: Routledge, 1976.

Cooke, Michael. *Acts of Inclusion: Studies Bearing on an Elementary Theory of Romanticism*. New Haven: Yale University Press, 1979.

Cross, Ashley. "Coleridge and Robinson: Harping on Lyrical Exchange." In *Fellow Romantics: Male and Female British Writers, 1790–1835*. Burlington, VT: Ashgate, 2009.

Cross, Ashley. *Mary Robinson and the Genesis of Romanticism: Literary Dialogues and Debts, 1784–1821*. New York: Taylor and Francis, 2017.

Cross, Ashley. "To 'Buzz Lamenting Doings in the Air': Romantic Flies, Insect Poets, and Authorial Sensibility." *European Romantic Review* 25, 3 (2014): 337–46.

Cross, Ashley. "The I Altered." In *Romanticism and Feminism*. Ed. Anne Mellor. Bloomington: Indiana University Press, 1988, 185–207.

Cross, Ashley. "Introduction." In *The Poems of Charlotte Smith*. New York: Oxford University Press, 1993, xix–xxviii.

Cross, Ashley. "Mary Robinson's *Lyrical Tales* in Context." In *Re-visioning Romanticism: British Women Writers, 1776-1837*. Ed. Carol Shiner Wilson and Joel Haefner. Philadelphia: University of Pennsylvania Press, 1994, 17–35.

Curran, Stuart. "Introduction." In *The Poems of Charlotte Smith*. Ed. Stuart Curran. New York: Oxford University Press, 1993, xix–xxix.

David, Alun. "Sir William Jones, Biblical Orientalism and Indian Scholarship." *Modern Asian Studies* 30, 1 (1996): 173–84.

DuPlessis, Rachel Blau. "Singing Schools and Mental Equality." In *Active Romanticism*. Ed. Carr and Robinson, 47–69.

Engell, James. *Biographia Literaria*. In *The Cambridge Companion to Coleridge*. Ed. Lucy Newlyn. Cambridge: Cambridge University Press, 2002, 59–74.

Engell, James and Jackson Bate. "Editors Introduction." In *Biographia Literaria*. Ed. Engell and Bate. Princeton, NJ: Princeton University Press, 1983, xli–cxxxvi.

Evans, Murray J. *Sublime Coleridge: The Opus Maximum*. New York: Palgrave MacMillan, 2012.

Everest, Kelvin. "Coleridge's Life." In *The Cambridge Companion to Coleridge*. Ed. Lucy Newlyn. Cambridge: Cambridge University Press, 2002, 17–31.

Faubert, Michelle. "Introduction." In *Mathilda* by Mary Shelley. Orchard Park, NY: Broadview Press, 2017, 9–38.

Follett, Danielle. "The Tension between Immanence and Dualism in Coleridge and Emerson." In *Romanticism and Philosophy: Thinking with Literature*. Ed. Sophie Laniel-Musitelli and Thomas Constantinesco. New York: Routledge, 2015, 209–21.

Ford, Susan Allen. "'A name more dear': Daughters, Fathers, and Desire in *A Simple Story, The False Friend,* and *Mathilda*." In *Re-visioning romanticism: British Women Writers, 1776-1837*. Ed. Carol Sher Wilson and Joel Haefner. Philadelphia: University of Pennsylvania Press, 1994, 57–71.

Freeman, Kathryn. *British Women Writers and the Asiatic Society of Bengal: Re-orienting Anglo-India*. New York: Routledge, 2014.

Freeman, Kathryn. *A Guide to the Cosmology of William Blake*. New York: Routledge, 2017.

Freud, Sigmund. "The Uncanny." In *The Standard Edition of the Complete Psychological Works of Sigmund Freud*. Trans. James Strachey, et al. Vol. XVII. London: Hogarth Press, 1948, 219–52.

Fruman, Norman. *Coleridge, the Damaged Archangel*. New York: G. Braziller, 1971.

Fulford, Tim. *The Late Poetry of the Lake Poets: Romanticism Revised*. Cambridge University Press, 2013.

Fulford, Tim. *Romantic Poetry and Literary Coteries: The Dialect of the Tribe*. New York: Palgrave Macmillan, 2015.

Fulford, Tim. "Mary Robinson and the Abyssinian Maid: Coleridge's Muses and Feminist Criticism." *Romanticism on the Net.* February 13, 1999.

Fulford, Tim. *Romanticism and Masculinity: Gender, Politics and Poetics in the Writings of Burke, Coleridge, Cobbett, Wordsworth, De Quincey and Hazlitt.* New York: St. Martin's Press, 1999.

Gallagher, Catherine. "Introduction: Cultural and Historical Background." In *Oroonoko or, the Royal Slave.* Boston, MA: Bedford Critical Edition, 2000, 3–25.

Gallagher, Catherine. *Nobody's Story: The Vanishing Acts of Women Writers in the Marketplace 1670–1820.* Berkeley: University of California Press, 1994.

Gilbert, Sandra, and Susan Gubar. *Madwoman in the Attic.* New Haven, CT: Yale University Press, 1979.

Goldsmith, Steven. "Apocalypse and Gender: Mary Shelley's *Last Man.*" In *Unbuilding Jerusalem: Apocalypse and Romantic Representation.* Ithaca, NY: Cornell University Press, 1993, 261–313.

Grant, Allan. "The Genie and the Albatross: Coleridge and the *Arabian Nights.*" In *The Arabian Nights in English Literature.* Ed. Peter Caracciolo. New York: St. Martin's Press, 1988, 111–29.

Handwerk, Gary. "Envisioning India: Friedrich Schlegel's Sanskrit Studies and the Emergence of Romantic Historiography." *European Romantic Review* 9 (Spring 1998): 231–42.

Hawley, Judith. "Romantic Patronage: Mary Robinson and Coleridge Revisited." In *British Women's Writing in the Long Eighteenth Century: Authorship, Politics and History.* Ed. Cora Kaplan. New York: Palgrave Macmillan, 2005, 62–75.

Hayter, Alethea. *Opium and the Romantic Imagination.* Berkeley: University of California Press, 1968.

Himmelfarb, Gertrude. *The Roads to Modernity: The British, French, and American Enlightenments.* New York: Alfred A. Knopf, 2004.

Hipolito, Jeffrey. "Coleridge, Hermeneutics, and the Ends of Metaphysic." *European Romantic Review* 15, 4 (December 2004): 547–65.

Hoeveler, Diane. *Romantic Androgyny: The Women Within.* University Park: Penn State University Press, 1990.

Holmes, Richard. *Darker Reflections, 1804–1834.* New York: Pantheon, 1999.

Holmes, Richard. *Early Visions.* New York: Viking, 1990.

Homans, Margaret. *Bearing the Word. Language and the Female Experience in Nineteenth-Century Women's Writing.* Chicago: University of Chicago Press, 1986.

Hunter, Ian. *Rival Enlightenments: Civil and Metaphysical Philosophy in Early Modern Germany.* Cambridge: Cambridge University Press, 2011.

Johnson, Barbara. *A World of Difference.* Baltimore: Johns Hopkins University Press, 1987.

Kaplan, Cora. *Sea Changes: Essays on Culture and Feminism.* London: Verso, 1986.

Keach, William. "The Shelleys and Dante's Matilda." In *Dante's Modern Afterlife: Reception and Response from Blake to Heaney.* Ed. Nick Havely. New York: St. Martin's Press, 1998, 60-70.

Kristeva, Julia. *Powers of Horror: An Essay on Abjection.* New York: Columbia University Press, 1982.

LeFebure, Molly. *The Bondage of Love: A Life of Mrs. Samuel Taylor Coleridge.* New York: Norton, 1986.

Lehmann, Winfred P. "The Impact of Jones in German-speaking Areas." In *Objects of Enquiry: The Life, Contributions, and Influences of Sir William Jones (1746-1794).* Ed. Garland Cannon and Kevin Brine. New York: New York University Press, 1998, 131-40.

Lowes, John Livingston. *The Road to Xanadu: A Study in the Ways of the Imagination.* Cambridge, MA: Riverside, 1964.

Lowes, John Livingston. *The Road to Xanadu: A Study in the Ways of the Imagination.* Princeton, NJ: Princeton University Press. 1927, 1986.

Luther, Susan. "A Stranger Minstrel: Coleridge's Mrs. Robinson." *Studies in Romanticism* 33 (Fall 1994): 391-409.

Mays, J. C. C. *Coleridge's Experimental Poetics.* New York: Palgrave MacMillan, 2013.

McFarland, Thomas. *Coleridge and the Pantheist Tradition.* New York: Oxford, Clarendon Press 1969.

McFarland, Thomas. *Romanticism and the Forms of Ruin: Wordsworth, Coleridge, and Modalities of Fragmentation.* Princeton, NJ: Princeton University Press, 1981.

McGann, Jerome. *The Romantic Ideology: A Critical Investigation.* Chicago: University of Chicago Press, 1983.

McGavran, James Holt. "Introduction." In *Time of Beauty, Time of Fear: The Romantic Legacy in the Literature of Childhood.* Ed. James Holt McGavran. Iowa City: University of Iowa Press, 2015.

McGrath, Patrick. "Afterword: The New Gothic." *Conjunctions*, no. 14 (1989): 239-44. www.jstor.org/stable/24515047(accessed August 5, 2020).

McLean, Karen. "Plotinian Sources for Coleridge's Theories of Evil." *Coleridge Bulletin.* New Series 20 (Winter 2002): 93-104.

McWhir, Anne. "Introduction." In *The Last Man.* Mary Shelley. Orchard Park, NY: Broadview Press, 1996, xiii-xxxvi.

Mellor, Ann. *Romanticism and Feminism.* Bloomington: Indiana University Press, 1988.

Mellor, Ann. *Romanticism and Gender.* New York: Routledge, 1993.

Mellor, Ann and Richard Matlak. "General Introduction." In *British Literature: 1780–1830.* Ed. Anne Mellor and Richard Matlak. Orlando, FL: Harcourt Brace & Company, 1996.

Metzger, Lore. "Modifications of Genre: A Feminist Critique of 'Christabel' and 'Die Braut von Korinth.'" *Studies in Eighteenth-Century Culture* 22 (1993): 3–19.

Modiano, Raimonda. *Coleridge and the Concept of Nature.* Tallahassee: Florida State University, 1985.

Moi, Toril. *Sexual/Textual Politics.* London: Methuen, 1985.

Moussa-Mahmoud, Fatma. *Sir William Jones and the Romantics.* Cairo, 1962.

Neff, D. S. "'Hostages to Empire': The Anglo-Indian Problem in *Frankenstein, The Curse of Kehama,* and *The Missionary. European Romantic Review* 8 (Fall 1997): 386–408.

Newlyn, Lucy, ed. *The Cambridge Companion to Coleridge.* Cambridge: Cambridge University Press, 2002.

Oxford English Dictionary. https://www.oed.com/browsedictionary;jsessionid=2 2E1EC0C6BAF50BAA7288094337FA5ED (accessed August 5, 2020).

Pascoe, Judith. "Mary Robinson and the Literary Marketplace." In *Romantic Women Writers: Voices and Countervoices.* Ed. Paula Feldman and Theresa Kelley. Hanover, New York: University Press of New England, 1995, 252–68.

Pascoe, Judith, ed. *Mary Robinson: Selected Poems.* Orchard Park, NY: Broadview, 2000.

Poovey, Mary. *The Proper Lady and the Woman Writer: Ideology as Style in the Works of Mary Wollstonecraft, Mary Shelley, and Jane Austen.* Chicago: University of Chicago Press, 1984.

Prickett, Stephen. "Romanticism and Philosophy." In *Handbook of British Romanticism.* Ed. Ralf Haekel. Berlin: de Gruyter, 2017, 104–15.

Richardson, Alan. "Romanticism and the Colonization of the Feminine." In *Romanticism and Feminism.* Ed. Anne Mellor. Bloomington: Indiana University Press, 1988, 13–25.

Richardson, Alan. *The Neural Sublime: Cognitive Theories and Romantic Texts.* Baltimore: Johns Hopkins Press, 2010.

Ricoeur, Paul. *Freud and Philosophy: An Essay on Interpretation.* New Haven: Yale University Press, 1970.

Robinson, Daniel. "From 'Mingled Measure' to 'Ecstatic Measures': Mary Robinson's Poetic Reading of 'Kubla Khan,'" *Wordsworth Circle* 26 (1 January 1995): 4–7.

Ross, Marlon. "Quest and Conquest." In *Romanticism and Feminism.* Ed. Anne Mellor. Bloomington: Indiana University Press, 1988.

Ross, Marlon. *The Contours of Masculine Desire: Romanticism and the Rise of Women's Poetry.* New York: Oxford University Press, 1989.

Schutz, Alexander M. "Divine Law and Abject Subjectivity: Coleridge and the Double Knowledge of Imagination." In *Mind's World: Imagination and Subjectivity from Descartes to Romanticism.* Seattle: University of Washington Press, 2009, 214–61.

Setzer, Sharon M., ed. "Introduction." In *A Letter to the Women of England and The Natural Daughter.* Orchard Park, NY: Broadview Press, 2003, 9–32.

Shaffer, Elinor S. "Iago's Malignity Motiviated: Coleridge's Unpublished 'Opus Magnum.'" *Shakespeare Quarterly* 19, 3 (Summer 1968): 195–203.

Sourgen, Gavin. "A Volatile Unity: Coleridge, Starling Mimicry, and Romantic Form." In *Mocking Bird Technologies: The Poetics of Parroting, Mimicry, and Other Starling Tropes.* Ed. Christopher GoGwilt and Melanie Holm. New York: Fordham University Press, 2018. https://books.google.com/books?id=mZWUDwAAQBAJ&pg=PT69&dq=coleridge%E2%80%A6born+along+like+smoke,+mist%E2%80%94&hl=en&newbks=1&newbks_redir=0&sa=X&ved=2ahUKEwjWkpyb9aPnAhWKuVkKHTerDJ4Q6AEwAnoECAMQAg#v=onepage&q=coleridge%E2%80%A6born%20along%20like%20smoke%2C%20mist%E2%80%94&f=false (accessed January 27, 2020).

Stabler, Jane. "Contemporaries (2): Coleridge, Byron, Shelley." In *John Keats in Context.* Ed. Michael O'Neill. Cambridge: Cambridge University Press, 2017, 2238–47.

Stelzig, Eugene. "'Spirit Divine! With Thee I'll Wander': Mary Robinson and Coleridge in Poetic Dialogue." *Wordsworth Circle* 35, 3 (Summer 2004): 118–22.

Stephen, Leslie. *Hours in a Library.* London: Smith, Elder. 1892. https://www.gutenberg.org/files/20459/20459-h/20459-h.htm (accessed August 5, 2020).

Stevenson, Warren. *Romanticism and the Androgynous Sublime.* Cranbury, NJ: Associated University Presses, 1996.

Struwig, Dillon. "'Schelling Puzzles Me Forever': Freedom, Evil, and Remorse in Coleridge's Critical Commentary on the Freedom Essay." *Coleridge Bulletin* 50 (2017): 69–83.

Sunstein, Emily W. *Mary Shelley: Romance and Reality.* Boston: Little, Brown and Co., 1989.

Taylor, Anya. *Erotic Coleridge: Women, Love, and the Law Against Divorce.* New York: Palgrave, 2005.

Taylor, Anya. "Coleridge's 'Christabel' and the Phantom Soul." *SEL* 42, 4 (Autumn 2002): 707–30.

Vallins, David. "Immanence and Transcendence in Coleridge's Orient." In *Coleridge, Romanticism and the Orient: Cultural Negotiations.* Ed. David Vallins et al. London: Bloomsbury, 2013, 119–30.

Vargo, Lisa. "The Claims of 'Real Life and Manners': Coleridge and Mary Robinson." *Wordsworth Circle* 26, 3 (July 1995): 134–7.

Verma, C. D., ed. *The Gita in World Literature*. New Delhi: Sterling, 1990.

Van Woudenberg, Maximiliaan. *Coleridge and Cosmopolitan Intellectualism 1794–1804: The Legacy of Gottingen University*. New York: Routledge, 2018.

Wheeler, Kathleen. "'Kubla Khan' and Eighteenth-Century Aesthetic Theories." *The Wordsworth Circle* 22, 1 (Winter 1991): 15–24.

Williams, Jeffrey. "Re-writing Literary History: An Interview with Elaine Showalter." *Symploke* 20, 1–2 (2012): 355–70.

Wilson, Carol Shiner and Joel Haefner. "Introduction." In *Re-visioning* Romanticism*: British Women Writers, 1776–1837*. Ed. Carol Shiner Wilson and Joel Haefner. Philadelphia: University of Pennsylvania Press, 1994, 1–14.

Young, J. E. "Perdita's Cottage: Mary Robinson in Mary Wollstonecraft Shelley's *Last Man*." *Notes and Queries* 64, 1 (March 2017): 83–6.

Index

abjection 8 n.17, 105 n.16, 114 n.2
  See also Kristeva, Julia
androgyny 11 n.21, 24, 59–60, 87, 117
  in *Christabel* 94
  in "The Eolian Harp" (Effusion XXXV) 36, 41, 104
  in *Frankenstein* 128 (*see also* gender; sexuality)
  in *Walsingham* 72–3, 76–8
Armstrong, Isobel
  See noncanonical literature
associationism 6, 8–9, 18 n.33, 21, 28, 46, 89–91
  See also fancy
  Hartley, David and 13–14, 23 n.42, 48, 90 (*see also* materialism; memory)
  Priestley, Joseph and 23 n.42, 35

ballad
  See genre
Barbauld, Anna Letitia 53–5
binaries
  See also androgyny; categorical imperatives; contamination; dualism
  gender 25, 75–7, 111, 114, 116, 128, 148 (*see also* genre)
  moral 53, 131–2
  subject/object 120
  systematic 3, 11, 20, 52, 95, 98, 106, 109, 143
Blake, William 10 n.20, 27 n.2, 62 n.10, 87 n.1, 108 n.21
Bloom, Harold 2 n.3, 4, 93
Byrne, Paula 61, 64, 73–4, 114 n.2, 117

canon
  Romantic 4–6, 8, 57–8
categorical imperative(s) 1, 7, 25, 28, 43, 88, 121, 128, 145
Chatterton, Thomas 58 n.1, 68–71
  See also "Monody" (Coleridge and Robinson)

Coleridge, Ernest Hartley 92, 96, 98, 108–9, 129 n.12, 134 n.15
Coleridge, Samuel Taylor
  Ancient Mariner, The 28, 39, 48–9, 53, 79, 91–3, 103, 123–4, 145 (*see also* contamination; gender; metanarrative; narrative)
  Anima Poetae 108
  "Apotheosis, or, the Snow-Drop" 73–4
  Biographia Literaria 16, 35, 43, 60–3, 65, 67, 101, 115 (*see also* Enlightenment, British; fancy; German philosophy; imagination; Kant; recreative; Schelling)
  Christabel 13, 52, 60, 90–9, 103, 128–36, 144, 148 (*see also* nondualism; patriarchy; perverse)
  "Dejection" 29, 70, 99, 101–2, 127
  "Eolian Harp, The" ("Effusion XXXIX") 8, 21, 29–31, 33–9, 44, 129 (*see also* androgyny; Coleridge, Sarah Fricker; dualism; recreative)
  "Frost at Midnight" 29, 36–7, 63
  "Kubla Khan" 19, 25, 32, 43–5, 61, 68, 73, 94, 138 (*see also* androgyny; eros; feminine; fragmentation)
  Lectures on Shakespeare 7, 16, 54 n.36, 110
  Letters 58 n.2, 92
  Magnum Opus (Opus Maximum) 87–8, 106–9, 112, 116, 129–40 (*see also* evil; fragmentation; nondualism)
  "Monody on the Death of Chatterton" 69–70
  Notebook Fragments 102, 108
  Notebooks 17, 29, 44, 96, 107 n.29
  "Ne Plus Ultra" 102, 103
  Poems on Various Subjects 32, 69
  Sibylline Leaves 138–9
  "Stranger Minstrel, A" 83
  Table Talk 46
  "To a Gentleman" 27–9

Coleridge, Sarah Fricker 27, 31, 99
contamination
   androgyny, gender, and 1, 23, 24, 59, 87
   in *Christabel* 9, 72, 92, 94, 125
   in *Frankenstein* 122, 128, 137
   in *Mathilda* 128–9, 132, 134, 136–7
   plague in *The Last Man* 25, 140, 144
   recreation and 114, 116
   in *Rime of the Ancient Mariner* 55–6, 147
Cross, Ashley 11, 58, 59 n.3, 69, 73, 117 n.6
Curran, Stuart
   See noncanonical literature

Dante Alighieri
   Divine Comedy (Matilda) 115 n.5, 135–6
decomposition (Jones, Ernest) 45 n.26, 95
Della Cruscanism 59 n.3, 74, 81, 92
dualism
   canon and 4, 6–7
   Cartesian 10, 14–16, 25, 35, 77, 87, 100, 104
   gender 90
   moral 1, 2, 110, 122
   nondualism and 10, 18
   patriarchy 38, 72, 78, 92, 94, 117
   Wollstonecraft, Mary and 113
   Wordsworth, William and 100 (*see also* binaries (systematic))

Enlightenment(s) 1 n.1
   British 2–3, 7–10, 14, 108
      Bacon, Francis, Sir 46, 108 n.21
      binaries and 23, 45, 62–3, 143
      humanism and 14, 137
      Locke, John 46, 108 n.21, 23 n.42
      materialism and 22, 25, 87, 104, 110
      Newton, Sir Isaac 23 n.42, 38, 46 n.28, 51, 108 n.21
      patriarchy and 18–19
eros (eroticism)
   creativity and 66, 93
   epistemology and 12, 44, 93
   female 10 n.20, 23, 67, 92, 102–3
   gender and 41, 72
evil
   binaries (dualism) and 1, 55, 109, 117
   creativity and 107–9
   in Coleridge, S. T. 15–16, 23–5, 70
   "motiveless malice" 54
   perverse and 78
   gender and 8, 89, 92–4 (*see also Magnum Opus*)
   in Robinson, Mary 76, 78, 82, 119
   Schelling, F. W. J. von on 20
   in Shelley, Mary 25, 137
      Frankenstein 121–2
      Last Man, The 139–40, 143
      Mathilda 130–2

fancy
   Coleridge, S. T. on 102 (*see also* memory)
   associationism and 31–2, 39
   in *Biographia Literaria* 47–50, 52, 63, 106
   Wordsworth, William and 28, 91
feminine (female)
   binary (gender) 5–6, 9–10, 23–4, 38–9, 58–9
   in Coleridge, S. T. 12, 14, 17, 103, 110
   recreative and 20–2, 36, 42–3, 65–6
   Robinson, Mary and 67–8
   in Shelley, Mary 117, 126–7, 138, 144
   in Shelley, Percy 127, 148
feminist criticism 2, 117
   See also Mellor, Ann
feminist psychoanalysis 8 n.17, 105 n.16
   See also abjection; Irigaray, Luce; Kristeva, Julia)
Fichte, Johann Gottlieb 17, 48 n.30, 105
fragmentation (fragment) 22, 31, 45, 75, 96, 106
   Christabel and 9, 95–6
   "Kubla Khan" and 12, 39–41, 63, 64, 66–7, 87–8
   Magnum Opus ("Opus Maximum") and 23–4, 109
   "Notebook Fragments" 102, 108
Freud, Sigmund 2, 8 n.17, 18 n.34, 45 n.24
   unheimlich, the 79 n.28, 103
Fulford, Tim 7 n.14, 11, 49 n.3, 67 n.16, 94

gender
   binaries 2, 13, 25, 41–2, 46, 58–9, 65, 97 (*see also* androgyny; eros)

Coleridge, S. T. and 7, 16, 22, 36, 72, 87, 107, 111 (*see also* patriarchy; recreative; subjectivity)
  contamination and 23–4, 137
  creativity and 61–2, 99
  genre and 3, 30, 73, 85
  Robinson, Mary and 25, 73–80, 82, 88, 119, 148
  Shelley, Mary and 117, 124, 128–9, 134, 138 (*see also* Godwin, William; Wollstonecraft, Mary)
generation 3–5, 30, 70, 111, 147
  See also lineage
genre 3, 22, 30, 36, 47, 71, 73, 85, 108
  elegy 68 n.18, 70, 84, 95
  epistolary 118
  gothic 58, 62, 68, 70, 72, 74, 81, 92, 122, 126
  "last man" novel 142 (*see also* Lyrical Ballads)
  monody 32, 69–71, 73–4 (*see also* narrative)
  narrative poetry 21
    ballad 75, 78, 95–7, 99, 102
  novel (sentimental) 148
    embedded poetry in 22, 125, 73, 81
  poetry 121–2
  German romanticism 14, 20–1, 38, 64
Godwin, William 24, 113–14, 116, 140
Goethe, J. W. 89 n.2
  Bride of Corinth, The 97
Goldsmith, Steven 137–8, 142

Hayter, Alethea 30 n.23, 45 n.25, 60 n.6, 99
hermeneutics (hermeneutical) 18 n.34, 77, 92, 95, 97, 120
Hoeveler, Diane 60, 93, 129 n.11
Holmes, Richard 8 n.18, 10 n.20, 21 n.37, 44 n.23, 65 n.14
Hutchinson, Sara 99, 101, 108
  See Coleridge, "Dejection"

imagination
  contamination and 96, 98
  dualism and 60, 63, 100
  eros, gender and 20, 23, 93, 97, 102
  fancy (distinguished from) 47, 49–51, 53–4, 84, 91
  German philosophy and 8, 17, 20, 106
  imaginatio (distinguished from *phantasia*) 17
  Kant, Immanuel and 16, 52, 107
  in "Kubla Khan" 19, 40, 43–4, 60, 65, 88–9
  malignity and 108
  Robinson, Mary and 67, 74, 82, 84, 119
  in *Rime of the Ancient Mariner* 53–4
  Schelling, F. W. J. von and 104, 115
  secondary 19, 31–2 (*see also* recreative)
  Shelley, Mary and 105, 148
  Wordsworth, William and 23–9, 44
Irigaray, Luce 10 n.20

Kabbalah (Cabala) 14–15, 104
  Shekinah 14, 103, 110 n.23
Kant, Immanuel 1, 13–18, 23 n.42, 48, 52, 89–90, 105, 107
Kristeva, Julia 8 n.17, 10 n.20, 114 n.2
  See also abjection

Leibnitz, Gottfried Wilhelm 18 n.32, 35 n.14, 104
Life-in-Death 25, 54, 112
  gender and 103, 128
  The Last Man and 140, 142–3, 145
lineage, literary 2, 10, 23, 142
  See also canon
  matriarchy (matriarchal) 7, 78, 137 (*see also* patriarchy)
Lyrical Ballads 25, 32
  as genre binary 22
  Christabel (omission) 91, 96, 100
  Preface (Wordsworth, William) 47–50, 98, 106
  Robinson, Mary and 72, 74

materialism
  associationism and 20, 37
  in Coleridge, S. T. (rejection of) 22, 29, 34, 48, 63, 87
  dualism and 3, 9–10, 14–16, 18, 104, 110
  gender and 9
  Priestley, Joseph and 35
McFarland, Thomas 12, 14, 19–20, 100, 108
Mellor, Anne 5, 59
memory
  associationism and 14, 37, 63, 91

Dante and 135
fancy and 106
in Robinson, Mary 81, 84–5, 99
in Shelley Mary 126 (*see also* Wordsworth, William)
metanarrative 1, 25, 75, 78, 96, 119, 133, 137
Milton, John 131, 135

narrative (story, tale) 22, 125, 128, 131, 179
contamination 22–4, 122, 134, 137–44, 147
epistemology and 32 (*see also* fragmentation)
gender and 23, 25, 97, 113, 116 (*see also* metanarrative)
narrative structure 24, 96
narrative frame 118
Robinson, Mary and 68, 72–4, 77, 79, 118, 120, 148
Shelley, Mary and 121–2, 125–6 (*see also* Shelley, Percy)
Newton, Sir Isaac
See Enlightenment
noncanonical literature
Armstrong, Isobel on 5–6, 11, 21, 57–9
Curran, Stuart on 57
Ross, Marlon on 57
nondualism (nonbinary) 21, 47, 50
Coleridge, S. T. and 16
Christabel and 72, 92, 95
"Kubla Khan" and 66
"positive negation" and 102, 104
dualism and 18, 20, 29, 59, 100
gender (androgyny, eros) and 22, 36, 38, 72, 92, 94
monism (distinguished from) 14–15
pantheism (distinguished from) 10
Robinson, Mary and 62, 72
Shelley, Mary and 116

opium (laudanum) 40, 44–5, 60–2, 64, 99

patriarchy
See also canon
Coleridge, S. T. and 8, 10, 19, 21, 23, 38, 43, 45 (*see also* lineage)
Robinson, Mary and 72, 75, 81
Shelley, Mary and 137, 140, 143–4

perverse
moral binaries and 24, 28, 53, 78, 109
fragmentation and 98, 102
plagiarism and 17–18
Robinson, Mary and 78–9, 81
Shelley, Mary and 123, 128–9, 132, 137, 143
plague
Last Man, The 25, 116, 137, 145, 147
Rime of the Ancient Mariner, The 55
plasticity 37–8, 47, 91
Poovey, Mary 113, 138

recreative 54
fragmentation and 114
gender, eros and 12, 17, 20, 42, 44
Robinson, Mary and 59–60, 67, 74, 82, 85, 115
secondary imagination and 8, 32, 88, 91, 102
Shelley, Mary and 116, 127, 138, 144, 148
Robinson, Mary
"Exile, The" 80, 147–8
"Haunted Beach, The" 22, 78–80, 83
"Maniac, The" 12, 60–4, 67–8, 83, 143
"Monody to the Memory of Chatterton" 69–74
"Ode to the Snow-drop" 73–4
"Stanzas to a Friend, Who Desired to Have My Portrait" 84
"To the Poet Coleridge" 12, 62–3, 66
Walsingham
Coleridge and 72, 78
embedded poems in 22, 69–71, 73–5
gender (androgyny) and 73, 148
satire in 72
Shelley, Mary and 24–5, 116–18, 121
Wollstonecraft, Mary and 117
Rousseau, Jean-Jacques 74–116

Schelling, Friedrich, Wilhelm Joseph von 14, 19–20, 48, 52, 89, 104
Shakespeare, William 7, 110–11, 139
Shelley, Mary 1–3, 7–10, 12, 14–15, 21, 110, 147–8
Frankenstein 115–18, 122–7
fragmentation 22
gothic in 62
lineage and 78

Last Man, The 138–45
Mathilda 128–36
recreative in 116
Shelley, Percy 4, 6, 24, 68, 113–15, 128, 137, 140
   epipsyche 124, 126, 130, 148 (*see also* Shelley, Mary)
Southey, Robert 4, 23, 98
Spinoza, Baruch 23, 104
subjectivity
   Coleridge, S. T. and 8, 24, 31–3, 43, 65, 97, 105, 108 (*see also* binaries; Wordsworth, William)
   gender and 5, 11, 14, 16–17, 21, 36–9, 42, 46, 58–9 (*see also* dualism; Wollstonecraft, Mary)
   Robinson, Mary and 62, 68–9, 71–4, 77–9, 88, 118
   Shelley, Mary and 121–2, 130, 135–6, 139, 143

subject/object binary 3–4

Wollstonecraft, Mary
   and Mary Robinson 24–5, 76–7, 81, 115–17
   and Mary Shelley 2, 113–14, 130, 135
Wordsworth, William
   associationism and 13, 20, 47–9, 106
   canon (patriarchal lineage) 4–5, 7–8, 16, 23, 113–14
   dualism 32, 66, 99–102
   in "Ebon Ebon Thalud" (Coleridge) 44–5
   in *Frankenstein* 122, 127–8
   memory and 9–10, 31, 52, 54
   "Nutting" 41–2
   Preface to *Lyrical Ballads* 50, 91
   Prelude, The 27–8